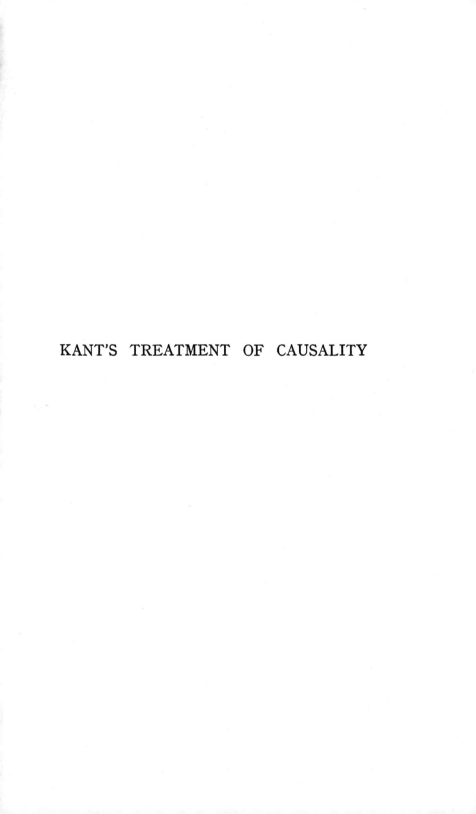

KANT'S TREATMENT OF CAUSALITY

Kant's Treatment of Causality

By
A. C. EWING

ARCHON BOOKS
1969

First Published 1924
Reprinted 1969 with permission
Routledge & Kegan Paul, Ltd.
in an unaltered and unabridged edition

SBN: 208 00733 4
Library of Congress Catalog Card Number: 69-15791
Printed in the United States of America

PREFACE

WHILE the number of general commentaries on Kant is legion, I know of no English book devoted to expounding his thought on a single category abstracted from the rest. Causality, as the chief of the categories and the centre of one of the main philosophical controversies of the period, seems especially to invite the attempt. The subject is, in a sense, a very specialised one, but Kant's treatment of causality is essential to one, at any rate, of the chief sides of his thought, and appears to me to convey a very valuable message that has often been lost sight of in recent philosophy. It would surely be of great philosophical importance if a real proof of the principle of causality could be given, and, while Kant's statement of his proof is too much bound up with other parts of his particular system of philosophy to have given general satisfaction, it seems to me that it may be re-stated in a form in which it can stand by itself and make a good claim for acceptance on all schools of thought. And the close connection of "causality" with many other fundamental problems must be obvious to the reader. The intricacy, as well as the importance, of the subject is such as to make me feel very diffident in submitting my work to the ordeal of publication, but by the kind help of University, Oriel and Magdalen Colleges (Oxford), where I held an open exhibition, research scholarship and senior demyship respectively, and the Committee for Advanced Studies at Oxford, I have been encouraged, as well as enabled, to do so.

The book was accepted as a thesis for the degree of Doctor of Philosophy at Oxford in March, 1923, and has been revised since, but without fundamental alterations. In its composition I am indebted, above all, to Prof. Kemp Smith's *Commentary on Kant;* the other writers whom I found most useful for the purpose were Profs. Caird, Adamson, Cohen, Riehl, Vaihinger and Mr. Prichard. I am responsible for the translations from Kant given in the text, but have made free use of the translations of the three Critiques by Max Müller, Abbott and Bernard respectively, also, where possible, of the translations of various passages given by Prof. Kemp Smith and Mr. Prichard in their commentaries.

A. C. EWING.

Oxford.
March, 1924.

CONTENTS

ABBREVIATIONS

A= Original pages in the first edition of the *Critique of Pure Reason.*
B= Original pages in the second edition of the *Critique of Pure Reason.*
H= Hartenstein's edition of Kant's works.
Berl.= Berlin edition of Kant's letters.
G= Gerhardt's edition of Leibniz's works.

KANT'S TREATMENT OF CAUSALITY

CHAPTER I

Causality in Kant's Predecessors

For Kant the problem of causality constituted the crucial test of his philosophy. It was Hume's attack on causality that first aroused Kant from his " dogmatic slumber " ; it is in regard to the category of causality alone that the all-important argument from objectivity to necessity is worked out in detail, and, if causality is not, as Schopenhauer held, the solitary and unique form of understanding, it seems at any rate much the most important of the Kantian categories. As the clearest and most indispensable instance of a synthetic *a priori* principle causality was the obstacle before which both empiricism and rationalism had been brought to a complete standstill. The rationalist was set the very difficult task of demonstrating a principle which is indispensable for science and practical life, and cannot but be assumed to be true, and yet the opposite of which is not, at any rate *prima facie*, self-contradictory, and he was further confronted with the very awkward fact that the particular causal laws in nature which together make up one of the principal parts of human knowledge are not intelligible or demonstrable *a priori*, but can only be discovered by means of induction from particular experiences. The empiricist, on the other hand, if he wished to be consistent with his first principles, was bound to set himself the still more difficult, nay impossible, task of deriving the universal and necessary principle of causality from a mere enumeration of particulars, and so deriving it without assuming any principle of induction which could not itself be derived by induction from particulars. If Kant's philosophy fails here, it has failed in what the author declares to be its main task, the proof of those synthetic *a priori* principles which cannot be regarded as self-evident, and yet are indispensable for natural science. In causality Kant had found a principle which could be proved neither by the empirical nor by the rationalist philosophy, but which both were bound to assume if they were to stand at all. It was Kant's claim that his philosophy alone could prove the truth of this principle, that his philosophy alone could solve the antinomies to which this principle gave rise. The main question for us to ask is simply this—does Kant succeed in proving this principle ? Causality is a test-case in a larger issue. " [1]Hume and Leibniz are the two protagonists that dwarf all others. They realised, as neither Malebranche, Locke, nor Berkeley, neither Reid, Lambert, Crusius, nor Mendelssohn ever did, the really crucial issues which must ultimately decide between the competing possibilities. Each maintained, in the manner prescribed by his general philosophy, one of what then appeared to be the only two possible views of the function of thought. The alternatives were these : (a) Thought is merely a practical instrument for the convenient interpretation of our human experience ; it has no objective or metaphysical validity of any kind ; (b) Thought legislates universally ; it reveals the wider universe of the eternally possible ; and prior to all experience can determine the fundamental conditions to which that experience must conform. Or to interpret this opposition in logical terms : (a) The fundamental principles of experience are synthetic judgments in which no relation is discernible between subject and predicate, and which for that reason can be justified neither *a priori* nor by experience ; (b) all principles are analytic, and can therefore be justified by pure thought.

The problem of Kant's Critique, broadly stated, consists in the examination and critical estimate of these two opposed views.   There is no problem, scientific, moral, or religious, which is not vitally affected by the decision which of these alternatives we are to adopt, or what reconciliation of their conflicting claims we hope to achieve, . . .   Kant was a rationalist by education, temperament, and conviction. Consequently his problem was to reconcile Leibniz's view of the function of thought with Hume's proof of the synthetic character of the causal principle. He strives to determine how much of Leibniz's belief in the legislative power of pure

[1]Prof. Kemp Smith, *Introduction to Commentary* XXXII, XXXIII.

reason can be retained after full justice has been done to Hume's damaging criticisms. The fundamental principles upon which all experience and all knowledge ultimately rest are *synthetic* in nature : how is it possible that they should also be *a priori* ? Such is the problem that was Kant's troublous inheritance from his philosophical progenitors, Hume and Leibniz."

To show more fully what Kant's " troublous inheritance " in regard to the problem of causality was we must begin with a short survey of the views of his chief predecessors on the subject. In so doing, at the risk of seeming arbitrary, we shall practically confine ourselves to the Locke-Berkeley-Hume tradition and to the Leibnizian philosophy, which were the two main streams of influence that affected Kant's metaphysical thought.

Locke. Locke's account of causality is perhaps the least satisfactory part of his philosophy. In introducing the conception of cause he speaks as though causation were a possible object of perception like colour or shape, and so could be discovered by observation, without inference or the use of a general *a priori* principle. " In the notice that our senses take of the constant vicissitude of things we cannot but observe that several particulars, both qualities and substances, begin to exist, and that they receive this their existence from the due application and operation of some other being. From this observation we get our ideas of cause and effect."[1] Yet he insists on the mysterious and unknowable character of the causal nexus. Since we can only observe sensible " ideas " or qualities in external objects, a power can only be known as the potentiality of producing or undergoing changes in these sensible qualities, a mysterious something that can only be described in terms of its effects.[2] The real ground in nature of even such fundamental laws as the cohesion of matter and the communication of motion by impact is unknown to us. Hence the mathematical method must give way to empirical induction in dealing with powers, which powers in fact constitute the greater part of our idea of the physical world. For, apart from the primary qualities of extension, etc., revealed by our senses, we cannot attribute to matter any qualities save the power to produce certain sensations in our mind and certain changes in other bodies which in their turn affect our mind.

[1] *Essay concerning Human Understanding* II., 26, 1 ; *cf.* II.,2 1, 1.
[2] II., 23, 23-28.

Hence the idea of spirit is no more unintelligible to us than that of matter[1] ; in fact, as regards causation, we acquire a better idea of active power from introspection than from the observation of physical changes, for in the latter motion is only transmitted, not generated, as by the will, and also we can acquire no idea of the second active power, thought, from our observation of matter. (The two kinds of active power are motion and thought, in the wide, Cartesian sense of the word.) Perhaps it is unfair to press too far the words of Locke quoted above, but we may point out that, if causation can as such be observed, causal powers cannot have the unknowable character ascribed to them. The view that we can observe one thing causing another and not only infer that it does so seems to involve a confusion between sequence and causation—we see B follow A, but we do not see A cause B. Causation is a relation of implication between events and not a sensible quality.

To prove the validity of the general principle that every change must have a cause Locke makes use of the argument that it is obviously impossible for nothing to produce something. " Men know by an intuitive certainty, that bare nothing can no more produce any real being than it can be equal to two right angles."[2] The circular character of this argument is partly concealed by confusing causal connection with connection by logical identity, to say that nothing is something involves a flagrant violation of the law of non-contradiction, to say that something occurred with nothing precedent to cause it involves no such contradiction, for it is essential to causality that cause and effect should be distinct and not capable of logical identification. The plausibility of the argument depends partly on this confusion, partly on the principle that " nothing " as such is incapable of being a cause. This principle is true enough, but cannot be applied without already assuming universal causality. For if the causal principle is denied the conclusion is not that things are caused by nothing, but that they are not caused at all. It is only because Locke assumes the universality of the causal principle that he can assume that, if an event is not caused by something, it must be caused by " nothing," yet it is just this universality that he is seeking to prove.

The problem of freedom is less closely connected with that of causation in Locke than in other writers, for he does not

---

[1]*Essay concerning Human Understanding*, II., 23, 30–32.   [2]IV., 10, 3.

attempt to solve the problem by a distinction between mechanical and spiritual causation or a denial that the category of cause is adequate when applied to spiritual beings, but by a criticism of the common habit of viewing faculties like the will as independent agents, which gives rise to the meaningless question " Is the will free ?," not " Is the man free ? " This criticism is very effective and valuable as far as it goes, but it can hardly be said to reach the root of the problem—How far, if at all, can the category of mechanical causation be applied to psychical development ?

Berkeley. Berkeley, while assuming without proof the general principle that every change must have a cause, denies that causal connection between physical phenomena the nature of which Locke had already asserted to be unknown. He thus makes another step forward in the direction of Hume. Berkeley's philosophy leaves in existence only spirits and their ideas ; our ideas cannot have causal efficacy, because we cannot perceive any such quality in them, and by its intrinsic nature an idea in my mind cannot have any qualities beyond those I am conscious of.[1] But, since we must suppose the changes in our ideas to have some cause, and there are many cases in which we cannot suppose this cause to lie in ourselves, we are driven to postulate a spiritual being, infinitely more powerful than ourselves, namely God, to account for these changes.[2] Thus Berkeley makes use of his novel views of matter to arrive at a new and, to his mind, more convincing proof of God than any yet discovered.

In dealing with the "material" world he substitutes for the relation of cause and effect the relation of " sign " and " thing signified."[3] Thus " the fire which I see is not the cause of the pain I suffer upon my approaching it, but the mark that forewarns me of it." We find by experience that ideas succeed each other in such a regular manner that we may frame laws of nature and use these laws for predicting future events, but this orderly succession is not dependent on any causal influence of one idea on another, but on nothing save the direct will of God. Natural science consists in the reduction of the multitudinous observed sequences to a few simple and universal laws of sequence, not explicable further except by an appeal to final causes,—in the discovery of a simple alphabet of signs from which the whole complicated natural

---

[1] *Princ. of Human Knowledge*, 25.   [2] *Ib.*, 26.   [3] *Ib.*, 65.

system is built up, just as a language with many thousands of words is ultimately reducible to different combinations of twenty-six letters. The main innovation lies in suggesting that the results of science express not truths about an objective physical world existing independently of being perceived, but truths about the sensations we should experience under given conditions. Even if the material world exists as a system of ideas in God's mind[1], Berkeley could not admit that this world in God's mind was either causally connected with our sensations, which are ascribed to the immediate action of the will of God without the intervention of particular " ideas " in God's mind, or an object of our perception, since it is a cardinal doctrine of his philosophy that we cannot perceive anything but ideas in our own mind. It is therefore not the world with which science deals and which surrounds us in our everyday life, but a world supposed to correspond to that world, and itself in no way connected with us.

Locke had ascribed causation to unknown " powers," Berkeley denied that such unknowable and imperceptible powers could be real qualities and reduced all so-called physical causation to necessitated, not necessitating, sequence. Since, however, there was no " activity " involved in what we regard as physical causation, he denied the title of causation to the latter altogether, satisfying himself by ascribing the necessary " activity " to God. As with substance, so with cause, Locke declared it to be unintelligible to us, Berkeley relegated it from the physical to the psychical, Hume denied altogether the possibility of justifying it, Kant justified it but on lines that involved a fundamental change both in the conception itself and in the general view of objective reality.

Hume. Hume, in carrying the principles of Locke and Berkeley to their logical conclusion, directs his main attack against causality, as being the foundation of knowledge of a physical world. He assumes as first principles that we can be immediately conscious of nothing save our own ideas, and that there is no simple idea not derived from a precedent impression of which it is an exact copy. The former was admitted by all schools, being based on the physiological account of sensation and the difficulty of explaining the subjective element in perception on any other theory ; the latter was the cardinal principle of pure

[1]As Berkeley suggests in the 2nd dialogue between Hylas and Philonous (*Everyman* ed., p. 248).

empiricism. Of neither principle does Hume give any proof whatever. In laying down the maxim that every simple idea must be copied from a precedent impression he first challenges his opponents to produce a simple idea that has not a corresponding impression or *vice versa*, and then asserts that, as no such idea or impression can be found, we are forced to explain the resemblance by supposing the ideas to be all derived from their corresponding impressions, since experience tells us that it is always the impression which precedes the idea. This no doubt follows if by impressions are understood sensations and emotions, but the first point, that every simple idea has a corresponding impression, is nothing but an arbitrary assumption. To assert, as Hume does, the validity of the principle on the ground of failure to produce an idea that does not conform to it, and then, later in the argument, when such an idea, namely the idea of causality, is introduced, to deny that it is a real idea, because it does not conform to the principle, is a breach of the most elementary rules of logic.

Hume's treatment of causality in his larger work resolves itself into four main parts : (1), an attempt to show that the general principle of causality is incapable of proof ; (2), an attempted reduction of reasoning on particular cases of causation to mere association of ideas, due to past contiguity in experience ; (3), a corresponding theory of probability ; and (4), an attempt to reduce the necessary character of the causal law, as conceived by us, to a determination of the mind by custom, the feeling of which we misinterpret as representing a real necessary connection in the object itself.

Of these the first-mentioned is perhaps the most important, for it was the discovery of the synthetic character of the causal nexus that provided Kant with a starting-point for the revolutionary change he brought about in philosophy.[1] Certain knowledge, Hume says, is confined to the " agreement and disagreement of ideas," which is the same as saying that it is only found in what can be deduced from the principle of non-contradiction and immediate experience of ideas as copies of impressions. Therefore, if the general principle that every change must have a cause is to be proved, it can only be by showing that its opposite is self-contradictory. That this cannot be shown " we may satisfy ourselves by considering, that, as all distinct ideas are separable from

[1] *Treatise* I., 3, 3.

B

each other, and as the ideas of cause and effect are evidently distinct, it will be easy for us to conceive any object to be non-existent this moment, and existent the next, without conjoining to it the distinct idea of a cause or productive principle." There can be no self-contradiction in imagining the effect to occur without the cause since the effect certainly does not include the cause in itself or *vice versa*. That all reasoning is analytic is, of course, assumed. The arguments usually advanced to establish the proposition that every change must have a cause, on the ground that otherwise something would be caused by nothing, or by itself, or that, all the points of space and time being " equal " a cause is necessary to determine where and when anything shall begin to exist—Hume points out, all presuppose what they set out to prove, for the difficulty in each case only arises if we have already denied that anything may occur without a cause.

Hume now proceeds to the examination of reasoning about particular causes. (In the Inquiry he only discusses this question and not[1] the question of the validity of the general principle of causality.) The connection between a particular cause and effect, he maintains, can be discovered neither by rational insight nor by observation—not by rational insight because, each being a distinct idea, it involves no contradiction to suppose one existing without the other, not by observation, because powers of production are not sensible qualities. However much we talk of forces or powers of production we cannot by that means explain causality, for a " force " already presupposes a causal relation.[2] Nor can we argue from the fact of sequence in the past to sequence in the future because such an argument implies the principle of induction, i.e., that future events will resemble past events, and this principle can neither be proved by reason because we may without contradiction suppose a change in the order of nature, nor be shown to be probable by experience because it is itself the foundation of all probability and all arguments from experience. Now, Hume continues, there are two kinds of relation between ideas—that discovered by reason and that based on association. It has been shown that the causal relation does not belong to the former class, therefore it must belong to the latter. Now causal arguments always proceed from an impression present to the senses or memory to an

---

[1]Except perhaps by implication.   [2]*Treatise* I., 3, 6.

idea which is the copy of an impression conjoined in past experience to impressions similar to the present one. It is an obvious empirical fact that ideas or impressions tend to call to mind by association both similar ideas and ideas conjoined with them in past experience. The causal relation may thus be explained by a double association of ideas—the impression calls up the idea of a similar impression in the past ; this idea calls up the idea of an impression conjoined with the previous impression in experience—two stages which custom makes us resolve into one. There is still to be explained the attitude of belief which we adopt towards the idea thus called to mind, but belief does not consist in the addition of any fresh idea to those already entertained by the mind, and consequently can be nothing beyond a certain feeling with which we conceive the idea, a feeling best described as " a more vivid, lively, forcible, firm, steady conception of an object than what the imagination is ever able to attain." This feeling is the same in character as that which accompanies a present impression, and experience shows that such an impression may communicate its vivacity to any idea which it calls to mind by the ordinary laws of association. It follows that our sentiment of belief may be explained by the theory that the idea of the cause, being called up by a present impression, has some of the vivacity belonging to the latter.

It remains to explain our consciousness of necessity in the causal connection.[1] This consciousness cannot be derived from any particular sense-impression, and similar difficulties to those already discussed arise when we try to derive it from the impression of willing. But it has the strange characteristic of resulting from a repetition of similar instances. Such a repetition cannot change the instances nor enable us to extract a new idea from them by reasoning, for no reasoning can give us an idea underived from impressions, but the consideration of it by the mind produces a new impression of reflection, or feeling of the emotional order, the feeling that upon the appearance of one of the objects the mind is *determined* by custom to consider its usual attendant, and to consider it in a stronger light upon account of its relation to the first object. This feeling is then identical with the necessity in the causal sequence, which thus, instead of being an objective connection discernible by reason,

[1] *Treatise* I., 3, 14.

becomes, as far as known by us, an unavoidable but logically unjustifiable tendency of the mind to pass from one idea to another and regard the latter with a certain feeling which we call belief. Hume's theory of probability is elaborated by working out the same principle; it treats a judgment of probability as the result merely of conflicting, involuntary tendencies of the mind to fix its attention on and vividly conceive one or other of the alternatives presented.

On the representative theory of perception all arguments for an external world seemed to depend on the principle of causality, consequently Hume's criticism of the latter involved the abandonment of any hope of logically proving the former. Not only, as Berkeley had held, was the assertion of an objective physical world unjustified, but (on Hume's principles) the argument to a deity or any being external to our own mind was equally without logical justification, since any such argument was held to presuppose the principle of causality which Hume had proved to be incapable of demonstration by any known method. But it was still necessary to give some explanation of the undoubted fact that we make a distinction between the subjective and the objective, between the world of our own feelings and ideas and the world of objects. In view of the fact that Kant's vindication of causality depends largely on the argument that the distinction between the subjective and the objective already implies real causal necessity, it will be well here to quote Hume at some length in order to show what characteristics he regarded as the distinguishing mark of objective as opposed to subjective phenomena. "After a little examination we shall find that all those objects, to which we attribute a continued existence, have a peculiar *constancy*, which distinguishes them from the impressions whose existence depends upon our perception.[1] Those mountains, and houses and trees, which lie at present under my eye, have always appeared to me in the same order, and when I lose sight of them by shutting my eyes or turning my head, I soon after find them return upon me without the least alteration. My bed and table, my books and papers, present themselves in the same uniform manner, and change not upon account of any interruption in my seeing or perceiving them. This is the case with all the impressions whose objects are supposed to have external existence, and is the case with

---

[1]*Treatise* I., 4, 2.

no other impressions, whether gentle or violent, voluntary or involuntary. This constancy, however, is not so perfect as not to admit of very considerable exceptions. Bodies often change their position and qualities, and, after a little absence or interval, may become hardly knowable. But here it is observable, that even in these changes they preserve a *coherence*, and have a regular dependence on each other, which is the foundation of a kind of reasoning from causation, and produces the opinion of their continued existence. When I return to my chamber after an hour's absence, I find not my fire in the same situation in which I left it, but then I am accustomed, in other instances, to see a like alteration produced in a like time, whether I am present or absent, near or remote. This coherence, therefore, in their changes, is one of the characteristics of external objects, as well as their constancy." Hume here unjustifiably makes use of terms involving conceptions which he had denied ; thus, to be consistent, he should have spoken not of " objects " like " books and papers " presenting themselves in the same uniform manner but of " a succession of similar perceptions," not of " dependence " but of " uniform sequence." As a matter of fact in explaining our belief in an external world he takes the account in that sense. Proceeding from the above distinction between different kinds of immediate experience, he accounts for this belief by " tendencies to feign " conditions of which we have no real idea. This was indeed the only course open to him, since he was bound to deny not only that the categories of cause and substance can be shown to carry with them any objective validity, but that we have any idea of cause or substance at all, since there are no corresponding impressions. The tendencies he appealed to are two in number ; first, the tendency[1] to seek uniformity in the sequence of phenomena, even beyond what is given in experience. This leads us to suppose that where one impression, which has in the past always been preceded by another, occurs without that other preceding, the latter has really occurred unperceived by us, forgetting that an impression cannot exist except as perceived. Secondly,[2] he alleges a tendency to confuse a sequence of closely resembling perceptions with an identical, unchanging perception. Our perceptions being obviously interrupted, this leads to a clear contradiction, which is evaded by distinguish-

---

[1] *Cf.* " coherence " alone.   [2] *Cf.* " constancy " alone.

ing between *objects* which remain identical and the *perceptions* of them which do not.

It is a further corollary from Hume's principles that there can be no distinction between moral and physical necessity. Causal necessity has been analysed as involving (1) the constant conjunction of " cause " and " effect " in past experience, (2) the consequent necessary passage of the mind from one to the other, but it is obvious that both characteristics may belong to those actions which are called free. Similar events are in human life, as elsewhere, followed by similar; human nature is fundamentally the same at all times and all places ; at every moment of life we act and think on the assumption that human nature is uniform and calculable ; if a man leaves a purse full of gold on the pavement at Charing Cross at noon " he may as well expect that it will fly away as a feather, as that he will find it untouched an hour later." This account of necessity, of course, implies, not that each psychical event is caused mechanically by the train of preceding events, but that psychical events are shown by experience to follow on each other with a certain uniformity which is not really incompatible with a belief that *some* acts are not *wholly* determined.

Hume established two important points in metaphysics : (1) that the causal principle is synthetic in character, (2) that empiricism must lead to scepticism. Both of these were whole-heartedly adopted by Kant and formed the starting-point of the *Critique of Pure Reason*, which was primarily an attempt to find a new logical basis for those principles, which, though incapable of demonstration from the law of contradiction or induction from experience, yet were implied in all, even so-called empirical, knowledge of the objective world. Hume strongly emphasised the dependence of all scientific and empirical reasoning on the principle of causation, but he did not take the further step and discover that the principle was implied in all experience of objects in time. His philosophy must be regarded rather as a confession of the bankruptcy of empiricism than as an attempt to establish a doctrine of complete scepticism, which latter is indeed, as the philosopher himself saw, impossible to human nature. He did not deny causality, in fact he admitted that we must believe in it, what he denied was that our belief in it is capable of justification on logical grounds. Hence he was not guilty of inconsistency in attempting to explain our belief in causality by a psychological theory which in itself involves the assumption of causality. His psychological explanation of causality is no doubt open to a good deal of criticism—it may be pointed out that it is rather unusual than usual occurrences that imprint on our minds the consciousness of necessity; that the judgment of causal connection, which must be distinguished, if only as a psychological fact, from the mere feeling of it, implies a synthesis of perceptions which is not possible for a mind that is itself nothing but a series of separate perceptions ; that, as we generally only look at an object at disconnected moments and not continuously, the number of times in which we observe the effect without the cause is probably much greater than the number of times we observe both ; that, although for example we generally in the morning see the objects around us lighted up before we see the sun, we do not for that reason infer that the light is the cause of the sun but *vice versa* ; that the judgment of probability cannot be either a feeling or an estimate of our feelings, because we may often feel as though a future event were unlikely and remote while judging it to be likely and imminent. However, the value of Hume's metaphysical work lies much more in his criticism of earlier positions than in his psychological theory, which, as he fully realises, is a way of inquiry that could never establish the logical validity, as opposed to the historical origin, of any belief. But the breakdown of empiricism rendered it necessary to reconsider its fundamental doctrine that all ideas are the copies of detached sensations or feelings, a doctrine which ruled out from the beginning any principle like causality. Hume did not attempt to conceal, but rather to emphasise, the failure of the empirical principles on which his philosophy was based, he did not, for instance, try to reduce causality to constant sequence, but insisted that we needed something more than that for scientific reasoning. But by stating in its acutest form the fundamental difficulty connected with the principle of causality he at the same time suggested a solution.

In a sense it might actually be said that Hume's deficiency lay in not carrying his sceptical principles far enough. Had he pushed his atomistic sensationalism to its logical conclusion it would have been shown to be quite inconsistent with the very possibility of cognition, and so would have provided its own refutation ; had he shown that the synthetic, indemonstrable principle of causality was implied in all our empirical knowledge and not only a foundation for all scientific arguments he would have, by this means, provided as good a proof of causality as could be given for any principle, namely, by showing that we must either believe it or believe nothing at all. This was, in fact, the work of Kant. Hume came very near to it—he emphasised the importance of causality as the basis of practically all non-mathematical inference, and pointed[1] out that it is through this principle alone that we can convince ourselves of the existence of external objects. "We readily suppose an object may continue individually the same, though several times absent from and present to the senses ; and ascribe to it an identity, notwithstanding the interruption of the perception, whenever we conclude that, if we had kept our eyes or hand constantly upon it, it would have conveyed an invariable and uninterrupted perception. But this conclusion beyond the impression of our senses can be founded only on the connection of *cause and effect* ; nor can we otherwise have any security that the object is not changed upon us, however much the new object may resemble that which was formerly present to the senses." We may note also the importance that Hume attaches to the demand for coherence as a basis of our belief in the external world, meaning by this the demand for a greater regularity in phenomena and a greater facility in formulating causal laws than can be attained if we confine ourselves to the consideration of sense-perceptions and do not introduce external objects characterised by an endurance in time which we cannot assign to our individual perceptions. Without trying to minimise the difference between this position and Kant's argument that objectivity implied necessity, we cannot but note that in both knowledge of (or, according to Hume, logically ungrounded belief in) objects is held to depend on causality. We must, however, note that Hume rejects "involuntariness " (cf. Kantian "irreversibility ") as the criterion of objectivity on the ground that pain, which we do not ascribe to the object, is equally involuntary. We may contrast Berkeley, who makes independence of our will the main distinguishing mark of those ideas which are held to represent the objective, physical world, i.e., "ideas of sensation."[2] In this respect Berkeley comes nearer to Kant than Hume does.

[1] I., 3, 2. *Cf.* " Of these three relations, which depend not upon the mere ideas, the only one that can be traced beyond our senses, and informs us of existences and objects, which we do not see or feel, is causation."—*Ib.*   [2] XXIX., *Princ. of Human Knowledge.*

To sum up, Hume showed that empiricism led to scepticism and even that awareness of objects depended on causality, but he did not realise that this was at once a refutation of empiricism and a proof of causality. It was left to Kant to work out the positive implications of the sceptical doctrine. Kant himself holds that Hume's scepticism was due to failure to extend his principles to the whole field of *a priori* knowledge and speaks as though it were his own task just to realise the implications of his predecessor's thoughts. " I admit frankly it was just the remembrance of David Hume, which, many years ago, first interrupted my dogmatic slumber and gave my investigations in the field of speculative philosophy quite a new turn.[1] I was far from accepting his conclusions, which were only due to the fact that he did not set his task before him as a whole, but only dealt with one part, which, without reference to the whole, could give him no means of advance. If we begin with a well-founded, although undeveloped thought, bequeathed to us by another, we may well hope as the fruit of continued meditation to develop it further than the keen-sighted man whom we had to thank for the first spark of this light."

I do not propose to deal at length with the well-worn subject of the time and manner of Hume's influence on Kant. Kant's thought on causality between 1760 and 1770 runs on lines similar[2] to Hume in the *Essays*, but he does not seem to have realised the difficulties involved in the general principle of causality till after 1770. This can be accounted for by the plausible conjecture that it was the passages quoted from Hume in Beattie's *Essay on the Nature and Immutability of Truth*, first translated into German in 1772, that first gave Kant an adequate idea of the wider implications of Hume's thought on causality, and that prior to this time Kant was only acquainted with the *Essays* of Hume. With this remark we shall pass on to the rationalist philosophy in which Kant was brought up.

Leibniz. Although in his " critical " position and his refusal to extend metaphysics beyond possible experience Kant has much in common with Hume, by temperament and training he was essentially a rationalist. Not only does he try to beat the Wolffians with their own weapons

[1]*Prolegomena*, 260. [2]For the view that, as regards the aim of the arguments used, there is a considerable difference between Kant and Hume, Prof. Caird has made a good case (*Critical Philosophy* I., pp. 120 ff.).

in the Dialectic, but the reconstruction of philosophy within the bounds of experience is undertaken in a thoroughly rationalistic spirit, which is perhaps exhibited most strikingly in his cumbrous architectonic and his doctrine that all metaphysics must be *a priori* and absolutely certain or else mere illusion, and made quite clear by an outline comparison of his avowed and practised method with that of the Wolffian school. Kant's method was analysis of what is implied in the possibility of experience in general, the orthodox rationalist method was analysis of what is implied in the possibility of existence in general, and without under-rating the great importance of the substitution of " experience " for " existence " or ignoring the greater fruitfulness of Kant's inquiries we must admit that the difference between the two methods is far less than that between the Kantian and the empirical method, which consisted in investigating the origin of our knowledge on the assumption that it was wholly explicable as the result of particular experiences and did not imply from the beginning general principles incapable of derivation from any collection of such particular experiences. The attempt to substitute psychology for theory of knowledge, either like Locke with the mistaken idea of testing the validity of our knowledge by this means, or, like Hume, in despair of any theory which would justify our first principles, was never made by Kant ; and nothing could be further removed from the principles of the Critiques than Hume's exaltation of feeling and his attack on the necessity of mathematics.[1] (So much so, that Kant, not knowing the passage referred to, regarded it as inconceivable that anybody could impugn the necessity of mathematical deductions, though he might be unable to give a theoretical explanation of it, and remarks that if Hume had realised the destructive effects on mathematics of his general doctrine he would have been led to reconsider his position[2].)

Now, on turning to the rationalists, taken in general, we find that their treatment of causation was characterised by an attempt to make it a sub-species of the logical relation between ground and consequent. The impossibility of deducing particular effects from their causes *a priori* and the unintelligibility of the relation between mind and body left philosophy in an impasse and led the occasionalists to deny any causation except by the immediate will of God.

[1]*Treatise* I., i, 2.   [2]20 B.

But, instead of solving the problem, they only threw it further back. For the action of mind on matter is no less a mystery, if ascribed to God only, than if made universal, and the logic of identity is as incapable of deducing *a priori* the general law that every change must have a cause, as it is of deducing that this particular change must have this particular cause.

So, too, Leibniz saw that the effect could never be deduced from analysis of the cause taken alone, but did not extend this conclusion to the general principle of causality itself. His treatment of the subject, was, however, markedly original and drew a distinction very like that of Kant between analytic and synthetic. According to the principle of sufficient reason no fact can be true and no being existent without a reason adequate to explain *a priori* why it is just what it is. In some cases the truth may be found to follow from the law of contradiction, which is then its " sufficient reason," but in other cases no amount of analysis will show the denial of the truth to involve a contradiction. In the former case we have a necessary truth of reason, in the latter a contingent truth of fact ; in the former case the opposite is impossible, in the latter possible. However, the proof of both contingent and necessary truths involves analysis, only in the case of contingent truths the analysis can never be completed. " Il y a une infinité de figures et de mouvements présents et passés qui entrent dans la cause efficiente de mon écriture présente, et il y a une infinité de petites inclinations et dispositions de mon âme présentes et passées qui entrent dans la cause finale. Et comme tout ce détail n'enveloppe que d'autres contingents antérieurs ou plus détaillés, dont chacun a encore besoin d'une analyse semblable pour en rendre raison, on n'en est pas plus avancé, et il faut que la raison suffisante ou dernière soit hors de la suite ou série de ce détail des contingences, quelque infini qu'il pourrait être. Et c'est ainsi que la dernière raison des choses doit être dans une substance nécessaire, dans laquelle le détail des changements ne soit qu' éminemment, comme dans la source, et c'est ce que nous appelons Dieu."[1] The difference between necessary and contingent truths is that necessary truths follow wholly from the law of non-contradiction, while contingent truths follow from the goodness and wisdom of God, which must have led to the creation of the best possible universe. Conse-

---

[1] *Monad.*, 36–38.

quently, where we cannot deduce a known fact from the law
of non-contradiction, we must account for it by supposing that
it is an integral part of the best possible universe such that
without it the universe would be inferior to what it is. Both
contingent and necessary truths could only be proved by
analysis, but in the case of contingent truths, first, the analysis
could never be completed by a finite mind, because the
relations involved are infinite in number ; secondly, the
ultimate ground of the truth is moral, not logical, the opposite
is not self-contradictory but incompatible with the absolute
goodness and wisdom of the deity.

The doctrine that all the predicates of a subject must be
included in the notion of that subject may be regarded as
one of the fundamental doctrines of Leibniz's philosophy.
But there is one exception—the predicate of existence, (if
it can indeed be called a predicate), is only allowed by Leibniz
to be included in the notion of the subject in one case, that of
God, and this inconsistently. Hence, with this exception,
existential propositions are for Leibniz " contingent," but
they, for all that, may be proved by analysis, since analysis
of the subject would, if fully carried out, reveal that it, as
a substance, was in itself good to a certain more or less limited
extent and not incompatible with the best universe possible.
But this would be the same as saying that it was bound to
exist, for God must, owing to his inherent goodness, bring
everything of value into existence, provided only it does
not conflict with the realisation of greater good.

The contingency of existential propositions, of course,
involves the contingency of all propositions about actual
occurrences in time, and of laws governing all the moments
of actual, as opposed to possible, time. Whether contingent
can be identified with synthetic is a doubtful question, and
Leibniz[1] certainly held the predicate to be always in some
sense contained in the subject (excepting perhaps existential
propositions),[2] but he seems to have considered the relation
between cause and effect, as successive moments in a changing
substance, to be synthetic.[3] For, although the notion of
the substance, according to Leibniz,[4] contains the notion of
all its states at different times, this does not mean that its
state at one time can be deduced from its state at another
without taking into account the whole notion of the substance
or the principle of unity which welds its successive states into

[1]G., VII., 199.   [2]G., VI., 319.   [3]G., II., 52.   [4]G., III., 645.

one connected whole, moreover the judgment that the notion of the subject[1] (or substance) contains all its predicates is hypothetical and only means that, if the subject is given as existent, the existence of its predicates will follow. Now the existence of the substance is contingent, therefore the existence of the attributes is contingent also.

But Leibniz apparently does not recognise the synthetic character of the general causal principle ; thus, in writing to Des Bosses he says that a power of determining oneself without any cause implies a contradiction as does a relation without foundation, and adds " but from this the metaphysical necessity of all effects does not follow.[2] For it suffices that the cause or reason be not one that metaphysically necessitates, though it is metaphysically necessary that there should be some such cause." (" Metaphysical necessity " for Leibniz was always analytic and dependent on the bare principle of non-contradiction.) Also in writing to De Volder he says that, to conceive the essence of a substance, " we require the conception of a possible cause, to conceive its existence we require the conception of an actual cause."[3] But, according to Leibniz's philosophy, no truth about " essences " can be other than " metaphysically necessary," and elsewhere he argues that, for a notion to be a notion for possible existents, there must be another notion, which, if existent, would be a sufficient reason for the former to exist.[4] Leibniz's doctrine that the " notion " of the substance always contained all its attributes led him to deny real causal connection between different substances, hence arose the need for a pre-established harmony. A " created thing," he held, was to be considered the cause of something in another just in so far as it contained in a more perfect form that which was imperfect in the other, for the imperfect was always to be explained by the more perfect, inasmuch as in adjusting the pre-established harmony God must have adapted the imperfect to the perfect and not *vice versa*. Everything except God was partly active, partly passive, active in so far as it contained the explanation of what was less perfect in other beings, passive in so far as it contained elements which could only be explained by the more perfect form in which they existed in another being.[5]

In discussing freedom, Leibniz, like most other thinkers,

[1]Leibniz virtually identified logical subject and substance, thus falling under the criticism of Kant. [2]*G.*, II., 51. [3]*G.*, II., 225. [4]*Monad.*, 49-52. [5]*G.*, II., 420.

sought to find a middle term between the equally unacceptable doctrines of an irrational and capricious indeterminism and a strictly mechanical determinism. Indeterminism, in the sense of uncaused action, would have been inconsistent with the principle of sufficient reason and the doctrine of a pre-established harmony, while the second alternative would have destroyed the ethical theology which played such a pre-eminent part in his system. Leibniz sought to escape by a distinction between metaphysical and moral necessity. Every action he held to be determined, but it was determined by an inclining, not a necessitating, cause ; that is, all acts are motived but cannot be deduced logically by the law of non-contradiction. This distinction was backed by the classification of all actual events as contingent. Freedom for Leibniz consisted in contingency with intelligence and without external constraint, (or rather that relation to another being which is interpreted in the phenomenal world as constraint), and its degree varied in proportion to the reasonableness of the motives determining it. Mechanism he held to be universal among phenomena but not to affect real existence.

We may now sum up the chief points of agreement and disagreement between Kant and Leibniz in regard to causality. They agreed in recognising the synthetic character of the particular laws of nature and in making mechanism universal among physical phenomena while leaving room for freedom in the reality behind phenomena, and the Leibnizian distinction between necessary and contingent truths naturally suggests the Kantian distinction between the logical principles on which analytic reasoning is based and the synthetic principles which are valid only as conditions of possible experience. Leibniz differs from Kant : (1) in failing to recognise the synthetic character of the general principle of causality ; (2) in denying the possibility of necessary *a priori synthetic* propositions ; (3) in his " dogmatism " which leads him to see in the causal connection a phenomenal representation of a real connection in the thoughts of God ; (4) in admitting degrees of freedom and in his more distinctly deterministic position ; (5) in making our apprehension of spirit an apprehension of reality, and so not admitting the distinction between the phenomenal and the noumenal self—these specified differences being, of course, quite apart from the fact that he did not anticipate the revolutionary method of the *Critique of Pure Reason*.

Wolff.

The Wolffian philosophy, in which Kant was brought up, while modelled on that of Leibniz, toned down or eliminated the most original and striking suggestions of the latter, like the doctrine of the pre-established harmony. Wolff attached far more importance to the principle of non-contradiction than to the principle of sufficient reason. He makes an attempt to prove the latter from the former by arguing that " nothing," being that to which no notion corresponds, cannot be said to cause or logically account for " something " without contradiction.[1] This is practically the same argument as that used by Locke and has been already dealt with. It assumes that a change must be *caused*, either by something or nothing, and then, because for " nothing " to be a cause would be self-contradictory, it concludes triumphantly that " something " must be its cause. But, that a change must be caused, is just what the argument was intended to prove.

Wolff also explicitly makes cause a sub-species of logical ground and explains a particular cause as that from which the effect may be logically deduced.[2] He allows the pre established harmony to fall into the background, practically confining it to the relation between soul and body, and allowing real interaction between physical objects, at any rate as a more probable hypothesis.

We have now dealt with the Leibnizian school. This school, while rightly repudiating the principle that all ideas can be accounted for by sense-impressions, failed to realise the necessity of the empirical element for any real, as opposed to formal, knowledge, and, like the empirical school, assumed that all necessary judgments must be analytic.

As applied by Leibniz to causality this principle was interpreted in a way which suggests the view that analysis of the cause will give us the effect not because the effect is already part of the cause, as abstracted from the flow of other events, but because no analysis of the cause could be complete without involving the whole of the universe ; but as the principle presented itself to Kant in its common, narrow interpretation, it was not only quite incapable of application to causality but should logically have led to the invalidity of all judgments except mere tautologies, if these can indeed be called judgments.

---

[1] *Ontologia*, 56–70. [2] *Ib.*, 870–880.

Spinoza. Kant hardly ever refers to Spinoza and does not acknowledge any debt to this great thinker. We may therefore be excused in practically ignoring him in a short preliminary summary of this description. Perhaps the most remarkable point in which Spinoza and Kant resemble each other is in the important conception of the timeless causality of God as ground standing in sharp contrast to the natural causality of science. Further, despite his extreme monism, Spinoza recognised in the case of causality the difficulty in accounting for the particular by means of the universal. He points out that a finite thing cannot be determined by the " absolute nature " of an " attribute of God," for otherwise it would be infinite and eternal. A finite thing implies other finite things of the same genus limiting it ; a thing not limited by anything in the same genus, but possessing, so to speak, all there is of the attribute characterising that genus would be not finite but infinite.[1] At any rate, as a matter of fact, there are finite things of the same genus existing together with different determinations. But these cannot be all due to the attribute of God which forms the basis of that genus, taken in itself, since otherwise they would all be the same, e.g., the nature of different things in space cannot be determined by the general nature of space, since all propositions that follow necessarily from the general nature of space would apply equally to all things in space and so would not account for their difference. Similarly, since all the attributes of God are eternal, anything that follows necessarily from any attribute of God must itself be eternal, otherwise the attribute would exist without it for a certain time and therefore it could not be a necessary consequence of the attribute. So " idea rei singularis, actu existentis, Deum pro causa habet, non quatenus infinitus est, sed quatenus alia rei singularis actu existentis idea affectus consideratur, cujus etiam Deus est causa, quatenus alia tertia affectus est, et sic in infinitum."[2] This involves a recognition that the characteristics of a particular object cannot be logically deduced from purely general propositions about the nature of the whole, but can only be accounted for causally by reference to other such objects, which, if regarded as a mode of real explanation, leads to an infinite regress. How the unity of God's attributes could ever be reconciled with the diversity realised in the finite world is not explained by

[1] *Ethics*, I., 21.   [2] *Ib.*, II., 9 v., I., 28.

this, for, even if the characteristics of particular objects may be explained causally by reference to other such objects, this does not show how the undifferentiated unity of the whole could give rise to any different objects at all. The reference to another object only puts the difficulty a stage further back. With this remark on an interesting anticipation of the problem we may leave our brief historical sketch and pass on to Kant himself.

c

CHAPTER II

The Development of Kant's Conception of Causality up to the Critique of Pure Reason.

It was the discussion of the Leibnizian conception of force that first brought Kant into touch with the problem of causality, just as it seems to have been later the consideration of the interaction of opposing physical forces that first suggested to him (in the treatise on negative quantity) the synthetic character of the causal nexus. In his earliest published work, *Thoughts on the True Valuation of Active Forces* (1747), he defended Leibniz's doctrine of an internal force, which, though an attribute of all extended objects, is itself not deducible from extension. At the same time he insisted that this force ought to be called not " vis motrix " as heretofore, but " vis activa " on the ground that it was exerted just as much in pressing against an object as in actual motion, indeed more so, since in motion there might be little resistance to overcome.[1] He claimed that this view removed the main difficulty concerning the interaction of soul and body, for it was only because force was looked upon as nothing but a capacity to produce motion that it seemed inconceivable that it should affect an immaterial soul, while similar difficulties presented themselves with regard to the action of soul on body.[2] But if it were recognised that the one inevitable result of the exercise of force was change in the internal state of the object on which it was exerted, and that motion was only one of the possible results of that internal change the difficulty would vanish. In fact mind and body must interact, otherwise they could not be in the same space, for on analysis of the conception of space we find that it means nothing but the interaction of substances.[3] Causal are thus conceived as prior to spatial relations, a doctrine which was repudiated in favour of the Newtonian view of absolute space in 1768, only to be quickly replaced in its turn by the critical

[1]*H.*, I., 16.   [2]*Ib.*, 18, 19.   [3]*H.*, I., 19.

doctrine of space as an *a priori* form of our sensibility.   In
the present work Kant goes so far as to suggest the possibility
of a metageometry which would deduce the three-dimensional
character of our space from the laws of motion and show what
kinds of space would result from other possible laws of motion.[1]
The laws of motion Kant here regards as contingent so that
other laws could have been equally well-established by a
fiat of the deity.

In the *Monadologia Physica* (1756) Kant develops further
his doctrine of the dependence of space on force and uses this
doctrine to reconcile the reality of space with the Leibnizian
monadology.   He argues that occupation of space by a
body implies nothing beyond the possession by that body of
a force which excludes from a given extent of space all other
bodies.[2]   Hence the infinite divisibility of space does not involve the infinite divisibility of the bodies which occupy it, for
you could not divide a monad by dividing the space it occupies
any more than you could divide God by dividing the created
world.   However, as in his first work, Kant insists that the
monads cannot be held to exercise a force of repulsion only,
you must postulate a force of attraction also to account for
the cohesion of matter.   Thus we find Kant modifying the
doctrine of Leibniz on Newtonian lines.[3]

Meanwhile in the *Nova Dilucidatio* (1755) Kant had
attacked the doctrine of a pre-established harmony.   Change,
he argues, is impossible in any substance unless that substance
is first acted on by others.[4]   Suppose a substance causally
unconnected with the rest of the world.   Then, if that
substance has a quality, A, at a given moment, that quality
must be wholly determined by internal reasons, i.e., by the
qualities of the substance other than A.   But suppose
A to change to A1.   Then, if the other qualities of the
substance have remained unchanged, the same causes determine it as both A and A1, which is absurd; if they have
changed, the same difficulty occurs over again in trying
to account for their change.   Kant used this difficulty to
refute " idealism " (or, rather, the form of " idealism "
according to which external causes had no part in producing
our perceptions), on the ground that the changes in our perceptions cannot be accounted for by internal causes only.[5]
However, he thinks at the same time that the complete
individuality and independence of each substance precludes

[1]*Ib.*, 21-23.   [2]*Ib.*, 464-6.   [3]*H.*, I., 468.   [4]*Ib.*, 393-4.   [5]*Ib.*, 395.

the view that its external relations are involved in its essence, and hence the only way of accounting for the interaction of substances left open to him is by the introduction of the deity as an external unifying principle to hold the substances in relation by a continuance of the same action which brought them into existence.[1] In the same treatise Kant takes the important step of repudiating the ontological proof (in the form generally accepted) and substituting for it an argument from the nature of possibility.[2] In other sections of the treatise he defends determinism,[3] and denies the possibility of a change in the total quantity of reality (except by miracle) on the ground that the effect cannot contain anything beyond what was already contained in the cause.[4]

A separate current of thought as regards causality which we may trace through all Kant's work consisted in a revolt against the prevailing ideas of teleology. This first found expression in the *General Natural History and Theory of the Heavens* (1755). Here he goes beyond Newton and argues that the same mechanical laws which the latter had used to account for the movements of the planets might also be used to account for their formation. He insists that the mechanistic conception of the physical universe must not be regarded as taking anything away from the idea of God since the laws of nature themselves spring from God. It is the opposite view, he says, that shows a very poor notion of God, because it implies that nature in itself would produce chaos unless corrected by a perpetual miracle, and therefore that God is using means not properly adapted to the end in view.[5]

In *The Sole Ground for a Demonstration of the Being of God* (1763) Kant adopts an attitude towards the argument from design very similar to that of the first Critique. The argument is recommended as clear, natural and convincing, all the more so because it can appeal to the evidence of the senses in citing numerous instances of wonderful adaptation. Subtle metaphysical proofs, he says, as in the first Critique, cannot give us a living faith in God, and it would be absurd to try to base our whole happiness on abstruse subtleties which cannot be understood without a training in metaphysics.[7] What we need is an argument that is intelligible and convincing to all, and this need is supplied by the argument from design. But the latter falls short of a demonstration, for it

[1]*Ib.*, 396 ff. [2]*H.*, I., 375. [3]*Ib.*, 382–7. [4]*Ib.* 389–91. [5]*Ib.*, 315. [6]*H.*, II., 160. [7]*Ib.*, 109.

could, at the most, prove great, not infinite, wisdom and power in God, and it cannot demonstrate the existence of a single creator as opposed to a plurality of creators, though the unity of nature, as far as observed by us, may form the basis of a merely *probable* argument to the unity of its ground.[1] Further, as commonly formulated, it only gives us an architect, working on materials which may be of alien origin ; it does not prove an omnipotent creator, who is the source of matter itself, not only of the form imposed on it.[2] However, Kant proposes to remedy this defect by a modification of the argument in a mechanistic direction. He had departed from the view expressed in his first work so far as to hold that the laws of motion were not contingent but a necessary consequence of the existence of matter. The existence of matter is itself contingent, but, given the existence of any kind of matter, the laws of motion follow necessarily so that it would be impossible to deny them without self-contradiction. " Likewise the laws of motion itself are so conditioned that without them no matter could ever be conceived, and they are so necessary that they can be deduced without the least difficulty and with the greatest clearness from the general and essential properties of any matter."[3] However, the harmonious system of natural laws presupposes a common ground, for it is inconceivable that such a system should have resulted fortuitously from the interaction of heterogeneous elements. Kant was especially impressed by the fact that the same natural law may serve a number of different purposes. For example, the same properties of the air, which enable us to breathe, also make it possible for young animals to be fed by their mother through sucking, enable operations like pumping to be carried out, secure winds from the sea in daytime in hot countries, thus rendering the climate endurable, and ensure the formation of clouds, which, besides adding greatly to the beauty of the sky, enable the land to be watered by rainfall. A similar harmony is observable in knowledge, for we are often able to make the most various deductions from a single property of space or a single law of nature. Such a harmonious system, he argues, surely implies a wise being as its ground, whether the laws are conceived as flowing out of the nature of matter or as imposed on it from without. Only, in the first case, the argument proves not only an architect but a

[1]*Ib.*, 203.   [2]*Ib.*, 165, 167   [3]*H.*, II., 142 , v., also 143, 146, 148.

creator, for if, as Kant has already concluded, the laws of motion are bound up with the existence of matter so that one could not be asserted without the other ; then the being who is the ground of the laws must at the same time be the ground of the existence of matter.   Matter is brought into existence by the divine will, but its " essence," with the system of natural laws it involves, must be regarded as flowing from the divine nature in Spinozistic fashion, and not as being the product of God's choice, i.e., God cannot have conjoined the fundamental laws of nature to matter by a special act of will.[1]   However, in the organic world there are clear signs of a contingent order implying purposive choice on the part of the creator, although even here we have by analogy the right to expect a greater unity between the different laws than has yet been disclosed by science.[2]   We may compare the view of Leibniz, that all the changes undergone at different times by a substance are involved in its essence, and that the choice of God was only exercised in determining which of these essences should be realised in existence. With the more " metaphysical " proof of the existence of God given in this treatise we need not concern ourselves, because it is based not on causality but on the notion of logical possibility, but it is interesting to note that Kant's criticism of the three established arguments for the existence of God corresponds very closely to that given in the first Critique.

This work is one of the group (1763–66) in which Kant definitely broke with the Wolffian philosophy.   We may trace three main lines of thought in the period.   First, while he confesses himself a devoted lover of metaphysics in general,[3] and in a letter to Mendelssohn says that, since he has come to realise the true nature of metaphysics and its place in human knowledge,[4] so far from disparaging it, he has been convinced that the true welfare of the human race depends on it, he is discouraged and irritated by the chaos of conflicting systems, none of them thoroughly grounded.[5]   In *The Only Possible Ground for the Demonstration of the Existence of God* he compares metaphysics to " a dark ocean without lighthouses or shore " ; in *The Inquiry regarding the Evidence of the Principles of Natural Theology and Morals* he likens philosophical discoveries to meteors which shine brilliantly for a moment and then die out, while

[1]*H.*, II., 144 ff., 168–9.   [2]*Ib.*, 150, 161, 168.   [3]*Ib.*, 375.   [4]*Berl.*, I., 6, 7.   [5]*H.*, II., 110.

mathematics *lasts*.[1] But with his despair of existing metaphysical systems is combined the hope of a new metaphysics, which will do for the subject what Newton did for physics, giving philosophers an agreed method and sure criteria of truth. In a letter of 1765 to Lambert, Kant says that he is at last sure of the right method to follow in philosophy, " if we are to avoid that mirage of knowledge which makes the seeker think every moment that he has attained his goal, and, as often as he thinks so, forces him again to retrace his steps."[2] From the failure to observe this method, he holds, springs " the ruinous discord of would-be philosophers, for there is no common standard to bring their endeavours into harmony." The method he now observes is in principle and outline that which is characteristic of the critical philosophy, it is marked by the preliminary investigation of the possibility and conditions of attaining knowledge of the solution of a given problem. " From this time onwards I have always investigated the nature of every task which is set me, so as to see what I must know in order to answer any particular question, and what degree of knowledge is fixed for me by the data." Then the opinion—tentatively expressed in *The Dreams of a Spirit Seer*—grows up, that this new metaphysics must be preceded by a study of the nature and limits of the human intellect, a propaedeutic which was eventually developed into the *Critique of Pure Reason* and in its final form was thought to render any metaphysics beyond itself impossible.[3]

Secondly, he condemned the use of the mathematical method in philosophy. This is the main thesis of the *Inquiry regarding the Evidence of the Principles of Natural Theology and Morals* (1764). Mathematics, he argues, represents its propositions in concreto, i.e., in sensible form, while metaphysics represents them in abstracto, i.e., by means of universal concepts, a distinction which forms the starting-point of the line of thought expressed in the Aesthetic. Further—and this is the most important point of difference —the method of metaphysics is essentially analytic, the method of mathematics essentially synthetic. The mathematician starts with the definition, because he creates the object of his study by the very process of defining it, and does not need to ask whether his definition describes anything real, for he cannot be refuted by the objection, e.g., that there

[1]*Ib.*, 291.   [2]*Berl.*, I., pp. 52–3.   [3]*H.*, II., 375.

are no real triangles given in experience. In metaphysics, on the other hand, the definition, as distinguished from a mere verbal explanation for the sake of clearness, should not come at the beginning, but rather, one might almost say, at the end, for the object of metaphysics is not to make deductions from an assumed and uncriticised basis, but to discover the real, its definitions must describe something objective, otherwise they are fictions, not explanations but arbitrary inventions. The mathematician begins with a simple irreducible conception, involving, if possible, the possession of only a single property like triangularity, and proceeds to make deductions from that (with the help perhaps of other equally simple conceptions), the object of his study thus becoming more and more complex by the addition of new knowledge. The metaphysician starts with a complex, not a simple, conception, which, although frequently applied in common life and thought, is only confusedly known, and by analysis reduces it to a collection of simple and indemonstrable propositions, indemonstrable in fact just because they are simple and so cannot be reduced to or expressed in terms of any other propositions. We do not know the definition to begin with, but this need not prevent us proving with certainty many properties of the concept, and when we have done so we may quickly arrive at the definition, for the latter is but the sum-total of its properties. Metaphysics consists mainly in analysis of the given, mathematics in laying down an arbitrary hypothesis and then seeing what will follow necessarily. Not that Kant then[1] held synthesis to be impossible to the human intellect in metaphysics, on the contrary he suggested the hope that, when the process of analysis had gone far enough, it would be possible to deduce the complex originally given from the simple concepts found to be involved in it.[2] But, in his view, the time had not arrived for that in metaphysics, as it had long ago in mathematics, and meanwhile he could say that " nothing has harmed philosophy more than mathematics, that is, the imitation of mathematics in its method of thought, where it cannot possibly be used."[3]

I have dwelt on this distinction because there is no point in Kant's philosophy where the difference between the Kantian and the Wolffian (or mathematical) method is more clearly shown than in their treatment of causality. Wolff

---

[1]Though he did later.   [2]*H.*, II., 298.   [3]*H.*, II., 291.

starts with a definition,[1] incidentally circular, of the principle
of sufficient reason and then tries to establish its universality
by a proof, also circular.[2] Cause he then defines as " princi
pium actualitatis," " principium " being understood as
logical ground.[3] Now it obviously follows from this definition
plus the analytic view of inference, that the cause contains
the effect in the same sense as a substance contains its attributes so that " posita actione causae efficientis sufficientis
ponitur effectus," but that this definition represents the real
nature of the causal nexus is an assumption not justified
by its author.[4] That the efficient cause is the *logical* ground
of the event it causes and that the consequence is always
actually part of the ground, so that it can be deduced from
it by purely analytic reasoning, is assumed, not proved.
Yet Wolff certainly viewed the connection between cause and
effect as thus analytic. Further he makes a quite unjustifiable
transition from logical to temporal priority,[5] arguing that
because the ground contains in itself that from which the
consequence can be deduced it must " precede " it, precedence
having been defined already as temporal priority.[6] He then,
taking the main point as proved, devotes himself to defining
the different kinds of cause and effect and making deductions
of a tautological nature like—cause being a species of ground
(principium),[7] and the ground of anything being either
internal or external, the cause is internal if the ground is internal, and external if the ground is external,[8] or a contingent
thing must be produced by a cause because by definition the
contingent is that which has the reason of its existence in
something else.[9] Kant, on the other hand, without deciding
in advance the nature of causation by an arbitrary definition,
analyses, in the first Critique, the character of temporal
experience in general and finds that it involves causation
in the sense of necessary sequence. He thus bases his proof
of the universal validity of the principle of causality (in
phenomena) on the analysis of something admitted as given
by all philosophers and not on a definition worded by himself
and simply asserted as valid without any attempt at justification. Nor does he dogmatically lay down what the concept
of causation implies till he has shown in just what sense
causation is involved in all possible experience.

Thirdly, Kant came to realise the synthetic character of
the causal nexus. He starts from a distinction between

[1]*Ontologia*, 56. [2]*Ib*., 60–70. [3]881. [4]898. [5]867. [6]*Ontologia*, 882.
[7]*Ib*., 862. [8]908. [9]310.

logical and real opposition which is first suggested in *The Only Possible Ground for the Demonstration of the Existence of God*[1] and worked out fully in the treatise on Negative Quantity (1763). Logical opposition, he maintains, is impossible in real existents, for nothing that exists can be self-contradictory, real opposition of conflicting forces is not only possible but universal.[2] Logical opposition results in mere negation, real opposition, even when the opposing forces are exactly equal, has a sensible result, i.e., rest or inaction. In logical opposition the predicates cancel each other, in real opposition the conflicting tendencies both remain present in the object and only cancel each other's effects. Further—and this is the most important distinction of all—logical opposition can be discovered *a priori*, real opposition can only be discovered empirically. We can easily see by logical analysis that, for example, the predicate of eternity, when applied to God, must exclude that of mortality, but we cannot see *why*, and so, prior to experience of it, even *that* the movement of one body should prevent the movement of another. We cannot avoid the difficulty by saying that the reason is the attribute of impenetrability which all bodies possess, because that means nothing beyond what we already know, namely, *that* a body excludes all other bodies from the space which it occupies, and does not in the least explain *why* one body should thus exclude others.[3]

The consideration of this last point of difference leads Kant to the similar distinction between logical ground and real ground (or cause). The connection between cause and effect, he concludes, is quite as inaccessible to the logical reason as the connection between opposing forces. " I see very well how a consequent is deduced from its ground according to the law of identity, namely, because it is discovered through analysis of concepts to be contained in the ground.[4] Thus necessity is a ground of immutability, composition a ground of divisibility, infinity a ground of omniscience, etc., and I can clearly understand this bond of union between ground and consequent, since the consequent is really identical with part of the conception of the ground, and inasmuch as it is already contained therein is posited with the ground according to the law of identity. But how something can follow from something else otherwise than in accordance with the law of identity, that is something I should

[1]*H.*, II., 129–130.   [2]*H.*, II., 75–81.   [3]*Ib.*, 105.   [4]*Ib.*, 104.

like to have made clear to me. I call the first kind of ground the logical ground, because its relation to the consequent is logical, i.e., can be clearly realised as following from the law of identity, the second kind of ground I call the actual ground, because, while this relation belongs to my true concepts, there is no judgment possible about its nature." The result of all this is " that the relation of an actual ground to something that is produced or annulled thereby can never be expressed by a judgment but only by a concept.[1] This concept we can indeed reduce by analysis to simpler concepts of actual grounds, but only in such a way that in the final stage all our knowledge of this relation is reduced to simple and unanalysable concepts of actual grounds, the relation of which to their consequents cannot be made intelligible." In other words, we can only discover and simplify, not explain or logically deduce, natural laws. Kant might have added that the mere fact that the effect is often, perhaps always, posterior in time to the cause, proves that it cannot be derivable from the latter by any analytic proccess of thought, for, if it were thus derivable, it would actually be contained in the cause, and the two would therefore exist simultaneously. The relation of cause and effect is certainly not to be made a species of the relation between subject and predicate.

" A relation of the logical ground and consequent always constitutes an affirmative judgment, in which the predicate is the consequent and the subject the ground.[2] In the actual relation of cause and effect this is never the case." The non-logical character of the connection between cause and effect, or at any rate of our knowledge of it, seems to have been already realised by Kant in the period to which Benro Erdmann gives the name of " Dogmatismus," (i.e., prior to 1762), as, in one[3] of the " Reflexionen " published for that period it is remarked that we can only know the connection of cause and effect a posteriori, not a priori. There was nothing new in the recognition that we are unable to see a priori what there is in special kinds of causes which produces a special kind of effect ; what is new in Kant and Hume is the thoroughness with which this line of criticism is carried out and its logical grounding on the absence of identity between cause and effect, which debars the latter from being deducible a priori by means of the law of non-contradiction, also its extension to the general principle

[1]H., II., 106. [2]Ib., 719. [3]Erdmann, Reflexionen 727, (period of critical empiricism).

that every change must have a cause. This last, the most important step, had, however, not yet been made by Kant in the period we are considering. In the Dissertation of 1770 he does not think it necessary to prove the general principle of causality and seems to apply it without question to things-in-themselves, not only to things as they appear to us in space and time ; and in the works we have just been discussing he likewise makes no reference to the problems connected with the general principle. As yet ignoring these difficulties, Kant now concludes : " There are synthetic propositions derived from experience, so ' principia prima synthetica,' to these belong also the axioms of the mathematics of space, ' principia rationalia ' cannot possibly be synthetic."[1] The reason for this conclusion is that repeated briefly in the passage at the end of the Analogies of Experience where Kant says that a dogmatic proof of the analogies, i.e., a proof by analysis of concepts, is impossible because " we may analyse as much as we like, we shall never pass from one object and its existence to the existence of another, or to the mode of its existence, by means of these concepts only,"[2] and in *The Dreams of a Spirit Seer*—" For our laws of reasoning (Vernunftregeln) only apply to comparison according to the principles of identity and contradiction.[3] In so far as something is a cause, then as a result of something there is posited *something else*, and therefore there is no relation of identity to be found between them. So likewise, if I refuse to regard the same event as a cause, no contradiction arises, for, when something is posited, to deny something else involves no contradiction." In all this, as in Kant's difficulties with regard to the possibility of proving the general principle of causality, as we have already seen, the influence of Hume may be traced.

The Dissertation of 1770 marks a great step forward in Kant's view of space and time, but not in his view of the categories. As regards the former he takes up practically the position of the Aesthetic, but he still believes in the possibility of discovering positive and significant truths about the thing-in-itself. He distinguishes between real and logical reasoning : in real reasoning we create our concepts by pure thought, in logical reasoning thought accepts them as data and is limited to the functions of subordinating them to each other and bringing them together subject to the law of

[1] *Erdmann, Reflexionen*, 498.   [2] *Critique of Pure Reason*, B., 264.
[3] *H.*, II., 378.

contradiction.[1] Of phenomena we can only have a logical, not a real, understanding,[2] but of things as objects of pure thought we can have both a logical and a real understanding.[3] We can, however, only think of them by means of general concepts and can never hope to realise their nature as individual, because in order to realise anything as individual we must first subject it to the conditions of space and time, which in this case is quite illegitimate.[4] Metaphysics consists in the study of the principles governing the use of pure intelligence and should be preceded by a propaedeutic fixing the distinction between intelligible and sensible knowledge.[5] The concepts of metaphysics are discovered by abstracting the general laws according to which the intellect proceeds in thought and are not to be deduced from a study of sensible experience. Examples of these concepts are existence, possibility, necessity, cause, substance. Nevertheless Kant recognises apparently that the relation of cause and effect always implies time, and, in the case of external objects, space, an admission quite inconsistent with his inclusion of cause among "metaphysical" concepts.[6] In the last section there occurs another significant anticipation of the Critique. There he calls postulates like the assumption of science that everything in the physical world occurs according to natural laws, the principle of parsimony of causes and the principle of the indestructibility of matter, "subjective" principles of reason and says that they are rules of method which we must observe in research if we are to obtain the best results, but not, necessarily, valid truths about the objective world, thus suggesting the *Ideas of Reason* of the Dialectic. It is interesting to note that he even goes further than the Critique in calling a "subjective" principle of reason what he in the Critique claims to prove *a priori* as the real meaning of the category of substance or at any rate its most important application, i.e., the indestructibility of matter. However, as mentioned above, he continues to regard causality as a principle uniting things-in-themselves, and his theory regarding it here is very similar to that given in the dissertation of 1755. Thus he argues from the unity of the world to an "ens extramundanum" as common cause, on the ground that the essence of a substance can never determine its causal relations with other substances.

[1]95. [2]12. [3]6. [4]10. [5]8. [6]*H.*, II., 412. [7]92, 16–22.

The points of difference between the view of the Dissertation and the view of the Critique as to causality are patent. In both the concept is held to be due to a creative activity of mind, but in the Dissertation it nevertheless tells us the truth about a reality totally independent of human experience, though knowable, at least partially, by human intelligence ; in the Critique it is only valid for experience in time, just because without it such experience would be impossible. According to the Dissertation there is only a logical use of concepts possible in relation to phenomena but a " real " use also in relation to things-in-themselves ; according to the Critique there is only a logical use of concepts possible in relation to things-in-themselves but a " real " use also in relation to phenomena, i.e., as determining the conditions of all possible experience—the exact opposite of the earlier view. According to the Dissertation the *a priori* concepts like cause are discovered by abstracting from all sensible experience, according to the Critique their apriority depends on the fact that they underlie and are implied in all sensible experience.

While not satisfied with the positive results of the Dissertation, Kant held that he had now laid the foundations of the new metaphysic in the sense that he had discovered the way to the goal and had only to march forward along the newly opened route to reach it. In a letter written to Lambert in September, 1770, he says—" I flatter myself that about a year ago I attained conceptions that I need never seek to change but only to extend, conceptions by which all manner of metaphysical problems can be tested by quite sure and easy criteria and a certain decision reached as to how far they are soluble or not."[1] Certainly it was in the Dissertation that Kant first entered on the " critical " path, if, as seems right, we understand by the " critical " method the solution of difficulties by means of the principle that our knowledge must be interpreted as knowledge of objects of possible experience, for the Dissertation is, in the main, an attempt to solve the difficulties involved in the conceptions of space and time by pointing out that space and time have no meaning except in reference to our experience. Nor did Kant ever retrace the main step made in the Dissertation.

But the letter to Herz of February 21st, 1772, represents a still more important change in Kant's position.[2] The

---

[1]*Berl. ed.*, I., p. 93. [2]*Berl. ed.*, I., pp. 124–5.

Dissertation, he here points out, has left unanswered the questions as to how the reference of our representations to objects can be justified and in particular how we can justify the application of categories, or forms of our thought, to objects. Knowledge would be quite intelligible if we were either wholly active or wholly passive—if we either created the objects of knowledge by representing them, or, alternatively, if these objects merely impressed their likeness on us, and our mind did not actively add to the representation but merely accepted what was given. But neither is the case —our mind is partly active in that it assumes the applicability to things of its own laws of thought, partly passive in that it cannot have knowledge unless it has data given from without. To put it in different words, concepts like substance and cause are essential factors in all knowledge, yet neither substance nor cause are given as data of sense, therefore we must suppose them to be laws of thought ; but, if they are only laws of our thought, how can we justify their application to a reality external to our individual selves ? Such concepts seem neither to produce nor be produced by the objects to which they are applied. " The pure concepts of understanding can then neither be abstracted from sensations, nor express our receptivity of representations through sense, but must have their source in the nature of the soul, though only in so far as the latter is neither affected by the object nor produces the object itself. In the Dissertation I was content to express the nature of intellectual representations in merely negative terms, by saying that they were not modifications of the soul through the object. But how a representation can refer to an object at all without being in any degree caused by it I omitted to discuss. I had said, sensible representations present things as they appear, intellectual representations as they are. But how are these things presented to us, if not through the way in which they affect us ? If such intellectual representations depend on our inner activity, whence comes the agreement they are to have with objects, objects which have yet not been produced by them ? How can we hold the axioms of pure reason to agree with these objects except on the basis of experience ? " We must note that Kant does not yet distinguish the application of categories to things-in-themselves from their application to phenomena.

From here onwards to the first Critique the movement of thought depends on the twofold discovery that the categories presuppose perception for their application, and that perception of objects presupposes the categories. Conception without perception is empty, *i.e.*, without content, perception without conception blind, *i.e*, not cognition at all, and hence no possible foundation of judgment. Since blind perceptions and concepts without content cannot be real facts, this view, carried to its logical conclusion, implies that the separation between conception and perception cannot be absolute, that neither can ever be totally out of relation to the other, though Kant would be chary of admitting this.

How he proposed to meet the difficulty involved in the application of the categories at the time of the above letter he does not say, but he expresses a rash hope that he will be able to complete the Critique, as far as regards the theoretic reason, in three months. As a matter of fact he took nine years and was driven to hurry through the final stages of its composition by the fear of never completing it at all. This delay he ascribes mainly to the difficulties involved in the transcendental deduction of the categories.

We may conclude by summarising the development of the critical idea in Kant's own words. "This has not always been my view of this branch of learning" (*i.e.*, the old metaphysics). "At first I learnt from it what most commended itself to me. In some points I thought I could add something original to the common treasure, in others I found something to improve, but always with the purpose of thereby extending the scope of dogmatic knowledge. For that doubt, proclaimed with such boldness, seemed to me to be so very like ignorance in the guise of reason, that I gave no hearing to it. If you strive in your meditations with real earnestness to attain truth, there comes at last a time when you no longer spare your own work, even though it may seem that you deserve well of science for it. You subject unconditionally to criticism whatever you have learnt from elsewhere or thought yourself. It was only after a long time that I discovered by these means that the whole dogmatic system was dialectical.[1] But I still sought some certainty, if not in regard to objects, at any rate in regard to the nature and the bounds of this mode of knowledge I found gradually that many of the propositions which we regarded as objectively valid are really only subjective, i.e., include the conditions, under which alone we can have insight or understanding of the objects. It was this alone that

---

[1]*I.e.*, based on subtle fallacies.

made me cautious, but it did not yet teach me the truth. For since there really are *a priori* items of knowledge, which are not merely analytic but extend the bounds of our knowledge, I suffered from the lack of a systematised Critique of Pure Reason, and above all a canon for the latter, for I still always hoped to find the method of extending dogmatic knowledge by pure reason. For this purpose I needed the understanding how *a priori* knowledge in general is possible. Before the Disputation" (Dissertation, 1770) "I had already the idea of the influence of the subjective conditions of knowledge on the objective, and after that of the distinction between sensible and intelligible, but the latter was with me merely negative. By this treatise[1] of mine the value of all my previous metaphysical writings is totally destroyed. I shall only strive now to save the correctness of the general idea."

[1] *I.e.*, the *Critique of Pure Reason.*

D

CHAPTER III

The Transcendental Deduction

WE shall now proceed to the mainspring of Kant's philosophy, namely the *Critique of Pure Reason.* While the special proof of causality occurs in the Analytic of Principles, it presupposes the results of the transcendental deduction, and we must therefore first summarise the latter. The main purpose of the deduction is, in a word, to show that knowledge of succession implies self-identity on the one hand and knowledge of objects on the other, that self-identity and knowledge of objects likewise imply each other, and that the unity in both depends on necessary laws of connection, which are therefore the indispensable conditions to which all objects of experience (*i.e.*, empirical knowledge) must conform. The last point is not fully developed till the Analogies, and little more than suggested here ; the main weight of the deduction is thrown on the second point, the close relation and interdependence of self and objects, especially in the second edition.

There can be no doubt that the passage with which we are about to deal is one of the most important in the whole history of thought. It appeared at a moment when philosophy had been brought to a complete standstill and was in the sorest need of some such new light. Both the German rationalists and the English empiricists had failed, not only to supply a rational justification of such fundamental beliefs as the existence of a world independent of the individual consciousness or the principle that every physical change must be caused, but even to explain the very possibility of acquiring fresh knowledge (as opposed to particular unconnected experiences), so that philosophy seemed to be incapable of anything but either formulating analytic judgments which were known already or inventing synthetic judgments which, just because they were synthetic, seemed unjustified and unjustifiable. Not only was philosophy held up by contradic-

40

tions at every turn but had no glimpse of a method which seemed to provide even a possible chance of progress. Now Kant claims to have, at one stroke, justified the fundamental presuppositions of science and ordinary life, and discovered a totally new method of procedure in philosophy, a method by which it is possible to prove, with what he regarded as mathematical exactitude and certainty, a system of really synthetic *a priori* principles and to establish a complete philosophy of all that concerns human experience directly. Of this philosophy the foundation is the transcendental deduction of the categories.

Kant introduces the deduction proper by pointing out that there are only two conditions under which representations could correspond to their objects, and so correspond as a necessary consequence of their nature.[1] They might do so if they were wholly determined by their objects and impressed on our mind without any activity on our part so that we could be sure we had not illegitimately tampered with the evidence about the external world. This is the case with that element in experience which we call sensation, but we cannot hold it to be true of the *a priori*, for it would be inconsistent with the necessity of the latter. Or again, if we by a mere act of representation determined the existence of the object represented, the problem of the correspondence of representation and object could not arise. Now it is obvious that we do not create things by representing them, but unless they are capable of representation they cannot be known by us. To be known by us they must conform to the conditions. without which awareness of them would be impossible to use But awareness involves two factors—(1) perception, (2) the thought of an object to which we refer our perceptions. The *a priori* forms of sensibility condition perception and are therefore valid for phenomena. Similarly, if it can be shown that the categories condition the thought of an object, they too will have been shown to be valid for all phenomena. Further, such a deduction alone can solve the problem of the categories, for no empirical deduction could possibly be consistent with their necessity, yet this necessity is a fact, since it is the basis of a body of truths whose reality we cannot deny, *i.e.*, the *a priori* principles of pure science (among which the primary position would be held by the principles of substance, cause and reciprocity).[2]

[1] B 125-6 (=A 92-4).   [2] B., 128 ; contrast, *e.g.*, B., 120 (=A88).

Now as the deduction, at any rate as given in the first edition, is by no means a homogeneous structure but is probably made up of parts composed at different times, a discussion of the relations of which is not necessary for our present purpose, it seems best to proceed by giving a summary of the main lines of the argument as a whole, taking the versions of both editions together as supplementing and correcting each other and trying to follow its logical order and implications rather than the actual order of its statement.

Kant's primary datum is that we are aware of a changing manifold. Now, although Descartes' " I think, therefore I am," as it stands, cannot be held to prove the existence of a self in the sense of a permanent subject for our changing perceptions, it does prove the impossibility of doubting the occurrence of immediate experience. A man cannot doubt whether there is anything at all, because the doubt itself is something. Nor can it be doubted that there is succession, at least in what we call our immediate experience, at any rate no sceptic has been found to doubt it. So, as succession obviously implies plurality, we are conscious of a manifold, and this at least is a certainty. We can at least make the judgment, " There is a manifold passing away in time."

But, Kant argues, we cannot be conscious of a manifold as a manifold unless we can combine its diverse elements in thought. To do so, a threefold synthesis is required.[1] The manifold being in time, its perception must occupy a period of time, we must perceive first a, then b, then c, before we are aware of $a\ b\ c$, but we must also be capable of combining our different perceptions into a single whole. This Kant calls " the synthesis of apprehension in perception " (Anschauung). But, if we had forgotten a when we came to be conscious of b, we obviously could not think of a and b together. Therefore, for awareness of the manifold to be possible, each perception must recall the preceding ones in memory. Hence we get a second synthesis, " the synthesis of reproduction in imagination." But it would be useless remembering a, if I were not conscious that it belonged to the same process as b ; in order to go on counting I must be conscious not only that I have already counted 1, 2, 3, 4, but that the four units are linked together in a single process which I am to continue. This gives us " the synthesis of recognition in concepts." (In summarising this chapter later

[1] A 99–103.

Kant described the three empirical syntheses as belonging to empirical perception, association and recognition, respectively, with a transcendental synthesis corresponding in each case, namely pure perception, the pure synthesis of imagination and transcendental apperception, and it is impossible to harmonise the two classifications perfectly ; but this makes no difference to the main principle of the argument.)[1]

This passage constitutes the chief part of what Kant in his preface to the first edition calls the subjective deduction. There he describes it as psychological and consequently disparages its importance. "This discussion, which is somewhat deeply grounded, has two sides.[2] The one refers to the objects of pure understanding, and is meant to establish and make intelligible the objective validity of its *a priori* concepts ; just for this reason is it indeed essential to my purpose. The other is meant to deal with the pure understanding itself, its possibility and the cognitive faculties on which it depends, and so to treat it from the subjective side. Now, although this exposition is of great importance for my main purpose, yet it is not an essential part of it. For the main question always is—What and how much can understanding and reason know without the help of experience,[3]—and not—How is the faculty of thought itself possible ? " Now we shall later have to criticise the psychological elements involved in the deduction, and we shall then do well to remember this warning and not think that we can refute its fundamental doctrines by pointing out the defects of its psychology. Here, for instance, the important point about the doctrine of the synthesis is not its actual occurrence as a psychical event, but the discovery that consciousness of its results is implied in consciousness of succession. Being a condition, not an object of, consciousness and therefore unconscious, or at the most semi-conscious, itself, the threefold synthesis can only be described in terms of its results for consciousness. It is only as the unification of the manifold for consciousness that the synthesis has any meaning at all. But while we should be careful not to overstress the importance of what is purely psychological in the deduction, this does not mean that we should ignore those portions of it which are couched in a psychological form. We cannot rigidly divide the deduction into two parts, one

[1]*A.*, 115. [2]*A.*, X. XI. [3]*C.f. H.*, IV., pp. 364–6 (footnote).

epistemological and essential, the other psychological and unessential, for important epistemological truths are sometimes
expressed in psychological form.   This is especially the case
with the present passage, and in the remark in the preface
about the " subjective " deduction which we have quoted,
Kant hardly seems to do justice to his own argument.   For it
is not by empirical introspection only, or ordinary hypothetical reasoning, that he arrives at the threefold synthesis,
but by logical analysis of what must be involved in any
possible experience, an analysis in principle the same as that
which characterises the " objective " deduction ; and the
proof of the occurrence of the synthesis is essentially a proof
that consciousness of the manifold as connected, or as having
a synthetic unity, is necessary if we are to be conscious of
the manifold as a manifold at all.   Further, it is the clearest
statement of this doctrine in the whole deduction, and
although in other passages the synthesis is formally different,
this does not alter the validity of the proof that cognition
of anything always involves consciousness of it as a connected
object of thought.   Without such consciousness judgment
would be impossible, for to judge about anything we must
recognise it as " so-and-so," we must know it as it is or at
least ascribe some definite character to it, whether rightly or
wrongly.   But since what we judge about is never anything
absolutely simple and unrelated, internally and externally,
the consciousness that accompanies judgment always
involves the holding together by the mind of a diversity in
unity, it is always consciousness of something as having
different but related aspects, in other words, it is consciousness
of an object.   Without such consciousness we might still
feel, like animals, but we could not know our feelings as
feelings and consequently we could not judge either about
them or about anything else.   A philosophy that denied
this consciousness would be forced to be a dumb philosophy,
and so would be a contradiction in terms.

Now for Kant the presupposition of all consciousness is
self-identity (the transcendental unity of apperception).
On this he lays great stress, and it is treated almost as an
axiom by him.   This unity of self-consciousness clearly
follows from the twofold doctrine that we can know nothing,
even our perceptions, except as an object held in unity by
the relating activity of the mind, and that self-identity is
for us only expressed in this unity, might in fact almost be
described as but another aspect of this unity.   " This

complete identity in the apperception of a manifold, given in perception, involves a synthesis of representations, and is only possible through the consciousness of this synthesis.[1] For the empirical consciousness, which accompanies the various representations, is in itself dispersed and has no reference to the identity of the subject. This reference does not consist in the fact that I accompany each representation with consciousness, but in the fact that I *add* one representation to another and am conscious of their synthesis. So it is only because I am able to combine a manifold of given representations in a single consciousness that it is possible for me to represent to myself the identity of my consciousness in these representations." In other words Kant held that the only path to knowledge of our self-identity was through knowledge of the connection of diverse elements in all objects of our thought, but if it is the only path, it is obviously *a* path to the knowledge of self-identity. Our identity as conscious selves is for Kant no unproved assumption, but is deduced from the possibility of being conscious of anything related as such—and all cognition is of the related. The argument just quoted may by mere reversal be turned into an argument from our cognition of representations (*Vorstellungen*),[2] *not* merely physical objects, to the transcendental unity of apperception as the condition necessarily presupposed therein. The passage on the threefold synthesis shows how all cognition, even if what is cognised be a mere manifold, involves consciousness of a related diversity. But to be conscious of anything as constituted by a relation of diverse elements we must clearly be conscious of these elements as united, and this means that they must be united in a single consciousness, which is just what is meant by the transcendental unity of apperception.

According to this view, then, the logical starting-point of the deduction is consciousness of a manifold of perceptions succeeding each other in time, and neither consciousness of physical objects nor consciousness of self, or rather, we should say, the starting-point is consciousness of a manifold in time, for the expression " consciousness of a manifold of perceptions " seems to imply that they are already referred to a self as its perceptions. The view seems supported by general consideration both of the text of the transcendental deduction

[1]B., 133. [2]The footnote, to B., 133, also seems to imply that the transcendental unity of apperception is realised not only in awareness of physical objects but even in awareness of representations as such.

and of the main principles of the critical philosophy. It applies better to the first than to the second edition standpoint. In the first edition the problem of the physical objects is not introduced till it has been proved that consciousness of a manifold of representations involves a synthesis. While the argument for the threefold synthesis starts at A 99, it is not till A 104 that the question is raised as to what is meant by referring representations to objects, nor till A 107 that the transcendental unity of apperception is introduced at all. But even in the second edition, as in the first, Kant insists, for instance,[1] that consciousness of the " pure manifold " of perception, space and time, implies an *a priori* synthesis.[2] Also, as Professor Kemp Smith has pointed out, it is on the whole what are probably the later passages in the Critique —*i.e.*, the chapter on Schematism, the section on Inner Sense in the second edition deduction, the passage describing the threefold synthesis—that lay most emphasis on the temporal factor.[3]

Even judgments about mere perceptions certainly seem to imply the objective unity of apperception. As judgments about what is related it seems to us that they must express a unity in diversity and must imply a synthesis and the categories as much as any judgments. In saying this we are aware that we have touched upon a very difficult and disputable subject, but while it is one that we must not shirk we feel that in a later chapter we shall be in a better position to make some not wholly inadequate attempt to find our way through the chaos. Here we shall just state our position that, while the very possibility of judgments about mere perceptions implies a not-self in contrast to which we recognise our perceptions as " mere perceptions," yet, as taken in relative isolation, what Kant calls " judgments of perception " must be treated like judgments about the physical world, *i.e.*, be held to involve the transcendental unity of apperception, the transcendental synthesis or syntheses and the categories as schematised. Two objections may be raised to this point of view. It may be said (1) that so-called judgments of perception like " I see green " are not judgments at all. That is, they do not possess the essential characteristic of judgment, a claim to objectivity. (2) That it is impossible to apply the categories to the empirical self or, at the very least, impossible to justify such an application

---

[1] *V.*, below, p. 49.   [2] *B.*, 160-1, 154 ; *cf.*, *A.*, 100-1.
[3] *Commentary*, p. 242.

of them.   These objections we hope to discuss later when
we have seen something of the meaning of the categories
of relation and of the character of the proofs Kant gives
of them.   But in any case it seems impossible to deny that consciousness of perceptions, as consciousness of something involving
different elements in relation, implies a synthesis, in the sense
of holding together diversity in unity in one consciousness,
and this, as we have seen, implies the transcendental unity
of apperception.   The further question as to whether what
Kant calls " judgments of perception " are objective and
involve the categories we must postpone for the present.

To return to the proof of the transcendental unity of
apperception, we have concluded that this unity is meant
to be deduced from consciousness of a manifold of successive
irepresentations.   That the proof is not made more explicit
as strange, but Kant is less concerned with this aspect of the
argument than with the limitations of our knowledge of the
self and the deduction of an objective world involving necessary laws.   There was little need of defending self-identity
at the time, but great need of showing the dependence of self-
consciousness on consciousness of objects and the consequent
limitations of the former.   Further, Kant with his strong
private opinions on the spiritual and unitary nature of the
self was apt to treat self-identity as an axiom.

It is quite clear, however, that he means to argue that the
transcendental unity of apperception is implied in all consciousness of objects.[1]   But, if " objects " is taken in the
sense of physical objects, Kant is basing his whole argument
on a doctrine that had been challenged by Berkeley and
Hume and is not really starting from first principles.   He
shows both that self-identity implies consciousness of objects
and that consciousness of objects implies self-identity, but
unless there is an independent proof of the objective
validity of one or both of these correlated terms the argument
is based on a vicious circle.   For both self-identity and knowledge of the physical world had been attacked by the sceptic,
and the latter could not be refuted simply by asserting them
without proof even though this assertion was accompanied
by the demonstration that the two imply each other.   Such
a proof is, however, clearly implied in the doctrine, certainly
maintained here by Kant, that all cognition implies a syn-

[1] E.g., B, 137, 143 (footnote).

thesis.   This constitutes as valid a proof as can be given of any principle, for it seems that proof must in the last resort rest on the dilemma—believe this or believe nothing—and, in this case, if it is shown that the transcendental unity of apperception is implied in the very possibility of knowledge, the alternatives are to believe it or to believe nothing.   It is only if the premiss of the deduction is the recognition of the manifold of perceptions as a manifold that it is based on a principle admitted by the sceptic.   The latter takes his stand on " judgments of perception " and refuses to go any further, so his position can only be turned by showing that even these imply self-identity, consciousness of an object[1] (i.e., the empirical self), and categories like causality.   Once this is done he is logically bound either to abandon belief even in " judgments of perception," and so in any judgments whatever, in which case he is no longer an adversary to be feared since he cannot criticise us without judging and he has debarred himself from the right of making any judgment whatever, or to accept all the main points which Kant was seeking to prove.   He must either become like other men or cease to speak at all.   So, unless consciousness of the manifold of perceptions as a manifold is the starting-point, the argument is inconclusive, and it seems impossible to believe that Kant can have failed to see either the logical necessity of adopting this as his premiss or the fact that the proof in question is actually implied in his doctrine.

There is no doubt that, in speaking of " objects," Kant was chiefly concerned with physical objects, but the view that even judgments as to our perceptions are held to imply the synthesis and the transcendental unity of apperception is supported by the following points in the actual text of the deduction in addition to the more general considerations adduced above.

1. In both editions the argument begins with the term " representations," not " objects."   In the first edition Kant expressly says that representations, as subject to inner sense, already imply a synthesis, whether they be produced by the working of external objects on us or not.[2]   In the second edition he opens with the phrase *Das Mannigfaltige der Vorstellungen,* and then argues for the necessity of their combination being effected by the understanding and not merely given in sense.[3]   In Section 16, which contains the

---

[1]In the sense of a necessarily connected system.   [2]*A.,* 98–9.   [3]*B.,* 129.

most essential part of the deduction, the word *Vorstellungen* occurs constantly, *Object* never, *Gegenstand* only once and then only in the remark that combination (*Verbindung*) cannot be given in the objects (*liegt nicht in den Gegenständen*), but must be contributed by the understanding, a point which is not involved in the present question.[1] In B 137 he also argues to the unity of apperception from " Vorstellungen " and not from " objects."

2. In both editions he insists that consciousness of the forms of perception, space and time, even apart from any particular perception of objects, implies the synthesis and the transcendental unity of apperception.[2] Synthesis is viewed as a condition by which alone perception itself is rendered possible.

3. In B 137 Kant tries to prove the unity of apperception by the argument that without it " representations of perception " could never be " combined " (*verbunden*) in a consciousness, " for without that nothing can be thought or known thereby, since the given representations do not have the act of apperception, *I think*,[3] in common,[4] and would not be held together thereby in a single self-consciousness." It is important to note here that—(1) the argument starts with " representations," not with objects, (2) the necessity of representations being *combined* is made the ground of the doctrine of the unity of apperception. This is also done explicitly in A 107, and in B 143 Kant declares that the proof of the transcendental unity of apperception given in Section 17 rests on the fact that " it is through this alone that the *unity* of perception (*Einheit der Anschauung*) is possible."

We must, however, distinguish between self-identity and *de facto* self-consciousness. It is the former rather than the latter that Kant was anxious to prove, and by it is meant that unity which subsists between the different elements contained in our field of attention, which unity alone makes it possible for us to unite them in any specific way. To put the argument in a few words—in order to know the particular relation between A and B I must think A and B as together, but to think A and B as together I must be the same self in thinking B as in thinking A. (This does not of course imply that the transcendental unity of apperception can be realised

----

[1] *B.*, 134. [2] *A.*, 100–2, *B.*, 154, 160. [3] For Kant " I think " practically = the transcendental unity of apperception. [4] *i.e.*, the act of apperception is not like an ordinary universal, which may qualify each one of many particulars taken by itself.

without there being any particular relation between A and B—that would be quite against critical principles—but that any particular relation there is between them is only thinkable as involving their combination by the transcendental unity of apperception.) The degree in which the knower is actually conscious of his selfhood depends on quite other factors, and Kant is always very careful to distinguish between empirical and transcendental self-consciousness. Transcendental self-consciousness (or unity of apperception) is simply the unity involved in representations being known as together or being joint members of the same field of cognition, empirical self-consciousness is the knowledge which comes from discriminating attention to that aspect of representations by which they constitute the self as discovered in introspection in preference to that aspect by which they represent the external world. That we are actually conscious of the transcendental unity of apperception—(whether in the way of " enjoyment " or of " contemplation," to use Professor Alexander's phraseology) —is not the point which it is necessary to prove. " It should be remembered that the mere representation, I, in relation to all others (the collective unity of which would be impossible without it) constitutes the transcendental consciousness.[1] It does not matter whether this representation is clear (empirical consciousness) or obscure, nor even whether it occurs at all ; but the possibility of the logical form of all knowledge necessarily depends on the relation to this apperception *as a faculty*." For this reason I have always chosen to use the term " self-identity" rather than " self-consciousness " as the equivalent of the transcendental unity of apperception.

But the main theme of the deduction is the close relation between self and objects. If the fact that we are conscious of objects proves self-identity, conversely self-identity can only be known as the presupposition of consciousness of objects, and has for us no meaning apart from the synthesis by which we unify the manifold so as to constitute consciousness of objects. (We do not understand by an " object " only a physical object but anything having that systematic diversity-in-unity which enables it to be known. In that sense of object the transcendental unity of apperception is only realised in consciousness of objects, for the unity is impossible without the diversity just as the diversity is impossible without the unity. That is, all objects of cognition must contain both a given, empirical and a formal, *a priori* element.) It is only in relation to the synthesis that the self can be regarded as identical, for its identity is only known as presupposed in the synthesis which is necessary to all knowledge.

It might be thought that this was only an appeal to ignorance, but that is not the case, for the unchanging identity of the self is no possible *object* of experience, and therefore, in relation to possible experience, at any rate, (whether any knowledge be attainable by us outside that sphere or not), it can only be known as the subject which is the presupposition of all experience, for to be known at all in relation to experience it must be either a particular object in the empirical content of our minds or a presupposition of all experience. Further it is just as true that, in order to be aware that in perceiving A I am the same self who perceived B, I must be conscious of the combination of A and B in a single process of thought as that, to be aware of A and B together, I must be the same self when I perceive A as when I perceive B. Besides, for Kant, the transcendental unity of apperception was an absolutely identical unity which could include no diversity, and we could therefore only be aware of it in opposition to the diversity of perceived data. Self-identity and consciousness of objects are strictly correlative and imply each other. This is shown by the very names applied to them, the former being called the analytic and the latter the synthetic unity of apperception. Neither can strictly be called prior to the other, and Kant quite legitimately argues at one time from self-identity to the consciousness of objects, at another from the consciousness of objects to self-identity, thus showing their mutal implication. The two are regarded as developing *pari passu* so that complete knowledge of self would be impossible without complete knowledge of the objective world. Among " objects " Kant includes the empirical self and not only physical objects but he also holds that explicit consciousness of our representations as ours, *i.e.*, consciousness of the empirical self, so far from being the psychological and logical starting-point from which we infer an external world, is logically correlative and psychologically posterior to consciousness of physical objects. Logically the two are correlative because

　　1. I can only be conscious of my representations as *my*

representations in relation and opposition to a not-self, just as I can only be conscious of the not-self in opposition to the self. The self, both transcendental and empirical, implies a not-self.

2. While the not-self is only revealed to me by means of my representations, it is equally true that my representations have no content apart from what is given by the not-self, though owing to the moulding action of the self as a whole the content is not what it is in the not-self.

Psychologically, it cannot be denied that the introspective self-consciousness implied in awareness of my representations as my representations is both in the individual and race a late development preceded by long reflection on the objects that surround us, although no doubt in a sense this consciousness is implied as latent in all consciousness of objects.

By this line of reasoning Kant sought to prove (1) that consciousness of my representations as such implies consciousness of physical objects ; (2) that self-identity and consciousness of the objective, empirical element in knowledge imply each other ; (3) that we can never hope to gain knowledge either of an object out of relation to all subjects or of a subject out of relation to all objects. (The agnosticism[1] of this last point need not worry us, for, even if there be such a subject or such an object, it can, by definition, have no significance for our world whatever and so need not be taken into account by us.)

He had already proved (4) that consciousness of any manifold as such implies a synthesis and the transcendental unity of apperception.

It has been objected that the argument involves a vicious circle because sometimes consciousness of objects is deduced from the transcendental unity of apperception, and at other times, *vice versa*, the latter is deduced from the former.[2] But, when two facts (A and B) imply each other it is quite legitimate to argue first from A to B and then from B to A, indeed this is the only way of proving that each implies the other. Of course this does not establish the actuality of either unless one or both has been independently proved, but this is the case, at any rate if we are right in our contention that Kant has shown both to be implied in the

[1]This is not meant as a denial of the value of the doctrine of the thing-in-itself as the *Whole*, a doctrine suggested but not developed by Kant.   [2]Mr. Prichard, *Kant's Theory of Knowledge*, pp. 191, ff.

possibility of making the judgment " There is a manifold in time," a judgment which even the sceptics would admit. While it must be remembered that the results of the deduction given above are presupposed in the argument of the Analogies, we shall now proceed to deal with points that more closely concern our special subject, causality. One of the main objects of the transcendental deduction is to prove the universality of necessary connection in phenomena, and of the categories of necessary connection causality is the most important. Hence the importance for our subject of the transcendental deduction as the basis of the special proofs of causality. Now from the position we have arrived at three lines of approach to the proof of necessary connection are suggested.

The first line of approach is not more than hinted at in the transcendental deduction. The development of the proof is left to the Analogies, especially the second. The point is that all judgment and all cognition imply a distinction between the objective and the subjective, and this in turn implies necessity.[1] In the second-edition deduction Kant adopts a new definition of judgment as " the mode of referring given cognitions[2] to the *objective* unity of apperception " (*die Art, gegebene Erkenntnisse zur objectiven Einheit der Apperception zu bringen*). The purpose of the copula is to distinguish between objective and subjective unity. The emphasis is here laid on the objective unity, and Kant here suggests, without establishing it in detail, that this objective unity implied in judgment would be impossible without principles of necessary connection. " For it "(the copula) " expresses the relation of the representations to the original (*ursprüngliche*) apperception and their *necessary unity*, even if the judgment is itself empirical and so contingent, *e.g.*, the bodies are heavy.[3] By this I do not mean that these representations belong *together necessarily* in empirical perception, but that they belong together *through the necessary unity* of apperception in the synthesis of the perceptions—that is, they belong together according to principles of the objective determination of all representations, in so far as knowledge may be derived from them. These principles are all deduced from the transcendental unity of apperception. Only thus does this relation become a *judgment*, by which is meant a relation that is *objectively valid*. Such a relation is sufficiently distinct from the relation of these very same representations, in so far as it has merely subjective validity, *e.g.*, according to laws of association of ideas. The laws of association only entitle me to say—' If I carry a body I feel weight '—not, ' It, the body, *is* heavy.' The latter statement means—these two representations are combined in the object, *i.e.*, regardless of the particular state of the subject, and are not merely together in perception (however often the perception be repeated)."

Kant evidently means by " principles of objective determination of all representations " the three Analogies, but why objectivity implies necessity is not made clear in this passage. For that we must wait till the second Analogy. The argument of the latter is more directly suggested by the clause in the last sentence, " regardless of the particular state of the subject," which indicates that objectivity implies necessary determination in my experience *independently of my subjective* states, but the passage is so condensed as to be unintelligible without reference to the main argument of the second Analogy which we shall deal with in our next chapter.

Similarly in the first-edition version Kant points out that the notion of an object involves a rule forcing our representations to follow a certain order—*i.e.*, necessary connection in experience. All knowledge, he says, demands the concept of an object. But the object has no content other than what is given in representations, it reduces itself to a mere X or unknown cause of our perceptions, but what can be the use of such an apparently barren idea ? The answer is that it gives a necessary unity to our perceptions. " Now we find that our thought of the relation of all knowledge to its object carries with it something of necessity, inasmuch as the object is looked upon as that which prevents our knowledge from being haphazard or capricious by determining it *a priori* in a definite fashion, since, inasmuch as its different elements have to be referred to a single object, they must necessarily conform to each other in their common relation to the object, *i.e.*, must have just that unity which is involved in the concept of an object."[1] Although in this passage Kant seems to be thinking rather of the thing-in-itself as the object, and does not recognise phenomenal objects, this does not alter the fact that in making objectivity consist in determination of our representations it anticipates the second Analogy. The concept of a particular object is, as in the schematism, identified with the concept of a rule uniting and controlling our representations.[1]

Secondly, all judgments involve a reference either to the physical world or to the empirical self or to both—the judgment " There is green " is unintelligible unless " green " is regarded either as a representation of the self or an attribute of a physical object. We must at any rate admit both a self, with its empirical and transcendental aspects, and a connected system of objects. We must admit processes in time capable of being thought together as one. But an object means a complex of *necessarily connected* attributes ; a process in time means a series of phenomena with causal continuity. We must think of both the empirical self and objects as enduring beyond any single perception of them, but there is no sense in saying that they endure in time unless either there is no change, which is not the case, or the successive stages in the change are each determined according to what has gone before. This argument holds whether a " subjectivist " or a more objective view of the physical world is adopted, only if the subjectivist view is taken what endures is simply a system of laws connecting perceptions. However, " laws " imply necessary connection still more obviously and directly than " objects " do. Further, to make the world really intelligible, Kant holds, we must extend this relative permanence till the world is reduced to one single system of change.[2] " There is *one single* experience in which all perceptions are represented as in complete and necessary (*gesetzmässigen*) connection." But any unity, not being mere identity without difference, must involve a necessary connection between the diversity within it, otherwise these diverse elements cannot possibly be said to belong together in unity. This seems to be the main thought behind one[3] of the two arguments for necessary connection in the first edition but it is nowhere adequately developed. " The possibility, nay, even the necessity, of these categories rests on the relation which the whole sensibility, and with it also all possible phenomena, have to the original apperception.[4] In this relation everything must necessarily conform to the conditions of complete unity of self-consciousness, that is, be subject to universal functions of synthesis, *i.e.*,

<hr>

[1]*A.*, 105–6.   [2]*A.*, 110.   [3]*A.*, 110–112.   [4]*A.*,111–112.

E

synthesis according to concepts, for there alone can apperception prove *a priori* its complete and necessary identity. Thus the conception of a cause is simply that of a synthesis (of what follows next in the time-series with other phenomena), a synthesis *according to concepts* ; and without such a unity which has its *a priori* rule and subjects phenomena to itself, we could not find complete and universal, and so necessary, unity of consciousness in the manifold of perceptions. But in that case these perceptions would belong to no experience, consequently they would have no object and be nothing but a blind play of representations, that is, something less than a dream." We shall have occasion to refer to this argument later.[1]

Thirdly, the first edition deduction is somewhat confused by the insertion of a different line of argument starting from the empirical law of association of ideas.[2] It is an empirical fact that one representation tends to call up another, even in the absence of the object to which the latter is attributed. This association is necessary if we are to frame an idea of a complete object, for, as the apprehension of the latter takes time, each stage in the process must recall to our mind the preceding stages so that they may all be connected in a single idea. This association must not be indiscriminate or it would not enable us to form ideas of particular objects ; there must be laws associating particular ideas in our mind. Further, it presupposes a certain " affinity " among phenomena, that is, they must follow each other according to certain laws, for we should not have fixed laws of association if any sensation or group of sensations might accompany any other with equal frequency. But it is impossible to believe that this " affinity " is contingent, for on it depends the possibility of knowing objects ; and if it depends on any principle as its necessary consequence that principle must be the transcendental unity of apperception. As a matter of fact it is easy to see that it presupposes this transcendental unity as the condition of all experience. Further, it can be deduced *a priori* from it, for the transcendental unity of apperception is only realised in the combination of representations so as to constitute objective phenomena, and combination without " affinity " is impossible. It follows that the affinity of phenomena is itself *a priori* necessary, *i.e.*, it is an *a priori* truth that all phenomena must be sufficiently connected

---

[1] *V.* below, I. 14, 157ff.   [2] *A*,100–1, 113–4, 121–2.

and sufficiently regular to make possible association according to certain definite laws. " It is clear that even this apprehension of the manifold, taken alone, would produce no image and no combination of impressions, if there were not present a subjective ground enabling us to recall in association with those that follow it a perception, from which the mind has passed on to another, and so produce whole series of perceptions, *i.e.*, a reproductive power of imagination, which is, however, only empirical.[1]

Yet, if representations reproduced each other indiscriminately just as they happen to come together, they would give rise to no coherent system but mere lawless agglomerations and so produce no knowledge. Consequently their reproduction must be subject to a rule according to which one representation is much more readily associated in the imagination with a second than with a third. This subjective and *empirical* ground of reproduction according to rules is called the *association* of representations.

Now, if this unity of association had no objective ground besides, so as to make it impossible for phenomena to be apprehended by the imagination otherwise than under the condition of a possible synthetic unity in this apprehension, it would be a merely contingent fact that phenomena should fit into a system of human knowledge. For, though we had the power of associating perceptions, yet it would remain a matter of uncertainty and chance whether they were actually capable of association ; and, in case they were not, a host of perceptions, or even a whole sensibility, might, while including a good deal of empirical consciousness, have it dissociated and not in connection with a *single* consciousness of myself, which is impossible. For it is only by ascribing all perceptions to a single consciousness (the original apperception) that I am enabled to say of all of them that I am conscious of them. So there must be an objective ground, (*i.e.*, one discoverable *a priori* independently of any empirical laws of imagination), on which the possibility, nay, the necessity, of a law immanent in all phenomena depends, namely the law that we are to regard them throughout as sense data of such a character as to be in themselves capable of association and subject to universal laws fully interconnecting them in reproduction. This objective ground of all association of phenomena I call their *affinity*, and this can be found nowhere except in the principle of the unity of apperception in relation to all knowledge which is to be mine. According to it all phenomena must so enter the mind or be apprehended that they conform to the unity of apperception. Without a synthetic unity in their connection, which is therefore also objectively necessary, this would be impossible. The objective unity of all (empirical) consciousness in a single consciousness (the original apperception) is thus the necessary condition even of all possible perception, while the affinity of all phenomena (near or remote) is a necessary consequence of a synthesis in imagination which is founded, *a priori*, on rules."

There are three points to be noted here :—

1. Association of ideas, which is necessary if we are to think of any diversity-in-unity and so have any knowledge at all, presupposes a certain minimum regularity in phenomena. It does not, however, in itself presuppose universal and necessary connection but only *de facto* regularity, and though he may not have distinguished the two clearly enough here Kant does not say that it presupposes the former. What he says, where he speaks of universal necessity, is that this universal necessary connection follows from the transcendental unity of apperception and explains the empirical affinity implied in the association of ideas.[1] The bare principle of causality does not itself imply a regularity in phenomena sufficient to differentiate, for practical and scientific purposes, particular causes and particular objects, but if there were not sufficient regularity in phenomena to enable us to do so to a certain extent knowledge would be impossible.[2] So we should, on Kant's principles, be justified in regarding the " affinity " of phenomena as a necessary condition of knowledge and hence as an *a priori* transcendental principle, even if it be held to be due to noumenal conditions, for if the noumena were not of such a character as to enable the law of causality to be applied to their phenomena knowledge and hence phenomena would be impossible.

2. But Kant was not content with this. He thought that such dependence on noumenal conditions would make knowledge a mere accident and so introduced the doctrine that transcendental affinity is the creation of the transcendental unity of apperception, thus for once ignoring the importance of the merely given in experience. This does

[1] *A.*, 114.   [2] *V.* below pp. 147-9.

not, however, really remove the contingency of knowledge, because for Kant transcendental unity of apperception is itself only a fact dependent on noumenal conditions and proved from empirical data, *i.e.*, the occurence of a manifold in time. Further by transcendental affinity is presumably meant the particular laws of nature, but unless phenomena are wholly created by the knowing self, a doctrine which Kant would be the first to repudiate, the conformity of phenomena to *these particular* laws presupposes another " transcendental affinity " which must be regarded as due to the noumenal conditions which help in determining the phenomena.

3. Kant's argument constitutes a reply to those who maintain like Hume that self-identity is a result of association of ideas. For, to be associated, ideas must first be both present to the transcendental unity of apperception, otherwise they would not be objects of consciousness at all and so not ideas. Consequently, so far from self-identity being due to association, association is only rendered possible by self-identity.

To pass on, there is one more main point left to prove, namely that the different forms of unity required as conditions of the possibility of experience are just the categories specified by Kant. In the first edition version of the deduction he makes no attempt to show this, but in the second edition Deduction he inserts an argument based on the new definition of judgment as " the mode of referring given cognitions to the *objective* unity of apperception.[1]" This definition implies that the activity expressed in judgment is the same as that which constitutes by synthesis a manifold into an object for consciousness, or rather the conscious and verbal expression of that activity. Judgment involves the application of a predicate to a subject, which must itself already be qualified in some way, for otherwise it would not be known, and so it means the unity of two different attributes in one subject, just that unity in diversity which is the invariable product of the synthesis prior to consciousness. So judgment expresses and is parallel to the activity of cognition not only in the sense that it brings to light the knowledge obtained by it, but also in the sense of being a conscious recapitulation of the process which constituted the nature of the synthesis. It is an expression not only of the results of cognition but of

[1]*B.*, 143.

the process by which they are attained. From this Kant tries to prove his second point, namely that the list of categories he has adopted is accurate and complete. If judging is simply the expression in words of the process of relating sensible data to the unity of apperception, then this process must conform to the conditions of judgment. Consequently each of the different forms or formal aspects of the synthesis must correspond to a function of judgment, so that we can deduce a list of the former from a list of the latter by simply modifying them somewhat so as to meet the different conditions involved, especially so as to enable them to deal with the " pure manifolds " of space and time, which are involved in all perception. Further, Kant assumed that the classification of judgments given by formal logic was final and complete and had, in fact, the *a priori* certainty of mathematics. It followed that this certainty was communicated to the list of categories deduced from the different forms of judgments (in the metaphysical deduction), so that it was known *a priori* that just these categories and no more were necessary. That Kant's assumption as to the perfect adequacy of the list of forms of judgment drawn up by logic was unjustified is made clear by the subsequent history of philosophy, but for the discovery of this inadequacy we have to thank nobody more than Kant himself, since by assimilating judgment to a synthetic process he really broke with the old view of it as analytic on which the formal logic of the day was based. His failure to realise that a radical change like this must affect every branch of that logic, which he regarded as having already attained mathematical certainty in all fundamentals, is a striking example of the frequent blindness of reformers to the full extent of the revolution which they have themselves effected. So the attempt to prove *a priori* the completeness of the list of categories given in the Critique breaks down, and it is indeed difficult to see how any such proof could be discovered.

From *The Metaphysical Foundations of Natural Science* it seems that Kant regards the argument, that the application of the categories in the synthesis is generically the same activity as judging, as the second edition substitute for the subjective deduction. For in this treatise, written shortly before the issue of the second edition of the Critique, Kant, after distinguishing the proof that experience involves the categories from the question how experience by the means of the categories is possible and declaring the former proof to be alone really essential to the deduction, adds, " this latter task," *i.e.*, showing how experience by means of the categories is possible, " although the fabric stands fast without it, has, all the same, great importance, and, as I now envisage it, is as easy as important, for it can be almost completed by a single conclusion from the precise definition of a judgment in general (as a process by which representations given to us first become cognitions of an object).[1] The obscurity which characterises my first discussion in this part of the deduction, an obscurity that I do not deny, is to be ascribed to the common fate of the understanding in research, inasmuch as the shortest road is generally not the first of which it is aware."

In section 21 of the second edition deduction Kant makes the extraordinary statement that the proposition, that " a manifold included in a perception, which I call mine, is by the synthesis of understanding represented as belonging to the necessary unity of self-consciousness and this takes place by means of the category," is only " the beginning " of the deduction, while in reality the proposition in question is a summary of the whole argument of the deduction. Elsewhere it is always just the synthesis, the necessary unity of apperception and the dependence of experience on the categories that Kant treats as essential. What Kant here treats these as merely preliminary to is the doctrine of schematism, but in general the place occupied by this latter doctrine is quite subordinate. Even in the section of the transcendental deduction referred to in section 21 as though it constituted its main part, he seems to treat[2] the deduction as already completed as far as its chief purpose was concerned. What remains to be shown, he says, is the possibility of applying the categories to our sense-data. In order to bridge the gap between the purely logical concepts and the mere manifold of sensation the schema is adopted, this schema being obtained by the application of the category to the pure manifold, *i.e.*, really time. (In the transcendental deduction Kant adds " space " but he does not attempt to carry out in detail the schematisation with regard to space.) The general effect of the schematism is, in most cases, to diminish the importance of the category as an independent and significant concept almost to vanishing-point. It is,

[1]*H.*, IV, p. 365 (footnote).
[2]*B.*, 159, where he refers to the transcendental deduction in the past tense.

in fact, the schemata, not the categories, which are proved to be valid of phenomena in the Analytic of Principles. In the case of causality, however, the bare category, " ground," as opposed to the schema, " necessary succession in time," seems to retain an independence and significance greater than that possessed by the other categories. But it is still the schema, (not the category), the validity of which is proved in the second Analogy. However, of the relations between ground and cause we shall speak later.

Two further points must be added to our summary of the deduction. In the first place, the categories deduced are only valid for an understanding which merely thinks, *i.e.*, effects the synthesis of a manifold given from outside, not a perceptive understanding such as we may suppose God to have, *i.e.*, an understanding which creates its own manifold.[1] Kant adds a remark which, although it is the logical result of his philosophy, might seem inconsistent with his view, expressed above, that the list of categories is known *a priori* to be fully adequate :—" But of the peculiarity of our understanding, namely, that it can only produce unity of apperception *a priori* by employing the categories and employing just this kind and number of categories, it is no more possible to produce any further reason than it is to give a reason why we have just those and no other functions of judging, or why time and space are the only forms of perception possible to us."[2] But the sentence should be understood as an admission not that the categories cannot be deduced *a priori* from the forms of judgment but that neither the one nor the other are deducible without the help given by analysis of actual experience, and that we cannot know why experience should involve just these categories, only that it does so. The forms of judgment, once found, might still then serve as a basis for the deduction of the categories. However, it follows from this admission that any attempt to find a completely *a priori* guarantee for the adequacy of the list must end in failure. We can have no ground for supposing that we have discovered all the categories and forms of judgment but our failure to discover more, and this failure may be only due to ignorance on our part or lack of discernment.

To return to the point, while the categories are held to be valid only within the realm of sensible experience, actual or possible, their validity is extended somewhat beyond that

<hr>

[1] *E.g.*, *B.*, 145.   [2] *B.*, 146.

of the laws of space and time, because, while the latter are valid only for beings with our peculiar mode of sensibility, the former are valid for all beings with sensible (not intellectual) perception ; but the extension is of no real value, for without sensible content the categories are only empty, useless forms, and sensible content can only be supplied to us by experience according to our own peculiar mode of sensibility.[1] To objects of non-sensible experience on categories can be applied, nor can their nature be specified further except by negatives denying all sensible qualities to such objects.

The second point is that, as is urged at the beginning and end of the deductions in both editions, the necessity of the categories could not be proved by any method other than that here adopted. For we could never hope to arrive at necessity by a mere induction from experience.[2] Consequently, if the objects of experience and knowledge were things-in-themselves, we could not possibly know that they must conform to our categories, and if we assumed them to do so as the result of a miraculous pre-established harmony their adaptation would be merely contingent and we could recognise no real necessity that they should so conform, only a subjective necessity that we should think them as conforming to our categories, an assumption which we could not prove to have an objective ground. The only way by which there could be any chance of proving the objective validity and necessity of our categories is by showing that without the categories in question any empirical judgment would be impossible, but to establish their necessity in this way involves the admission that the objects which conform to them are not things-in-themselves but phenomena.

We are now in a position to tabulate the main results of the transcendental deduction.

1. Cognition of any manifold, even only our representations, being always cognition of a diversity-in-unity, is impossible unless the different elements are present in a single consciousness. Thus even the judgment, " There is a manifold passing away in time," a judgment which no sceptic ventures to deny, involves the transcendental unity of apperception.

2. We can only regard the self as identical in so far as it holds together different elements in a single act of thought. This identity is a presupposition of all knowledge and not

[1]B., 148.   [2]B., 124–8 (A 92–4), A., 129, B., 166–8.

an empirical fact discoverable by introspection. By itself it would be a mere form without content, and is therefore not a possible object of experience except in so far as it is realised in the unity which must characterise all objects of our cognition. It must be regarded as strictly correlative to, one might almost call it only another aspect of, the synthetic unity of the presented.

3. Knowledge of self is strictly on a par with knowledge of objects, and the one is no more difficult to explain than the other. The doctrine that what we perceive is never anything but a state of the *perceiving* self is false, on the contrary we never perceive a state of our self except as the self is made an object[1] by a process similar to that implied in cognition of the external world, and, like the latter, involving the categories. If we strictly confine ourselves to immediate experience without introducing any more permanent element we do not even get solipsism but a relation without terms, an appearance without anything that appears or anyone that it appears to, nothing that can be an object of cognition at all ; if we go beyond immediate experience we have as much right to extend our knowledge on the object as on the subject side. (Just as the transcendental self, as far as it is knowable by us, implies an empirical content, so the empirical self implies objects independent of itself. For (a) it can only be known as one object among others, as a self in opposition to a not-self, (b) the whole content discovered in it by introspection is derived from objects.)

4. All judgment and cognition imply objectivity and unity, and in the case of experienced events this objectivity and unity can only be interpreted in terms of necessity. (This point is only suggested here, and not developed clearly or adequately till the second Analogy, which we shall shortly discuss.)

5. The act of judging and the act by which we hold together diverse elements in that unity which alone makes them a possible object of cognition are identical, or, at any rate, strictly parallel. From this it should follow that judgment is essentially synthetic, never merely analytic, but Kant left it to others to make this deduction, and only used the parallelism between the two to guarantee the adequacy of his list of categories, as purporting to be deduced from the forms of judgment. He did not realise that a classifica-

[1]This interpretation is of course, disputable, but the objections to it will be dealt with more adequately in a later chapter (VI).

tion of the latter based on the analytic view of judgment must be affected by a view which (though it still nominally admitted judgment to be analytic) assimilated it to a process which was regarded as essentially synthetic. The outline account we have given does not claim to be in conformity with all passages in the deduction ; it seeks to represent rather the logical results of the latter than the precise expression of them at every stage or the fluctuations of opinion traceable in the text. Since the work is not of a unitary character no interpretation of the line of argument can be reconcilable with all passages, especially if it adds criticism to interpretation and attempts to disengage the material from the immaterial, the tenable from the untenable, as given therein. We may be fairly charged with having neglected the subjectivist and the psychological portions of the deduction, but we can hardly hope to do justice to all aspects of the passage and we have consequently contented ourselves with selecting what we take to be the main line of argument, the part that Kant himself deemed essential to his purpose. But we cannot pass on without a criticism of the view of the synthesis as a psychological process and not as merely a logical characteristic of knowledge, a view which seems to have been held by Kant and which had a fatal effect on the understanding of his argument.

As Kant started with the analytic logic so he started with the atomistic psychology of his predecessors, and while he supplied the corrective to both he never wholly shook off either. In the case of the atomistic psychology the results were especially harmful both for the form and the understanding of the deduction. Because of this psychology, instead of saying that consciousness of representations implied consciousness of objective and hence necessary connection, he said that consciousness of representations as such could only be explained by a synthesis according to *a priori* categories, a defect which was partially, but not wholly, remedied in the second edition. The reason is that he started with the current view that what we are conscious of first are mere sensations which we combine into an objective world by some process of inference. He soon came to see that consciousness, at any rate in so far as it involves cognition, can never have for its object unconnected sensations, and that our actual consciousness could not be explained by generation out of such sensations, but he retained in the unconscious the sensations in their original, unrelated form, and the process by which we advance from sensations to objects, now in the form of a creative synthesis. This, besides encumbering us with a host of mythical entities and faculties, involves Kant in a hopeless contradiction.

For the theory makes the process of synthesis at once an event within and a generative condition of the phenomenal world. In regarding this process as a process analogous to conscious cognition, (or imaginative construction according to a rule), exercised by the self on the manifold of its sensations Kant makes it an event of the psychical order in the phenomenal world. For sensations are essentially phenomenal. But, if so, this process, apart from the fact that it should be the study of psychology not of epistemology' cannot be the presupposition and condition of the very possibility of that whole of which it is itself a part. Sensations are facts, among others, in the phenomenal world and cannot precede the existence of the latter, nor can the phenomenal world be held to have been created by a synthesis of a few of its constituent parts, *i.e.*, sensations. Kant is not able, as the realist or absolute idealist would be, to reply that it is not the objective world but consciousness of the objective world by individuals which is to be explained in this way, for to him the objective, but phenomenal, world, which is the only world we know, cannot be supposed to exist prior to the synthesis. The phenomenal world cannot be causally accounted for by a process which could only be real as a process in the phenomenal world itself.

If, on the other hand, the synthesis be taken as noumenal, then equal or worse difficulties arise. If it is noumenal, it is on Kant's own principles unknowable. We may deduce a *law* conditioning all experience from consideration of what is involved in the possibility of experience, but we cannot from the same premises deduce a process prior to all experience. We can, in any case, only describe the process in terms of its results for experience. Any further specification by analogy to conscious processes of our mind is illegitimate. It is not a possible object of experience and the very description of it as a synthesis is unjustifiable, for the process cannot be called a synthesis merely because the experience it gives rise to is complex, but only if we have reason to suppose that the complex experience originated through the combination of several simpler elements. We have reason to do so as long as we regard the process as one by which, beginning with sensations, we acquire experience of objects, but not when we regard the process as the noumenal condition of all phenomena including objects and sensations (as psychical events) alike.   In fact, it must not even be called a process at all, for a process implies temporal change, and time cannot be predicated of noumena.   Even if it could be shown that there was such a process—putting aside for the moment the contradictions involved in that supposition—we could only describe it in terms of its results, which are elements in experience, and the supposed synthesis dwindles down to the palest of abstractions, akin to the scholastic " faculties." The doctrine has value and meaning only in so far as it asserts the *results* of the synthesis, which are discovered by analysis of experience itself.   But if so, why try to go behind experience and not be content with the discovery that all human experience is of a certain form, and that without conforming to certain conditions (the categories) experience in this form would be impossible ?   As an analysis of what is actually involved in all experience in time the Critique is invaluable, but the attempt to account for experience psychologically by a synthesis only confuses the issue and obscures the results.

The doctrine of the synthesis as a psychological process, then, we have seen, acquires plausibility only because the synthesis is treated both as phenomenal and noumenal, as phenomenal when it is made a knowable psychical process, as noumenal when it is made a condition of the existence of the phenomenal world, but if noumenal it cannot be the former, and if phenomenal it cannot be the latter, yet it must be both if the doctrine is to be retained.   No doubt if Kant had taken the standpoint of subjective idealism, and made the self and its states the one reality, and the physical world a mental construction by the human self out of its own sensations, then the synthesis could be at once a knowable event and a presupposition of the existence of the physical world, in the only sense in which the physical could then be said to exist, but this certainly cannot be regarded as his view at any part of the " critical " period, for he is quite decisive as to the merely phenomenal character of the empirical self. That he sometimes approaches very close to that view in other respects I do not, of course, mean to deny, and in so far as he does so he assimilates the synthesis to the cognitive activities of the empirical self and to an event in the phenomenal world ; in so far as he approaches the opposing standpoint the transcendental unity of apperception is viewed, not as guaranteeing the existence of a separate unitary self but as a *de facto* unity which may, for all we can prove, be the resultant of a great complexity of grounds, and the synthesis thus tends to become the wholly unknowable process which constitutes such a unity (as in the Paralogisms). Another harmful result of Kant's psychological presuppositions is the rigid distinction between form and content, content being the material imparted by sensation and regarded as absolute diversity, and form being the order contributed by the mind so as to assimilate the presentation to its own absolute unity. It was an unquestioned assumption of Kant, stated at the beginning of the second-edition Deduction, that all relation is contributed by the understanding. But, as all sense-data of which we can be conscious contain a relational factor, and as experience was supposed to have begun from unrelated sensations, Kant concluded that there must have been a synthesis of these sensations, by which synthesis the relational factor was introduced. Content is thus conceived, not as inseparable though distinguishable from form, but as an element which existed before form and to which form was subsequently added. This was one of the reasons for Kant's agnosticism since if we change our perceptions in receiving them, he argued, we are not entitled to say that they tell us the truth about what is outside us, for they have, by the addition of subjective factors, been already transformed beyond recognition.

But the distinction between form and content, when it is made absolute in this way and content is viewed as actually, not only ideally, separable from form, involves Kant in two insuperable difficulties. In the first place, if all relation is imposed by the mind on an unrelated manifold there is no way of accounting for the difference between the countless individual relations in the world, or even perhaps between the different categories. This difference can be ascribed neither to the transcendental unity of apperception, for that is the same throughout, nor to a difference in the content related, for in that case the content would be already related implicitly, and so all relation would not come from the mind. To take a physical analogy, the relation imposed by me is the same whether I add water or oil to fire, but the results are different. This difference can then only be accounted for by a difference between the properties of water and those of oil. But the property which differentiates them in regard to the effects of their union with fire can only be described as a relation between water (or oil) and fire, or even if it could be deduced from other properties of water (or oil) not explicitly involving a relation to fire it would be because those properties already contained the same relation implicitly, otherwise there would be no ground in the premises for the conclusion. Similarly, since the transcendental unity of apperception is always the same, the fact, that *e.g.*, A causes B while C causes D, can only be explained as due to different properties in the manifold and the relation of causation to B and D respectively must always be contained, either explicitly or implicitly, in these properties. Or again, as my mind applies the same form of space to all physical objects, differences in size between particular objects can only be accounted for by differences in the manifold, not in the form of space which is the same in all cases. (By properties of A " implicitly containing the relation " I simply mean that, if it possesses these properties, A must be such that it cannot but stand in just this causal or spatial relation to B.) Particular relations can only be accounted for by qualities in the manifold, but, if the manifold has qualities which will account for these relations, it is itself already related, and so it is not true that all relation comes from a synthesis by the mind.

The second difficulty is that an absolutely unrelated manifold can have no meaning for us, it cannot be thought or perceived and no judgment can be made about it. But, if so, it has for us no real existence. The situation is not remedied by relegating it to the unconscious, for nothing in the phenomenal world can be absolutely unrelated, and if it is not in the phenomenal world it is no possible object of knowledge. If the whole synthesis be placed outside the phenomenal world altogether and made prior even to the transcendental unity of apperception, then, as we have seen, the whole process becomes unknowable so that we cannot call it a synthesis of the manifold of sense or even a process at all, in fact it becomes nothing but a mere unknown ground of the unity involved in experience. But the synthesis cannot be kept within experience, for, as Kant himself admits elsewhere, the absolutely simple is not a possible object of experience.[1] Even mere sensations are not absolutely simple and unrelated; neither for consciousness, because they do not exist as sensations for the latter till differentiated out of the complex whole of feeling, and when we have thus differentiated them we

---

[1] *B.*, 497, *A.*, 800.

have already recognised them as elements in objective reality with diverse relations ; nor as events in the physical world, since, as such, they are obviously related to the stimulus which caused them and to the other parts of the organism. Besides, most, if not all, sensations are rendered complex by the possession of the characteristic of extensity. Kant indeed rises above this atomistic view when he speaks of that on which the synthesis is exercised as a manifold or a *Gewühl* of sensations, but he never definitely repudiates the doctrine that all relation is added by the mind to a pre-existing content. Both difficulties are smoothed over by the introduction of the imagination, for this faculty is used to account both for the individual relations in the world as given in perception and for the connected character of sense-data prior to conception, but no solution can be reached in this way, for the imagination, if its activities are to be known at all, must be regarded as working on a number of unrelated sensations according to those very *a priori* principles which the understanding afterwards recognises as such, abstracts and consciously uses, so it only throws the difficulties further back. The one possible solution is to regard form and content as distinguishable but inseparable elements in all human experience, and not divide them by the impassable gulf between absolute unity and absolute diversity, and to make not mere analytic identity but unity-in-diversity the type of thought and the ideal of knowledge, so that, while on the one side the content ceases to be mere diversity, the mind likewise ceases to be mere unity. For a mere form of unity without any content to combine is just as impossible an abstraction as a content of mere diversity without relation or unity.

The conclusion of Kantian idealism should be not that the mind prior to experience somehow added relation to an unrelated content but that phenomena are unintelligible without the co-operation of subject and object, that the two elements of unity and diversity, form and content, found in all experience, are both inseparable from and irreducible to each other, that is, while neither is a possible object of knowledge without the other, neither can be accounted for by the other.

We have dealt with the transcendental deduction at length because it is naturally the basis of the argument of the Analogies. Of the objections brought against the deduction most are directed against its subjectivist and psychological aspects, which we have repudiated as both unessential to the argument and themselves untenable. The view we have put forward as representing what seems to us most important and valuable in the argument does not treat experience as generated by the actual combination by the mind of an absolutely unrelated manifold nor does it identify knowing with making, consequently it is not liable to the criticisms directed against views which adopt the doctrines in question. It asserts not that we create, or construct out of given materials, objects of our knowledge, but that objects can only be known as they are when in relation to some subject and subjects as they are when in relation to some objects. Whether this much " idealism " is a valid conclusion of the deduction we are not asking, it is enough for our purpose that all knowledge has been shown to involve (1) self-identity, (2) systematic unity (with necessary connection) in the object known. Some remaining objections will be discussed in the next chapter as specially applied to the case of causality.

CHAPTER IV

The Second Analogy[1]

THE deduction of the special categories presupposes consciousness of an *objective* order in time, this being held to have been proved by the transcendental deduction. With cause and reciprocity the method adopted is to show that we cannot distinguish subjective and objective order in time without the category in question.

As in the transcendental deduction, so again here it is most important to distinguish the logical implications from the psychological form of the argument, as stated in many passages. Having given this general warning, we shall now proceed to summarise the actual deduction of causality.

[1] With regard to the meaning of the term "analogy" two alternatives are suggested by Kant. In B 222 (=A 179) he indicates that the term is used in opposition to "axiom" (or "anticipation") and is meant to imply that we cannot, in the case of the relational categories, determine the nature of, *e.g.*, the cause *a priori* but only say of every fresh event that it must stand in the same relation to another event, *x*, as every known effect bears towards its cause, thus differing from mathematical analogies. If we are told that *x* is to 4 as 6 is to 3 we can exactly determine *x* thereby, but we cannot determine the nature of the cause, but only its relation to the effect, by help of the analogy alone without experience ; however its form is the same as that of a mathematical analogy, *i.e.*, it says that a known term, the effect, stands in the same relation to *x*, the cause, as two other known events bear to each other. But in B 224 Kant suggests that the term is used because the category of cause is applied to phenomena on the analogy of ground and consequent, but the remark has the appearance of an afterthought. Both accounts are unsatisfactory—the former because it suggests that we can foretell a definite "intensity" by the "Anticipations of Perception," which is of course false, the second because of the subjectivism it implies.

Kant gives no less than six separate proofs of
this category, but of these five represent approx-
imately the same line of argument. One,
however, the fourth stated in the first edition and
the fifth in the second edition, is of quite a different type and it will be convenient to take this

Statement of one Kantian proof of causality.

first. It occurs in B 244-6[1] and runs as follows :—
" If it is a necessary law of our sensibility and so a *formal
condition* of all perceptions that the precedent time necessarily
determines the subsequent (inasmuch as I cannot reach the
subsequent time except by passing through the precedent);
it is also an indispensable *law of the empirical representation*
of time sequence, that the phenomena of the time that is
past determine every existence in the succeeding time, and
that the subsequent phenomena, as events, do not take
place except in so far as the precedent phenomena determine
their occurrence in time, *i.e.*, fix it according to a rule.
For it is *only in phenomena that we can know empirically this
continuity in the coherence of times.*

" What is required for all experience and is needed to make
it possible is the understanding, and the first thing which the
understanding does is not to make the representation of
objects clear, but to make the representation of any object in
any degree possible. This takes place by the understanding
transferring the order of time to phenomena and their
existence, and by assigning to each of them, as itself a consequence, a place in time determined *a priori* with regard to
antecedent phenomena. Without this the phenomenon
would be inconsistent with time itself, which determines
a priori the place of all its parts. This determination of
place cannot be derived from the relation of phenomena to
absolute time (for that time can never be an object of perception), but, on the contrary, the phenomena must determine
for each other and render necessary their position in the time-
order. In other words, whatever follows or occurs must
follow according to a general rule on what was contained
in the precedent state. From this arises a series of phenomena, which, through the understanding, produces and
necessitates in the series of possible perceptions just the same
order and continuous coherence, which can be found *a priori*
in the form of inner perception (time) in which all perceptions
must have their place."

In brief, the argument is to the effect that, as the precedent

[1] $= A.$, 199-201, eleventh to thirteenth paragraphs of first edition.

parts of time determine the subsequent parts, and as phenomena must conform to the conditions of time, precedent
must likewise determine subsequent phenomena as regards
their place in time, which involves causality, understood as
complete necessary determination ; but despite the insistence
of writers like Kuno Fischer on the importance of this argument, we are bound to say that it does not seem to us to carry
with it the intended conclusion. There are two senses in
which the precedent parts of time, time being regarded in
abstraction from events in time, may be said to determine
the subsequent parts.

      In the first place, we must pass through the earlier
Criticism of period of time in order to reach the later period,
the proof. or the past cannot be experienced as after or
      simultaneously with but only before the future,
but this is merely saying that it cannot be future as well as
past. That is, successive periods of time constitute a series
in which no term can bear the same relation to that which
precedes as to that which follows it and the relation between
predecessor and successor is never reciprocal. (We might,
of course, have a series of which either did not hold, *e.g.*,
2, 3, 2, 3, 2, 3, 2—or 2, 2, 3, 2, 2, 3). If so, the only
condition that phenomena must observe in order to conform
to this characteristic of time is that a phenomenon which is
past in reference to some other phenomenon cannot also be
present or future in reference to the same phenomenon.
This is obviously involved in the nature of time, but it is
equally obviously not the same as saying that each phenomenon must be causally determined by other phenomena.
The assertion that the past must be experienced before the
future and not *vice versa* is very different from the assertion
that the same future (qualitatively) must follow on the same
past. The first is the assertion that the series of succesive
events in time is asymmetrical, the second is, roughly, the
assertion that if a particular time-series of events has occurred
once it must occur again whenever the relevant conditions
are the same.

      Secondly, the limit of any period of time is on one side
fixed by the time prior to it. Now, being a mere form of
relation for phenomena, a period considered as pure time is
of course wholly determined by its external temporal
relations, for it has no content of its own apart from these
relations. Thus 1924, considered merely as a period of time,
is wholly determined by 1923 and 1925. But when this

period is considered in its concrete reality as a series of phenomena, its external, temporal relations only comprise one subordinate aspect of its nature, hence the most that the argument could establish would be that *one* aspect of its nature is determined by *a* relation it bears to other phenomena, *i.e.*, the relation it bears to them as preceding or succeeding them in time. Further, since the aspect thus determined is just its temporal relation to other phenomena, *i.e.*, the relation it bears to them as preceding or succeeding them in time, this is a mere tautology and not a judgment describing a synthetic connection like causality at all. So, when understood in this sense, as in the former, the determination of subsequent by precedent periods of time referred to is quite different from causal determination and does not carry with it causal determination for phenomena. The events of 1924 are determined as regards their place in time by the events of 1923 in the sense that none of them can, while, belonging to 1924, fall in or before 1923 ; they are determined causally in the sense that given the state of the world in 1923 just these and no other events must follow. The former is a case of disjunctive exclusion following from the proposition that the same event cannot occur in two different times so that if it occurs in one year it is debarred from occurring in any other year ; the second alone is a case of causal determination proper. That the two are essentially different is shown by the fact that in the first sense the future determines the past, 1924 is determined as to its temporal position not only by 1923 but by 1925, *i.e.*, it is the period after 1923 but before 1925.

This argument, however, although, as stated, a failure, suggests two more profitable lines of advance. In its first paragraph Kant refers to that characteristic of time, on account of which the past determines the present, as *Continuität*. Now continuity as usually understood involves also the coherence of innumerable shorter times in one and the same time, and it is difficult to see how this continuity could be realised in phenomena without a causal connection between past and present. A similar argument is used by Kant to prove substance, but it seems better fitted to prove causation. However, more of that later.

Then the fact that phenomena have a definite objective order in time means that this order must be the same for all percipients in so far as the conditions are the same, which is just the real basis of the other arguments of this section, while the basis of the present argument is that the parts of time determine each other, from which fact Kant wrongly concludes that phenomena determine each other in quite a different way, *i.e.*, causally. The point to emphasise is not that the past can only be experienced before the present and so forms the limit on one side of the present, but that what is past must be past for all experients. The latter, however, is not a statement about the past as time determining the present at all, for that determination of different times by each other is never causal and conformity to it in phenomena does not itself involve causality.

Statement of main Kantian proof of causality. It is on this connection between objectivity and necessity that the remaining arguments turn. We shall now go through these step by step. The first proof given in the first edition begins with the assertion that the apprehension of the manifold is always successive. Now phenomena have a twofold existence. They may be regarded, first, as objects themselves in which case they are not distinguished from our acts of apprehension following each other in time, but secondly, they may also be regarded as standing for objects. But our representations can tell us nothing about things-in-themselves, only about phenomena. The question therefore arises as to what we mean by distinguishing between objective and subjective order in time, *e.g.*, what do we mean by saying that, while the apprehension of the manifold of a house is successive, the manifold of the house is itself not successive but co-existent? " What then can be the meaning of the question as to how the manifold may be connected in the phenomenon itself (which phenomenon is after all nothing in itself) ?"[1] Here we consider as representation whatever is contained in our successive apprehension, and as object of the representations the given phenomenon, though it is nothing but a complex[2] of these representations, with which my concept, drawn from the representations of apprehension, is to be in accord. As the accord between knowledge and its object is truth it is easily seen that here we can only ask for the formal conditions of empirical truth, and that the phenomenon, in contradistinction to the representations of apprehension, can only be represented as the object differing therefrom if it is subject to a rule, distinguishing it from every other apprehension and necessitating a certain kind of combination of the manifold. What in the phenomenon contains

[1]*B.*, 236=*A.*, 191.   [2]*Inbegriff.*

the condition of this necessary rule of apprehension is the object."
The argument so far is couched in subjectivist terms.[1] Phenomena are identified with representations, and representations are regarded as indistinguishable from acts of apprehending, except where by the establishment of necessary relations between them these representations are converted into physical objects, which thus become mere compounds of acts of awareness, so that there is no middle term between my acts of awareness and the thing-in-itself,—although in the last sentence quoted Kant seems to be feeling his way towards the phenomenal object.[2] However, the sentence, " What in the phenomenon contains the condition of this necessary rule of apprehension is the object," involves an ambiguity. Kant may mean by " rule " either the general principle of causality or the empirical content of a particular causal law, by "object" either the empirical or the transcendental object. But in any case the phrase suggests that by phenomenon is meant something more than a mere complex of subjective representations.

The problem is how the same representations can be regarded as both subjective and, in a different setting, objective, and how we can pick out of the subjective order of representations those which are also objective. The first paragraph of the proof states the difficulty and gives the answer in general terms, *i.e.*, that representations as objective are connected by necessary laws, the second applies the answer to the particular aspect of experience specially connected with the problem of causality, as understood by Kant, *i.e.*, the aspect of succession in time, and gives the answer for this aspect of experience only.

To proceed with the argument, change, Kant says, can only be observed as succeeding a phenomenal state in which the change in question had not yet arisen, for an event succeeding on empty time is no object of possible experience, any more than an empty time itself. Consequently all apprehension of objective change consists in a succession of perceptions. This alone, however, gives us no mark to distinguish it from other apprehension, for Kant has already laid down the principle that all apprehension of the manifold is successive. However, a distinguishing mark is provided

[1]Phenomena are said to be only a complex of representations and " the house " only a representation (B., 236=A., 191).
[2]B., 235 (*gar nicht unterschieden*).

by the following consideration:—" I notice that, if in a phenomenon which contains an event I call the precedent state of perception A and the subsequent state B, B can only follow A in apprehension, and the perception A cannot follow B but can only precede it.[1] I see, *e.g.*, a ship going down stream. My perception of its position lower down follows my perception of its position higher up the course of the river, and it is impossible for me, in the apprehension of this phenomenon, to perceive the ship first lower down and afterwards higher up the stream. Here, therefore, the order in the sequence of perceptions in apprehension is determined, and perception is kept bound to this order. In the previous example of a house my perceptions in apprehending it could begin from its summit and end at the ground, but could also begin at the bottom and end at the top, or begin at the left and end at the right, or *vice versa*, in apprehending the manifold of the empirical perception. Accordingly there was in the series of these perceptions no determined order, which necessarily decided where I had to begin in apprehension in order to combine the manifold empirically. This rule, however, is always to be found in the perception of what happens, and it makes the order of the successive perceptions (in the apprehension of this phenomenon) *necessary*." It is then a rule determining our perceptions that the objectively later event should succeed the objectively earlier, but such a rule obviously carries with it causal necessity. Only if there is such a rule can I say that there is a sequence in phenomena, as opposed to my apprehension of them, which means " that I cannot arrange my apprehension otherwise than in this very order of succession."

The second and third proofs are very similar to this. The second proof differs from the first in that it argues only from the absence of any possible distinction between subjective and objective succession except for necessary rules of connection, and not also, like the first, from the fact that where we apprehend an objective event the order of our apprehensions is always irreversible, thus involving necessary connection.[2] It bases its conclusion on the impossibility of finding any distinction unless the objective has just this characteristic (*i.e.*, connection by necessary laws), rather than on the fact that the characteristic in question is actually involved in objectivity. If our perceptions are invariably successive,

[1] *B.*, 237–8 = *A.*, 191–2.
[2] *B.*, 239–41, fifth to seventh paragraphs of first ed. *A.*, 194–6.

Kant urges, their actual order in time can afford no ground to distinguish between subjective and objective. Hence if it were not the case that the perceptions of the objective were determined by necessary laws, we could only say that two apprehensions follow each other, not that two states of objects do so. To this proof is added a remark on the well-worn subject of the impossibility of proving causation by empirical induction because of its necessity.[1] " The case is the same as with other pure representations *a priori* (*e.g.*, space and time,) which we are only able to draw out of experience as clear concepts, because we have first put them into experience, nay, have rendered experience possible only by their help. It is true, no doubt, that logical clearness in this representation of a rule determining the succession of events, as a concept of cause, becomes possible only when we have used. it in experience, but a reference to this condition of the synthetical unity of phenomena in time, was nevertheless the ground of experience itself, and consequently preceded it *a priori.*"

The third proof opens with a statement of the thesis to be established, namely that we never regard a succession as objective without the presence of necessary connection and that, further, this necessary connection alone makes the idea of objective succession possible.[2] For no extension or increased accuracy of our consciousness of our subjective representations can ever make them objective. " Objective meaning cannot consist in relation to another representation (of what one wished to predicate of the object), for, if so, the question would only arise again—how can this representation again reach beyond itself and receive an objective meaning in addition to the subjective one, which belongs to it as a determination of the mind ? If we try to find out what new quality or dignity is imparted to our representations *by reference to an object*, we find that it involves nothing beyond the necessary combination of the representations in a certain fashion, and their subjection to a rule ; and that on the other hand they receive their objective significance only because a certain order in the time-relation of our representations is necessary." " I know an object when I must assign it to a certain determinate place in time, which after the preceding state cannot be other than it is." So, as in the previous argument, objective order in time is shown to involve necessary connection.

[1]*B.*, 241.   [2]*B.*, 241-4, eighth to tenth paragraphs, 1st ed., *A.*, 196-9.

The next proof has already been dealt with. In the fifth proof of the first edition version and in the proof added in the second edition the argument is couched in terms of the synthesis. In the former Kant begins with the assertion that all empirical knowledge involves a synthesis of the manifold by imagination.[1] In this synthesis the representations are always successive and the order of sequence is not determined, without the category of cause there is no reason to be found in the synthesis why it should not be the reverse order just as well as that which it actually is. But if this synthesis is a " synthesis of apprehension "—(this phraseology seems to indicate that the synthesis of apprehension is here regarded as a species of the synthesis by imagination, not as a second synthesis subsequently imposed on it)—then the order is determinate, or rather the synthesis determines the order in such a way that it is fixed for all experience. It follows that, if my perception is to involve the cognition of a real event, it must be an empirical judgment in which one thinks the sequence as determined or each event as presupposing an earlier event on which it follows according to a necessary law, otherwise it would be only *ein subjectives Spiel meiner Einbildungen*. So the causal relation is a condition of the objective validity of all our empirical judgments and hence a condition of experience itself, and this being so all objects of experience must conform to causal laws.

The above proof should be read in conjunction with that added in the second edition.[2] As the latter is Kant's final statement of the argument it may be well to quote it at length. " I perceive that phenomena succeed each other, *i.e.*, that there is a state of things at one time the opposite of which existed in the preceding state. I therefore, properly speaking, combine two perceptions in time. Now combination is not the work of mere sense and perception, but is here the product of a synthetic faculty of imagination, which determines the inner sense in regard to relation in time. This can, however, combine any two states in two ways so that either the one or the other is first in time. For it is impossible to perceive time by itself and determine by reference to it, as if empirically, what precedes and what follows in the objects. So I am only conscious that my imagination sets one state first and the other afterwards, not that the one state precedes

---

[1]*B.*, 246-7, fourteenth paragraph, 1st ed., *A.*, 201-2.   [2]*B.*, 233-4.

the other in the object. Or, in other words, the *objective relation* of the successive phenomena is not determined by mere perception. For this to be recognised as determined the relation between the two states must be so thought that it is thereby determined as necessary, which of them is to precede and which follow, thus rendering the opposite order impossible. But the concept which carries with it a necessary synthetic unity can only be a pure concept of understanding, not something in perception, and this is here the concept of *the relation of cause and effect*, where the earlier determines the later in time, as the consequence, and not as something, which could come first in the imagination (or even not be perceived at all). So it is only because we subject the sequence of phenomena, and so all change, to the law of causality, that experience itself, *i.e.*, empirical knowledge of phenomena, is possible, hence phenomena themselves, as objects of experience are only rendered possible by that law."

We shall now try to abstract and summarise the main contention advanced in these arguments. In proving the principle of causality Kant starts with consciousness of *objective* sequence in time. This consciousness is a fact established by the transcendental deduction, but how can we be conscious of such sequence and distinguish it on the one hand from merely subjective sequence of our perceptions and on the other from objective co-existence ? The distinction cannot lie in the actual order of our representations, for these are always successive, yet there must be some distinction, for consciousness of such objective sequence, as distinguished from subjective sequence or objective co-existence, is a fact. On consideration, however, we find that, whenever we regard two events, A and B, as objectively successive, the order in which we perceive A and B is irreversible, that is, we can only perceive A before B, not *vice versa*. Whatever the subjective factors involved, our experience of A and B *must* have this order. We need not look, but, if we do look, we *must* see the boat higher up the river before we see it lower down and not *vice versa*. That is, under given conditions, the experience of B *must* succeed the experience of A both for the same individual at different times and for different human individuals. But, since A and B are nothing for us apart from human experience of them, this is the same as saying that A and B are connected by a necessary law such that under given conditions B can only succeed A and not *vice versa*. Or, to put the argument in somewhat different language, (as is done in the fifth first edition proof and in the proof added in the second edition), a synthesis by imagination without the category of cause will only give us subjective, not objective, sequence ; without this category I could only know that B followed A in my imagination, not that B followed A in the object. So awareness of objective sequence in time involves awareness of the successive events as connected by a causal law such that the second necessarily follows the first in all human experience occurring under given conditions.

We may generalise the argument and express it in the form that all objectivity implies necessity because the characteristic of perception of the objective is that the content of our minds is determined independently of our volition and determined necessarily in such a way that under given conditions we must have a given experience, *e.g.*, when we say that there is a house in a certain place we imply that, if we have normal eyesight and look at the place, we *must* have the experience which we describe as seeing a house. Whether they mean anything more or not, physical objects mean, at any rate, a system of necessary laws connecting and determining our experiences.

The form of statement of the argument is open **Criticism of** to one serious objection. Four out of the five **Kant's** statements of the argument from objectivity to **argument.** necessity start with the assumption that all apprehension of the manifold is successive. By this does not seem to be meant merely that there is always a succession in time involved in our experience, but that we can immediately apprehend only the successive and never the co-existent or permanent, and that all our representations are successive and never co-existent. For Kant implies that in subjective apprehension the distinction between the successive and the co-existent is not present. My representations of the co-existent are treated as always successive just like my representations of the objectively successive.[1] Kant denies it to be possible to distinguish the co-existent and the sequent in any single case by simply having representations that co-exist as opposed to representations that follow each other, and denies it on the ground that our apprehension is always successive. Yet the doctrine that all apprehension is successive, when interpreted in this sense, seems so groundless

---

[1] *E.g.*, B., 234 (=*A*., 189–190), 225, 261 (=*A*., 214–5).

and indefensible that we are very loth to accept the interpretation. We shall criticise the view directly but it is important while doing so to remember that the deduction is not dependent on it. It is, in fact, stated without this assumption in the passage added in the second edition. The second analogy is an attempt to show that causality is involved in the distinction between objective and subjective sequence and between objective sequence and co-existence, and though all perceptions are not successive there can be no doubt that such a distinction is made and that it is not determined by the actual order of our perceptions. It is quite unnecessary to back up this distinction by the assertion that our perceptions are always successive and that therefore the actual order can never give the co-existent or show any distinction between objective and subjective sequence, for it is, in any case, an obvious fact that, when our perceptions are successive, we yet sometimes deny objective sequence or actually assert objective co-existence. Further, this distinction cannot be regarded as merely the content of empirical judgments which might theoretically be wrong, but as a condition of all judgment or cognition regarding sequence in time. For all cognition, Kant held, implies objectivity and objectivity implies a distinction between objective and subjective order, that is, between sequence in the object of knowledge and sequence in the experience of knowing or perceiving. Now it is just this objective sequence that the deduction shows to be unintelligible except in terms of necessity. Kant does not show merely that our distinction between the subjective and the objective can only be psychologically accounted for by the presence of necessary connection but that the very concept of experienced objectivity implies necessity. (Kant, of course, claims that his argument does not rest on the analysis of concepts, but he means concepts taken apart from the possibility of experiencing the concrete fact expressed in the concept. The addition of the word " experienced " or perhaps we should rather say "intrinsically capable of being experienced by us," expresses the main difference between Kant's view and the old dogmatism. At any rate, it seems to us that the proof of causality of which we have given an account must be described as an analysis of the implications of objective sequence as a possible object of experience, *i.e.*, an analysis of the concept of experienced, or " experienceable," objective sequence.)

Now the view suggested by Kant that all representations

follow each other so that none co-exist with others and none are more permanent than others is not supported by any ground whatever but simply assumed without discussion, and it seems quite inconsistent with the empirical evidence of introspection, which shows that what we are conscious of, even as an object of explicit attention or cognition, involves co-existent elements and is not a mere " one-dimensional " succession. Psychology seems to have established a view of the field of consciousness as containing a diversity of elements, more or less attended to, ranging from objects of concentrated attention to slight sensations of which we are not aware in distinction from other elements, but which form part of our experience and help to constitute its general feeling tone. It may be said that these elements are not all objects of cognition or explicit attention, so that, although a diversity of elements is present in our consciousness, we can only attend to them, or know them, singly. But even that in the field of consciousness which we attend to specially —leaving aside the elements not explicitly attended to—is seen by introspection to be indeed always a unity, but a unity containing various and sometimes very diverse elements. So far from introspection always revealing the merely successive it never does so at all. The merely successive would be, at any given moment, the absolutely simple, a mere line without breadth, yet introspection always seems to reveal a certain complexity of simultaneous presentations, or at any rate simultaneous aspects and elements, even in the object of our special attention or cognition. Otherwise that object would always have only one quality. The data of introspection always seem to be further analysable, and it seems impossible to make this analysis merely an analysis into earlier and later sections of the specious present without introducing a second " dimension," simultaneity. If my experience were merely successive I should be aware only of the absolutely simple, though it would be a changing simple—if that be not a contradiction in terms—yet, so far from it being the case that our experience is at any moment absolutely simple, the absolutely simple is rightly said by Kant elsewhere not to be a possible object of experience at all.[1]   It cannot be objected that we are never conscious of a mere moment without duration, for to say that we are always conscious of something having duration is to say that

[1] *B.*, 497, *A.*, 800.

we are always conscious of something further divisible, which must mean for Kant that our representations of the different elements into which it is divisible *co-exist*.

Above all, if we are never immediately conscious of the co-existent, we can never be immediately conscious either of space or of representations of spatial objects, in other words we can never perceive or image anything spatial at all. For space always involves the presence of coexistent parts, our representations of spatial objects are always representations of a spatial whole not only ideally and theoretically but easily and actually divisible into different coexistent parts, which, I should think, is quite sufficient by itself to refute the doctrine that our experience is always merely successive. Indeed to deny that there can be coexistent elements in our experience seems to be inconsistent with the very possibility of knowledge, since, as Kant himself maintains—and this is one of the fundamental tenets of the Critique—knowledge is always knowledge of a complex held in unity by the mind, and this implies the simultaneous presence of different elements in our experience.

The only explanation of the extraordinary assumption, apparently made by Kant, that our experience is merely successive, seems to lie in a confusion between the undoubted truth that all our experience is successive and the falsehood that it is *merely* successive, *i.e.*, involves no coexistent elements at all. He does not expressly say that our representations are always *merely* successive, only that they are successive, and then treats this statement as barring the simultaneous presence to our mind of different representations—thus he says that we can find no difference in the time-relation of representations because they are always successive. However, as we have seen, the argument from the successive character of our representations is not necessary for the proof of causality.

Secondly, the relation between causality and objectivity must be conceived as logical, not as psychological. As in the transcendental deduction the doctrine is rendered misleading by the suggestion that the synthesis is an actual psychological process. This view must not be regarded as essential to the main argument. The point proved is not that we only come to apprehend the objective by a process in which we arrange phenomena according to necessary laws but that from the beginning objective sequence logically implies necessary connection between the precedent and the subsequent events. If the doctrine of the synthesis is regarded as fundamental, the argument is liable to all the objections already advanced against this doctrine in our account of the transcendental deduction. The argument shows that the cognition of necessary connection is implied in the cognition of objectivity, not that it must precede the latter as a psychical event.

Nor can we rightly say that in grounding his proof of causality on objectivity (or, as it is sometimes put, in assuming change and not merely succession) Kant was not critical enough but based his argument on an unproved though practically indispensable assumption. We must remember that the Analogies presuppose the transcendental deduction, and the transcendental deduction has already shown that even consciousness of our perceptions as a manifold presupposes consciousness of the objective. Scepticism must be a dumb philosophy, for, if it allows a single judgment, it admits the objective. All judgments imply the objective, therefore we cannot renounce the objective without renouncing all knowledge, even knowledge of our ignorance, which renunication is not a possible alternative. But the objective[1] as we have seen, implies necessity.

Defence of the general principle of Kant's argument against various criticisms. Kant's position may be made clearer by trying to answer certain objections that have been brought against him. We shall first take the four criticisms directed by Schopenhauer against the second analogy and contend that they all show a misunderstanding of the issue.[2]

(1) It will be remembered that Kant, in proving the principle of causality, took the cases of a house and of a ship moving down-stream, and pointed out that, while in the former case our perceptions could follow any order we chose—we could see the bottom first just as easily as the top, in the latter case we were constrained to see the ship at a point higher up the river before we saw it at a point lower down. Schopenhauer rejoins that the cases are quite analogous. In both cases the change in our perceptions is necessarily determined by the movement of a body, only in the case of a house it is our eyes that move

---

[1]In speaking thus I do not mean to limit " the objective " to the physical world as opposed to psychical states of human beings, though Kant expressly deduces causality only for the physical world. But this point will be discussed in the next chapter but one.

[2]*Ueber die vierfache Wurzel des Satzes vom zureichenden Grunde,* 323.

relatively to surrounding objects, in the other case it is the ship. Hence one succession is quite as objective as the other. To this we may reply that the movement of our body is still subjective in reference to the object of cognition, *i.e.*, in so far as our perceptions are determined by such movements and not by the object observed, they are not referred to that object. Thus we do not assign objectivity to the order in which we perceive the different parts of the house, because we do not regard this order as determined by factors external to our body, or as following an order which cannot be changed by our act of perceiving the house. If we were observing not the house, but our own movements, then we should assign objectivity to the latter, but in either case objectivity involves a necessary succession in our perceptions of what we call the object.

(2) That one event may succeed another without being caused by it, is Schopenhauer's second objection. If objective sequence and causal sequence are identified, then, he argues, night must cause day; if I come out of a house and a tile, immediately afterwards, falls from the roof and strikes me on the head, my coming out of the house must cause the falling of the tile—which is absurd.

But what Kant has proved is not that, if B succeeds A, it must be causally determined by A, but that the sequence A–B must necessarily be determined by some cause or causes,—that any given event is causally determined by some "as yet indeterminate correlate."[2] This is certainly the logical conclusion of the deduction, and is implied in Kant's frequent insistence on the point that particular causal laws can only be discovered by induction from particular experiences. Unfortunately in B 234 he speaks as though all objective sequence were causal, but against this we may set several passages in the actual proof of causality.[3] Further, the examples of objective succession given by him are not examples of cause and effect—the cause of water turning into ice is not the water, the cause of a ship going further downstream is not the presence of the ship higher up the river. It is indeed almost impossible to suppose that Kant consistently meant to hold a doctrine so palpably contrary to facts and so at variance with his repeated assertions that particular causal laws can only be discovered by induction from particular

---

[1] *V.* further below, ch. vi.   [2] *B.*, 244=*A* 199.
[3] *B.*, 239, 243, 244 (=*A* 194, 199–200) ; also first edition formulation of principle to be proved.

G

experiences, and there is certainly not the least need either to suppose that he actually held the view or that he logically ought to have held it as the consequence of his proof of causality.

It might be objected that according to the view expressed here causality is merely necessary sequence and that, therefore, to say that B necessarily succeeds A is to say that A causes B. But the Kantian view is not, strictly, that B necessarily succeeds A, for that would imply that B must always succeed A, but that, under the given conditions, B necessarily succeeds A, *i.e.*, that B necessarily succeeds A plus the sum-total of other relevant conditions. It is a task of science to suggest other conditions, C, D, such that we can formulate a law to the effect that B necessarily succeeds A, C, D, (or, often, quantitatively varies in a certain proportion to the variations of A, C, and D). This answer seems to meet Schopenhauer's objection—whether, as in the case of day and night, the successive events may conveniently be regarded as different states of the same substance, or, as in what we call a coincidence or fortuitous conjunction of circumstances, *e.g.*, a tile falling and striking me on the head when I go out of the house, they must be regarded as what Kant would have called states of different substances, *i.e.*, relatively disparate causal systems. The difference between Schopenhauer's two examples, *i.e.*, day succeeding night and the falling tile, is only one of greater complexity. In both cases, while the precedent does not itself determine the subsequent state, the succession must be determined by some cause and hence falls under the head of the analogy.

Schopenhauer also objected (3) that we can distinguish a real event from a phantom without knowing the particular causes by which it is determined, and (4) that Kant's admission that we can only discover particular causal laws by experience (*i.e.*, experience of objective succession) is inconsistent with the doctrine that we only recognise a succession as objective by discovering the causal laws which determined it. Such objections seem to confuse the consciousness of an event as causally determined by some, as yet unknown, law with the discovery of particular causal laws. Kant's contention is that, when we recognise a succession as objective, we, *ipso facto*, recognise it as causally determined by some unspecified and unknown antecedents, not that, before we can recognise it as objective, we must first find the particular causes by which it is actually determined. We are from the beginning conscious of objects, and the conception of the objective is found to be equivalent to the conception of necessary order in time, or, at any rate, to imply the latter as the most essential ingredient in its meaning. Hence consciousness of necessary order in time and so of causality is found to be implicit in human consciousness from the beginning. But this is not the same as saying that to be conscious of a given event as objective we must first come to know the particular causes which determine it. The point is not that objectivitiy is inferred from the discovery of a particular causal connection, but that it is simply another aspect of the same concept as necessity.

It is a remarkable and significant fact that the proof of causality which Schopenhauer substitutes for that given by Kant is in principle closely akin to that which it claims to supersede. Schopenhauer, like Kant, maintains that, unless we assume causality, knowledge of the objective world is impossible. He argues that sensation cannot give us objects unless we first, by a process of unconscious and intuitive inference, introduce an external cause to account for our sensations as effects on our sensibility, thus assuming that every change must be causally accounted for.[1] " Sensation of every kind is and remains a process in the organism itself, as such, however, is confined to the region underneath our skin, can therefore in itself never include anything which lies on the other side of this skin and so is external to us. A sensation may be pleasant or unpleasant—that is, have a certain relation to our will—but in no sensation is there any objective element...... It is only when the understanding, (a function, not of particular delicate nerve-ends, but of the brain, that brain, so cunningly and mysteriously built, weighing three and, in exceptional cases, up to five pounds only), becomes active and applies its single and unique form, the law of causation, that a mighty change takes place, by which subjective sensation is transformed into objective perception. The understanding, in fact, by means of its own peculiar form, and therefore a priori, .i.e, prior[2] to all experience (for experience is till then impossible),comprehends the given bodily sensation as an effect (a word which it alone understands), and realises that as such it must have a cause. It then immediately takes the form of outer sense, space, which is lying ready in the intellect, i.e., the brain, in order

[1] Ueber die vierfache Wurzel des Satzes vom zureichenden Grunde, 321.
[2] This indicates a confusion between temporal and logical priority.

to locate that cause outside the organism, for thereby first originates for it the external, the possibility of which is just space ; so that pure perception *a priori* must contain the foundation of empirical perception." The argument undoubtedly suffers from being couched in a psychological (and, still worse, a physiological) form, but is there any difference of principle between this proof and the Kantian proof which we have just outlined ? While Kant proves the principle of causality by showing that unless we recognised certain sequences in our experience as irreversible, *i.e.*, necessarily determined, we could not recognise them as bringing us into contact with an objective reality relatively independent of our act of perceiving it ; Schopenhauer proves it by showing that we could have no knowledge of a world of objects without inferring an external cause to account for our perceptions and so using the principle of causality. But what does the reference of sensations to an object as their cause mean, when interpreted in terms of our experience,—can it mean anything but that those elements in experience which we regard as objective are thereby regarded as necessarily determined independently of the individual perceiving subject ? Can the intuitive inference from our sensations to an external cause be anything but the recognition of certain elements in our experience as necessarily determined by that cause, and hence, in so far as thus determined, " irreversible " in order ? But it is just this irreversibility in experience on which Kant insists as a necessary pre-requisite of knowledge. It follows that the proofs of causality given by Schopenhauer[1] and Kant cannot really be separated but are, at the most, different aspects of the same proof.

All this time the realist may have been thinking : " This is all right as far as it goes, but it does not prove anything that we really wish to know. The principle of causality on which science is based tells us about states of physical objects, but you say nothing whatever about states of objects, only about our apprehensions. Consequently, you are flagrantly evading your self-imposed task of proving the principle of causality as an indispensable presupposition of science ; you are giving us chaff for grain, necessity in perceptions for necessity in objects." In the words of Mr. Prichard, " As soon as the real nature of Kant's vindication

[1]Whether Schopenhauer's language about the objects that determine our perceptions is reconcilable with his subjectivist attitude is a question that falls outside the scope of this discussion.

of causality has been laid bare, it is difficult to describe it as an argument at all. He is anxious to show that in apprehending A, B, as a real or objective succession we presuppose that they are elements in a causal order of succession. Yet in support of his contention he points only to the quite different fact that where we apprehend a succession A B, we think of the *perception* of A and the *perception* of B as elements in a necessary but subjective succession."[1]

I think this argument is, from the realist point of view, valid against the argument of the second Analogy as stated by Kant, but I also think that starting from the latter an argument which will establish causality for an independent physical world as well as for our experiences of perception may easily be developed. Let us accept the realist point of view, if only for the sake of argument—(and I certainly do not wish to reduce matter to a collection of particular human perceptions)—let us take the realist position and see what follows. As far as I can see, the realist must accept one of three alternatives.

(*a*) He may base our knowledge of the physical world on an immediate perception of it as physical. But how can this be ? It cannot mean that we perceive it as existing independently of our perception or existing when we are not perceiving it, that would be to say that we can perceive an object without the object being perceived, a palpable self-contradiction. It must mean that we are aware of our immediate object of perception as connected by law with other objective states not actually perceived by us and so as necessarily determined independently of us. In saying that we perceive an object as having such and such a quality or being in such and such a state we covertly introduce causality, and if we tried to get rid of the notion of causality we should find that without it the solid, physical bodies we " immediately perceive " vanished into thin air. We must regard the perceived physical state as a member in a system of physical states determining its position irreversibly so that under the given circumstances it could not be other than it is. To be qualities of *an object* the percepta[2] must be members of a system, for us to know them as qualities of something other than the

[1]Kant's *Theory of Knowledge*, p. 291.
[2]I use the term " percepta " to indicate what we immediately perceive as opposed to the so-called act of perception by which we perceive it, and without thereby prejudging the question whether what we immediately perceive is a representation or a physical state.

perceiving self we must know them as connected by laws, which are not determined by the acts of perception of that self but rather determine its percepta. We cannot see our perceptum existing independently of our perception of it, we can therefore only recognise its independence if we know it as part of a system in which it is determined independently of our act of perceiving it. If so, it is not true that Kant's proof of causality depends on the representative theory of perception, as is often said.

(*b*) The realist may base our knowledge of the physical world not on immediate perception itself, but on a causal argument from what we immediately perceive, and say—we do not perceive physical objects directly as such, but must infer their independent existence in order to account causally for our percepta. But (1) the necessity of accounting causally for our percepta presupposes that they are caused by something, and so still leaves causality the indispensable presupposition of all knowledge about the physical. (2) Physical objects will not account causally for percepta unless these physical objects are themselves subject to causality. (3) Further, Kant has shown that the very conception of an object, or a physical system, changing in time, implies universal causal connection between the precedent and subsequent states of the process. (4) It seems to us that on the premises of the realist who retains the representative theory of perception it can be logically proved that the possibility of inferring a perceptum B1, (whether actual or possible), by causal reasoning from another perceptum, A1, implies a necessary[1] connection between the states of the physical objects which cause A1 and B1 respectively. But, if so, any causal law which can be discovered connecting percepta (or " percipibilia ") implies a causal law connecting the states of the physical objects which determine the percepta (or " percipibilia "), and necessary succession in our percepta cannot be really separated from necessary succession in the object. But this point requires some further development.

[1]*I.e.*, a connection which enables us to infer one state from the other ; of course, to say either that two percepta or that two physical states are necessarily connected by causal laws is not to say that one is the cause of the other. Nor would our conclusion follow from the fact that A1 and B1 are necessarily determined, because they might be determined by objects unconnected with each other, but only from the fact that— as everybody supposes—percepta A1 and B1 are sometimes connected by causal laws.

To take a particular instance, I see two billiard balls and conclude that, if the first strikes the second, the second will move (barring external hindrances). Let us call the first ball A, the second ball B. In terms of experience the law connecting the movements of A and B means that the proposition, " an observer under normal conditions of perception would have a perceptum of A striking B," implies the proposition, "such an observer would have a perceptum of B moving." I mean by " normal conditions of perception " certain conditions specified so as to guard against sense-illusion (*i.e.*, good light, healthy eyes, etc.). Then the perceptum of B moving necessarily follows on the perceptum of A striking B (when observed under " normal " conditions of perception). Our object is to show that the necessary sequence of the perceptum of B moving on the perceptum of A striking B implies that the motion of B as a physical object follows necessarily on A striking B, provided the general position of the realist who holds the representative theory of perception—we shall call him the " critical realist " for short—be accepted. For it is to him that we are replying, we are not concerned here with attacks made from other philosophical standpoints.

We begin then with these two propositions : (1) the observer would have a perceptum of A striking B ; (2) the observer would[1] have a perceptum of B moving. The first proposition *ex hypothesi* implies the second. But the " critical realist " must hold that, if it is the case that under " normal " conditions of perception an observer would have the perceptum of B moving, B really does move, *i.e.*, that proposition (2), " the observer would have a perceptum of B moving," implies another proposition (3), " B will move." Therefore (1), " the observer would have a perceptum of A striking B," also implies (3), " B will move."

Further the " critical realist " must hold that, if A strikes B, an observer under " normal " conditions of perception would have the perceptum of A striking B, *i.e.*, that (4), " A strikes B," implies (1). But (1) has been already shown to imply (3) " B will move." Therefore, the proposition, " A strikes B," implies the proposition, " B will move." That is, the movement of B follows necessarily on the impact of A on B.

[1]We use the Conditional to cover cases both of actual and possible experience. By the observer is, of course, always understood " the human observer under ' normal ' conditions."

Similarly, it seems, it could be shown in all cases that, if realism be combined with the representative theory of perception, it logically follows that a law connecting percepta implies a law connecting the states of the physical objects which determine the percepta. And this seems to apply not only to laws connecting actual but to laws connecting possible percepta, for in our argument we have started not with the premiss, "an observer *has* a perceptum, etc.," but with the premiss, " a human observer under ' normal ' conditions *would* have a perceptum, etc." At any rate a realist who deduces the existence of physical objects in order causally to account for our percepta must *a fortiori* admit some causal laws connecting our percepta, and, as we have tried to show, any such causal law seems to imply a causal law connecting the states of the physical objects which determine the percepta. We shall not, however, lay most stress on this, but on the argument that the very conception of a physical object, whatever else it involves, involves at any rate the conception of a system of laws connecting perceived and perceivable physical states.

(*c*) The realist may not only repudiate the representative theory but also identify the act of perceiving with the object perceived and so with something in the physical world, as indeed a subjective idealist might. But he must still distinguish between perception and imagination, and it seems that it follows directly from Kant's argument in the second Analogy that these, from such a position, can only be distinguished by the introduction of necessity. From this point of view the objection that Kant had only proved necessity in our perceptions and not necessity in the object falls to the ground, for the distinction between perception and object has vanished. This line of argument seems to apply to any philosophy which identifies the physical object and the experience of perceiving it, whether it tends to eliminate the physical or the psychical side, or endeavours to preserve a balance between them. It thus applies alike to " subjective idealism," to " neo-realism " and to " radical empiricism."

If, however, the realist maintains the separation between the physical object and the experience of perception, it may be argued, in addition to what we have already said, that the idea of any definite physical object can only be reached by co-ordinating the experiences of different percipients and of the same percipient at different times, and this co-ordination is impossible without thorough-going causal determination in the object. I have an experience of seeing flames in the grate on leaving my room, I have no such experience on returning a few hours later but have the experience of seeing ashes instead. The two experiences are co-ordinated and their sequence explained by the thought of a fire which is independent of my experience and goes on burning when I am not there. But this can only be achieved if the fire I saw when I went out is causally continuous with the ashes I see when I return. The only explanation of my experience that can be given by means of physical objects or processes is causal explanation, and this can only be effected if there is a continuous causal connection between the physical states corresponding to the different experiences which are explained and correlated. If there is any break between, such that one stage or element in the process is not causally connected with the other stages or elements, the idea of a physical object or process does not connect the different experiences at all, because the stages of the process which determine the different experiences are themselves no longer connected. In referring different percepta to the same physical object we assert a necessary connection between these percepta, but since these percepta are either determined by or states of the physical object there cannot be a necessary connection between the percepta unless there is a necessary connection between the physical states of the object to which they are referred. And this argument seems to hold good on *any* theory of perception, whether representative or direct, that makes the physical world different from and independent of our experiences or acts of perceiving it. We cannot arrive at an idea of any particular physical object except by referring different percepta to it either as its effects (representative theory) or its states (direct theory), but to refer these percepta to the same object is to assert a necessary connection between them, from which it follows that any physical states which form intermediate links between the different percepta must be themselves causally connected and that the idea of a physical object derived from correlating different percepta involves thorough-going causal connection.[1]

The reader may feel that in all this we are straying very far away from Kant himself, but, if it could be shown that a proof of causality of the Kantian type is not incompatible with realism, the influence of the proof would obviously be

[1]This argument can be backed by the additional argument stated on p. 99.

far more widespread. The idea that Kant's conclusions on this subject are vitiated by their dependence on his particular system of idealism is one of the chief reasons that has led to the comparative neglect of the argument of the second Analogy in recent philosophy. It is, therefore, important to show, if possible, that the main principle of the Kantian proof of causality can be accepted not only without assuming Kant's particular system but without assuming any form of " idealism." We must, of course, admit that Kant takes an idealist standpoint throughout the argument, that he logically bases all his conclusions on the doctrine of " transcendental idealism," and that he supposed the acceptance of this doctrine to be necessary if the validity of the categories was to be proved at all, but it seems to us that it is not the doctrine but only the method of transcendental idealism, *i.e.*, the method of proof by appealing to the possibility of experience and knowledge, that forms the real presupposition and basis of the deduction of causality.

It has also been objected by Mr. Prichard that Kant's doctrine that the apprehension of an object consists in the apprehension of a complex (*Inbegriff*) of necessarily connected representations is untenable, because according to it the same representations are related both as physical and as psychical events, both as our apprehensions and as parts of the object apprehended, viz : a reality in nature.[1] Now the passage in which Kant speaks of the object as a complex of representations is extremely subjectivist in character.[2] But the fact that it is only the first statement of the proof should by itself warn us against laying too much stress on it, for the presence of five contiguous proofs of such a similar character points to their having been written at different times, and Kant would, in inserting them in the Critique, naturally put the earlier first, especially as he was apt to start with an inadequate point of view and then pass on to one more adequate. But the content of the passage itself clearly shows points characteristic of the earlier passages of the Critique. Its subjectivism, its reference to the transcendental object and its description of phenomena as representations connected by necessary " rules " all point to an early origin. Now in this passage Kant not only identifies a physical object with a complex of representations but also identifies

---

[1]Kant's *Theory of Knowledge*, pp. 209, 233, 281-2
[2]First paragraph of 1st ed. = third paragraph of 2nd ed. version of *Second Analogy*.

the content and the act of representation or perception so that the physical object becomes a combination of acts of our mind, a view which seems to me quite alien to the general trend of his philosophy. But, while dealing with Mr. Prichard's objection, we should remember a distinction that many realists much like to emphasise, the distinction between the perception and the perceptum, between the act of perception or " representation " and its content. It may be absurd to identify a physical object with acts of our mind, but it does not follow that it is absurd to identify it with the content of our experience. Kant, indeed, in the passage specially referred to (B 235) identifies the act and the content explicitly, but so far from this identification being anything in the nature of a cornerstone of his philosophy, the latter may rather be said to involve an excessive dualism between act and content. For the transcendental self is, roughly speaking, the act and the empirical self the content, yet who would dream of criticising Kant on the ground that he did not carry the dualism between the transcendental and the empirical self far enough? To make a physical object a complex of acts of representation would be, from the " critical " standpoint, to make it either a transcendental self or a set of categories without content!

We must, then, take " representation " in the sense not of a mental act but of a mental image in order to see whether, in that sense, we can describe a phenomenal object as a complex of representations.   Now such an object is certainly not said by Kant to consist of my or anybody else's private mental image of it as an element in his life-history, nor to be a sum of such images as psychical facts, forming parts of individual human minds.   All that can be said is that the physical has no content but that found in private images, actual or possible, and that it can only be understood as a mental image which is, however, public not private property. It cannot be objected, therefore, that the same representations are related both as private images and as objects, both as psychical and as physical events ; the identity is qualitative, not numerical, the same terms do not have to enter into two incompatible relations.

The material world is, for Kant, a conception produced by mind working on individual experiences, this conception being either, on the subjectivist view, only a logical fiction intended to express the fact that under given conditions different human experients will always have a given perception and

valuable as a means enabling us to discover and formulate laws governing experience ; or, on his more objective view, a representation of a reality other than itself which, though metaphysically only phenomenal, has for us a real substantiality and independence.   On the subjectivist view, logically carried out, there is nothing real for any representation of mine to stand in a relation to but minds and their other representations, although, by a logical fiction, it may be thought as an attribute of a physical object connected with other such objects ; on the more objective view physical objects have reality as a different class of being from private representations and are not composed of the latter.   In neither case do private representations exist both as parts of real physical objects and as psychical events in the life-history of individuals.

It remains to identify the physical world with "representations" in the sense of being a "public object" of knowledge or experience.   But this only means that to us it is nothing except as object of human experience, that, in so far as known, objects are known only through our representations, and that a physical object can only be conceived as an object represented, so that we could not say what it would be apart from all representation of it.   It does not mean that the same representations are, in different contexts, psychical elements in a human individual's private experience and elements in a real, physical world, or that the physical world is composed of private mental images.   Either, on the subjectivist view, there is no real physical world common to all observers, so that it is not necessary to regard our mental images as entering into two such disparate sets of relations as would be involved in making them at once members of an individual, psychical, and common, physical world, or, on the "phenomenalist" view, there is a really existent physical world but it does not consist of private, mental images.   In neither case are there two really existent worlds both composed of these images.

The account of the argument used to prove causality in the second Analogy should be supplemented by reference to the transcendental deduction.[1]   There Kant argued that all empirical cognition involved reference to an "object," and that an "object" could only be conceived as a necessarily connected system.   This general argument can, however,

---

[1] *V*. above pp. 55-6.

easily be turned into an argument for causality, since necessary connection between different stages in a process of change is for Kant identical with causality. Whatever else the being of a physical object may involve, it involves this at any rate, —a necessary connection between its different qualities or states. A state of an object unconnected with the other states of the same object could not rightly be called a state of that object at all, and connection of different qualities or states as qualities or states of one object without mutual dependence and so implication, *i.e.*, necessary connection, seems impossible. And for any object which changes in time this necessary connection must obviously involve causality. Further this seems to be an argument that will hold good *both* from a realist and from an idealist[1] point of view. In the transcendental deduction Kant had tried to show that all empirical knowledge presupposes systematic unity in the object known, but *system* obviously implies *necessary*[2] *connection*, and so causality in the sense of necessary succession.

Perhaps it might now be useful to end this chapter by summarily contrasting Kant's view of causality with the views held by different schools of thought. Hume held that causality was not a demonstrable principle, for reason, working by analysis, could not discern a connection between the cause and the effect as two separate events, and experience could not give us necessity. Kant met this criticism by showing that, while particular experiences could not form the basis of the proof of any strictly necessary principle, and reason could not discover by analysis any connection between the cause and the effect, yet there was another way of proof left open ; and a way of proof based on experience. He discovered an alternative method of proof to those suggested by Hume and so avoided the dilemma. The principle of universal causality could not be inferred by induction from particular experiences, but it could be inferred from experience in general, considered in its all-important aspect as experience of an objective order in time, an experience which the sceptic by the mere act of judging must admit as real. What is implied in all our experience must be admitted to be necessary,

[1]From the " subjective idealist " point of view this argument must take the form that the thought of a physical object is the thought of a system of perceptions connected by necessary laws, so that all judgments about physical objects are judgments about systems of laws connecting our experiences.

[2]*V.* below pp. 108ff. for the development of this argument in connection with the conception of " substance."

for without it there could be no experience of the kind we know. No more cogent proof can be given of any principle than by showing that we must either believe that principle or believe nothing, and this is the type of proof effected in the case of causality. Without assuming causality, no cognition or judgment about anything in time would be possible ; therefore causality is universally valid of events in time. It may be objected that the proof is after all empirical, because causality is deduced from the character of experience as involving sequence in time, and this character is simply taken as given empirically. In a sense this is true, but no *a priori* proof can be wholly devoid of empirical content, otherwise the concepts employed would be what Kant calls " empty " (*leer*). When a characteristic is selected which is given in all our experience and could not be removed without the total destruction of the latter as we know it, as is the case with the quality of objective sequence in time, and when it is found on examination that this characteristic implies causality, then causality may be fairly said to have been proved *a priori*. At any rate, if it has been proved, it is of little purpose disputing whether we are to call the proof *a priori* or empirical.[1]

Kant admitted Hume's contentions that the causal connection is always synthetic, and that we can have no insight into the connection between particular causes and effects, but he differed vitally from him in that he claimed to prove the general law of causality, whereas Hume held such a proof to be in principle impossible. Kant neither accepted causality without proof as " self-evident " but indemonstrable, nor sought to show its truth by an empirical induction ; nor regarded it as a merely " regulative " principle, partially confirmed by our progressive success in unifying experience by means of it, but incapable of strict demonstration. In this way he would differentiate himself from the various realistic and empirical schools of thought, while agreeing with the normal view of these in his reduction of causality in the physical world to necessary uniformity and his elimination of the notion of causal efficacy or activity,

[1] On Kant's usual view the conformity of the manifold to the principle of causality and hence the possibility of human knowledge depends on unknown noumenal conditions, so we cannot be theoretically certain that such knowledge might not cease to be possible, but we can know that, so long as such knowledge is an actual fact, then noumenal conditions must be such as to produce a manifold which conforms to the principle of causality.

as a peculiar quality in substances implied by causation, or of any notion involving an intrinsic connection between cause and effect as in any degree knowable by us. On the other hand, Kant was not an adherent of the extreme monism which is generally regarded as a leading characteristic of his idealist successors. His monism is purely formal and does not involve any assertion about the specific degree of connection between the parts of the whole, like the assertion that all individual minds are actually included in an absolute experience as its constituent parts, which, of course, to Kant would have been mere " dogmatism." The coherence view of reality, while insisting that everything is inter-connected and inter-dependent, does not exclude different degrees of connection between different particulars, nor can we logically deduce from the mere fact of inter-connection any proposition about the special degree and nature of the connection. Without abandoning monism Kant was always very careful to guard the rights of the individual, and the application, if not the very concept, of causality depends on a certain relative independence of the individual. It is strictly correct to say that a true cause cannot be anything less than the whole previous state of the universe, (or, perhaps rather, the whole previous series of events). But the practical and scientific application of the category depends on our ability to sort out particular causal links and distinguish them in the whole. In discovering " the causes " of any event an overwhelming proportion of the totality of events must be set aside as irrelevant or constant, although this irrelevancy and constancy are merely relative. We might conceive a universe in which, while the general principle of causality held good, we were unable to ignore parts of the whole as irrelevant, to anything like the extent we can do under present conditions, but, fortunately, experience has shown the world in which we live to be sufficiently pliable in this way. While it may be correct that no cause less than the whole can be the true cause in the full sense, yet the influence of by far the greater part of the whole on any given event is so small that it can be disregarded for practical and even scientific purposes. There are also certain factors in the whole like the motion of the earth round the sun, which, while of enormous importance for all events on the earth, can, on account of their constancy, be disregarded in determining the causes of any particular event. They are the same, relatively, for all events on the earth, and therefore their influence on any particular event may be ignored. The distinction between condition and cause might perhaps be reduced to a distinction between the more constant and the more variable factors.

As a matter of fact, the proof of causality given in the second Analogy proves that we can separate particular causal series from the whole just as much as it proves the general principle of causality. For we only arrive at consciousness of objective, physical succession by singling out a determinate series of events in our experience as belonging to the causal system which makes up the physical world and ignoring as irrelevant certain " subjective " factors (including in " subjective " both what is determined by psychological and what is determined by physiological factors). All experience of the objective is experience of particular objects, and I arrive at consciousness of particular objects by isolating that part in the total complex of my experience which I regard as determined by the physical object and ignoring the other elements as irrelevant. But this is just the isolation of a particular causal series out of a larger complex of events. Hence the possibility of this isolation is a presupposition of all cognition of objects.

But we must remember that causality, as proved by Kant, has lost a good deal of the content which it has in ordinary usage. What Kant proves is simply that all succession is necessary—the cause of an event is that event or events on which it succeeds necessarily. He makes no attempt to prove causality in the sense of dynamic activity on the part of the cause or of intrinsic logical connection, but tends to relegate the intrinsic connection or dynamic activity to the noumenal sphere. Cause and ground are very sharply distinguished, the object of studying causal laws is not to explain but to predict. The ultimate logical ground of a causal connection is for Kant only to be found in the non-temporal.

That causality is a phenomenal category, inadequate for the description of reality, Kant would have been the first to admit. He would not therefore be troubled by criticisms founded on the puzzles of relation and change, as causality is not for him an attempt to render events intelligible or to cure the vices of the relational mode of thought to which we are confined. His position was that we must accept relation and change as basic principles of all our experience and thought, while admitting their inadequacy to reality. In any case no special charge can be brought against the category of causality on these grounds, since whatever vices are inherent in a relational mode of thought must affect all judgments.

Kant himself pointed out the defects of causality as employed empirically—that it never gives a self-sufficient explanation or indeed an explanation at all, that it leads to an infinite regress, that the connection it establishes between phenomena is merely external. He should have added that the category cannot be applied without abstractions from the continuum like " events," " next states " or " momentary states," (according to Kant) " separate substances," that imply an atomism which, though necessary as a methodological fiction or working formula for certain purposes, is untenable as a theory of the nature of reality. Kant himself is liable to the charge of atomism in this as in other points, but it is important to insist that the argument of the second Analogy does not[1] prove any atomistic view of completely separable " causes," but only the bare fact that all succession is necessary.

Note on a point raised by Hume (Treatise Everyman's edition I, p. 188).

As we have seen earlier, Hume declares that involuntariness cannot be made the criterion of physical existence because pain and other feelings are quite as involuntary as the " impressions " we ascribe to objects.[2] But this criticism does not fit the proof of causality outlined above, because that proof is to the effect that all objective events are necessary, not that all necessary[3] events are objective, much less physical. Besides, pain itself has *objective* reality as a psychical fact. I do not make the pain I feel in toothache a quality of my teeth, because pain, as a feeling accompanying an act of perception, is essentially on the subject, not on the object, side in so far as this act of perception is concerned ; but pain, as a perceived fact, is applied to an object, *i.e.,* the empirical self. We must distinguish feeling pain from having a perception of the pain felt ; the necessity for this distinction is shown by the fact that I may positively enjoy recalling past pains, there pain is an object of perception but, so far from involving the presence of a subjective feeling of pain, the pain as object of perception rather produces the opposite feeling of pleasure.

[1]This might seem to contradict our remark above that the argument of the second Analogy proved the possibility of isolating particular causes in the whole, but it does not prove that this isolation must be absolute, and, in fact, it must always be only relative.

[2]*V.* above p. 14 ad fin.

[3]Kant certainly holds all necessary events to be objective, (though not always physical), but this is not the point on which the proof insists.

H

CHAPTER V

Substance and Reciprocity

THAT no discussion of Kant's treatment of causality can be adequate, if it altogether ignores the other two relational categories, is obvious, if only for the reason that causality is conceived by Kant as a relation between the successive states of a changing substance, and reciprocity as a relation derived from the combination of the two categories of substance and causality. But in our discussion of substance and reciprocity we shall, for the present, avoid one very important question, namely the question of the application of these categories to inner sense, as we have avoided it in the case of causality, intending to discuss the point at length in the next chapter with reference to all three analogies.

Kant's proof of substance. Now the main proofs of all three are based on the necessity of phenomena having an objective order in time. " This *synthetic unity* in the time-relation of all perceptions, *which is determined a priori*, is then the law : that all instances of empirical time-determination must stand under rules of universal time-determination, and the analogies of experience, with which we intend to deal now, must be rules of this kind."[1]

The argument of the first Analogy is stated in the second edition as follows :—" All phenomena[2] are in time. In time alone, as their substratum and the permanent form of inner perception, can *coexistence* and *sequence* alike be represented. Time, therefore, in which all succession of phenomena must be thought as occurring, remains and does not pass away, for time is that in which succession or coexistence can only be represented as its determinations. Now time in itself cannot be perceived. It follows that it must be possible to find in the objects of perception, *i.e.*, phenomena, that sub-

---

[1]*B.*, 220 (=*A* 177–8).   [2]*B.*, 224–5 (*cf.* B226–7).

stratum, which represents time in general, and in which all succession or coexistence can be perceived in apprehension through the relation of phenomena to it. Now the substratum of everything real, *i.e.*, all that belongs to the existence of things, is *substance*. In relation to this everything that belongs to being can only be thought as its determination. Consequently the permanent in reference to which all time-relations of phenomena can alone be determined, is the substance in the phenomenon, *i.e.*, the real element in the latter which as substratum of all succession always remains the same. So, as substance cannot change in being, its quantity in nature can neither be increased nor diminished." In the last sentence Kant passes from the metaphysical principle of substance to the scientific hypothesis of conservation of mass, hardly a legitimate transition.

Kant backs the argument quoted above by another to the effect that, since all our representations are successive, objective coexistence implies a permanent physical order. " Our apprehension of the manifold of phenomena is always successive, and is therefore always changing.[1] Consequently we can never determine by means of our apprehension alone whether this manifold, as object of experience, is coexistent or successive, unless there is something behind it (*zum Grunde*) which *always is*, *i.e.*, something *enduring* and *permanent*, of which all succession and coexistence are nothing but so many different forms (modi of time) in which the permanent exists. Only in the permanent, then, are time-relations possible (for simultaneity and succession are the only relations in time), that is, the permanent is the substratum of the empirical representation of time itself, and it is only in reference to it that any time-determination at all is possible."

Here again we must detach from the main **Criticism of** argument the false psychological assumptions **Kant's** with which it is cumbered. As in the second **argument.** Analogy, so here Kant makes the extraordinary[2] assumption that our experience is merely successive. We have already tried to show the complete untena-

---

[1] *B.*, 225-6 (first three sentences of first paragraph in first edition).

[2] As we have already pointed out in connection with the second Analogy, Kant confused the true statement that our experience is always successive with the false statement that our experience is merely successive. It is only if our experience is merely successive that the conclusion actually drawn follows, *i.e.*, that it can in itself give us no glimpse of the coexistent.

bility of this doctrine ; and whether it affects the validity of the argument here we shall try to see later.[1] We must also, in discussing the argument of the first Analogy, be careful to consider not only whether the proof of a " permanent " in the formal sense is valid, but also exactly what kind of permanence is presupposed by change.

Now Kant seems to have had in view in his deduction of substance four main points.

(1) He wished to assert the independent existence of the physical world, to assert phenomenalism against subjectivism, " substantia phaenomenon " against " empirical idealism." The application of the schema of substance, i.e., permanence in time, to phenomena implies that the phenomenal object is not identical with the fleeting individual representations of it, and so is quite inconsistent with subjective idealism in its usual sense. Kant meant to show that we can only be conscious of change in our subjective experience in contrast to a permanent order of physical objects ; but the argument representing this point of view is much more clearly stated in the second edition " Refutation of Idealism " than here.[2] However, the " phenomenalist " tendency in Kant, despite its important influence on his thought and on philosophy generally, is nowhere worked out with any approach to thoroughness and clearness.[3]

Further, of the three arguments into which the main thought of Kant's proof of substance can be analysed each would, if valid, really prove something different from the other two, as we shall see.

(2) Starting from his doctrine that all consciousness of events in time presupposes a single and, as he calls it, unchanging time,[4] Kant argues that the time in question cannot be itself regarded as an object among others but only as the form under which we perceive all objects. Hence all the characteristics which, by an act of abstraction, we are able to predicate of absolute time, can only be understood as characteristics realised in the general form of objects. The permanence, then, which we ascribe to time in the abstract, can only be understood as a permanence realised in objects. All propositions which we make about absolute time must be understood as propositions about the temporal relations of objects, so when we say that time does not change,

[1]P. 108 esp.   [2]B., 274 ff.
[3]V. Prof. N. Kemp Smith's *Commentary*, especially pp. 270 ff.
[4]*Die Zeit bleibt und wechselt nicht* (B., 224 *ad fin.*).

we can only mean that there is some unchanging element in objects. But the unchanging in objects is just what we mean by substance, and therefore a proof of the presence of an unchanging element in objects is a proof of substance. Supposing the assumption about the nature of time to be right, which is, of course, to say the least, disputable, what would follow? What would be the permanent element in phenomena proved by the argument? It could only be the temporal relations of phenomena by which absolute time is " represented " (*vorgestellt*), and the conclusion would be, therefore, that relations of phenomena, as far as they can be considered as purely temporal, must be of uniform structure. It is not, at any rate, the assertion of an unchanging substance behind phenomena, but of unchanging temporal relations. Such a law of uniformity should, however, come under the mathematical rather than under the dynamical principles, being strictly parallel to theorems based on the nature of Euclidean space, and may accordingly be neglected for our purpose, as we do not claim to give a full discussion of the first Analogy but only to deal with it in so far as it indirectly concerns the second. Kant came later to adopt the view that it would have been preferable to state the argument in terms of space rather than of time (*i.e.*, to argue from the fact of change in a single space), and such an argument would have served better to connect substance with the principle of conservation of mass.[1] What would be established in that case would be just a uniformity in spatial, as well as in temporal, relations.

(3) There is also the thought[2] that consciousness of any change as a change presupposes the consciousness of something that is not changing in order to measure the change, or even to recognise it as a change at all. Kant speaks as though what was needed were an absolutely permanent element, but surely the requirement is adequately met so long as all change does not proceed at the same rate (in which case it could perhaps hardly be called change). Then we can measure the different changes by each other, especially the less regular by the more regular, and be conscious of a particular change in contrast to something else which lasts for a limited time without changing or changes at a slower rate.

---

[1] *Erdmann, Nachträge* 79–81.
[2] On this argument is also based the second edition *Refutation of Idealism* (*B.*, 274 ff.), a much better statement of the case.

Kant also argues that we need something permanent to enable us to distinguish between coexistence and sequence, because our apprehension of the manifold is always successive.[1] We may sympathise with the view that even our subjective experience would be unintelligible if separated from consciousness of an objective physical world independent of this experience, but we cannot accept the argument given, for we have already seen that the successive character of our experience does not prevent us distinguishing between coexistent and sequent elements therein.[2] The argument cannot be described as an argument at all unless by " successive " is meant " merely successive," and the view that our experience is merely successive leads to such absurd conclusions that we find it hard to believe that Kant could have held it.

(4) Kant seems to hold the category of substance to follow directly from the continuity and unity of experience. But, while one argument would, if valid, prove the uniformity of temporal relations, and the next the occurence of motions sufficiently regular to measure change, this argument would prove something much more akin to what is usually meant by substance—and, what concerns us more, something involving *necessary connection* between present and past— namely identity in change. In a process the earlier stages must be connected with the later, because otherwise there would be an absolute break such that it would not constitute a continuous process at all. " Suppose an absolute beginning of something, then you would be bound to have a point of time in which it did not exist.[3] But to what will you attach this, if not to what is already there ? For an empty time preceding it is no object of perception. But, if you connect this beginning with things that were before and last up to the time of the object which now begins to exist, it follows that the latter was only a determination of the former, *i.e.*, the permanent. It is just the same with annihilation, for this presupposes the empirical representation of a time in which a phenomenon exists no longer." This argument suggests the second, subordinate proof of causality, the outlines of which we have already discovered in the transcendental deduction, but which is nowhere in the Critique made as explicit as we might desire. However, in the *Reflexionen*, published by Erdmann, Kant expressly bases

---

[1] *B.*, 225(=*A.*, 182). [2] *V.*, above, pp. 84-5 [3] *B.*, 231 (=*A.*, 187-8).

the proof of causality on the principle of continuity and identity in phenomena. " That everything contingent, everything which begins, has its ground follows from the fact that without a prior event there would be no continuity, and without a law no identity in phenomena."[1] Likewise, in the very next quotation, Kant says that the principle that the same antecedent must have the same consequent follows from the fact that " otherwise, without cohesion of its members (*Zusammenhang der Glieder*), there would be no continuum of phenomena," so that they can only be represented in a series through the principle of causality.[2] And the categories are very frequently said by Kant to be justified as the presuppositions of the *unity of experience* (*Einheit der Erfahrung*).

To sum up the argument for causality suggested by the first Analogy, the conception of an objective world involves the conception of objects undergoing a continuous process of change. Such an objective world has been shown in the transcendental deduction to be implied in the very possibility of knowledge. But, if the subsequent states of these objects were not determined by the precedent, the objects would lose their identity, and there would be not one world but an infinite number of successive worlds, each being absolutely annihilated and followed by the creation of a new one *ex nihilo* to take its place. The existence of a permanent element in the changing would not suffice to maintain identity in change, unless the non-permanent elements helped causally to determine those elements in the substance which succeed them. This identity is for us a necessary conception, because a mere state that is not thought as part of a connected whole is not a member in that objective unity which alone can fit it to be an object of cognition to us. What particular portions of reality we are to call substances remains a question of convenience and relative homogeneity.

But, whatever else the conception of substance implies, it certainly implies at any rate a system of necessarily connected states or qualities. Without necessary connection we cannot regard any two qualities or states as belonging to the same object, and an object with only one quality or state is a nonentity. A state of an object not necessarily connected with the object and its other states would not be a " state of the object " at all. Further the object to

[1]*Refl.*, 1074.   [2]*Refl.*, 1075.

which any empirical judgment refers must always be something that endures for a given time, yet it must be in some sense a unity. There must be a sense in which a thing may change while remaining " the same object." All our knowledge is of something with an " earlier " and a " later," but, to know it as such, we must grasp the " earlier " and the " later " as a unity. This unity, necessary to any knowledge, is achieved by thinking of all states or qualities as attributes of some object which remains in some sense identical in change. But, whatever else this identity means, it certainly must mean this at least, that the earlier and later states of the object are united by causality. That there should be such an identity is absolutely necessary for the conception of an object, since an object that does not exist any length of time is not an object at all. All empirical judgments qualify either the self or the external world, but in either case this qualification involves the reference of a fresh quality (or relation) to an " object " involving a system of qualities, yet a system implies necessary connection, and necessary connection in the case of changing states is causation. In the second and third Analogies Kant assumed *objective* sequence and coexistence as proved by the transcendental deduction and then proceeded to show what *objective* sequence and coexistence meant for our experience, and that their objectivity must be understood as involving necessity. He might have done better if in the first Analogy he had followed the same method, assuming an objective permanent order to have been proved by the transcendental deduction, and then devoting the Analogy to the purpose of showing what this objective permanence meant for our experience. Had he done so he might have again arrived at necessary connection, as the most important factor in the conception of substance. But instead of following this method he tried to prove objective permanence afresh by several very doubtful arguments and neglected to analyse the conception.

Further he continues to speak of substance as involving an absolutely permanent element in phenomena though none of his arguments would, even if valid, prove substance in this sense, but in four quite different senses. If they prove anything at all Kant's arguments for substance prove severally:—

1. The independence of the physical as against subjective idealism.

2. The uniformity of purely temporal (and perhaps spatial) relations.

3. A regularity in physical changes sufficient to serve the purposes of measurement.

4. A continuity in change involving causal connection. But Kant, in the main at any rate, still regards substantiality as consisting in the possession of an absolutely permanent element over and above the laws governing change. Now the only absolutely permanent element Kant could discover in the experienced world was mass. Hence he identified the principle of substance with the principle of conservation of mass, and shrank from admitting substance in the psychical sphere—but of the latter point more later. Here we shall just remark that the main reason for his well-known identification of substance with conservation of mass seems to have been just that he could find nothing else given in experience that could be regarded as absolutely permanent. It was certainly for this reason mainly that he found special difficulty in the application of the category of substance to inner sense. In *The Metaphysical Rudiments of Natural Science* he tries to justify the identification of substance and conservation of mass by the *a priori* argument that " in every kind of matter the movable in space is the ultimate subject of all accidents inhering in matter."[1] Since every part of a material body, however small, must be regarded as matter and as movable in space, it must be considered to be a substance, hence its destruction is impossible. This is his contention, but it is difficult to see how it can avoid the criticism brought by Kant himself against the orthodox argument for the substantiality and permanence of the soul, namely that it proceeds from the logical to the " real " sense of substance, while the application of substance in the latter sense to any given object can only be based on the empirical criterion of permanence. In any case the argument is, of course, no refutation of the presence of substance in inner sense, since it expressly limits itself to the question as to what the substance is for outer sense.

Kant insists that the proposition " substance is permanent" is analytic, and that the only, or chief, criterion of substance is empirical permanence.[2] It seems, especially from the

----

[1] *H.*, 4, p. 437.
[2] But in *B.*, 250 (=*A.*, 204–5) another empirical criterion, activity or force, is suggested. The subject of activity must be conceived as permanent, *i.e.*, substance, Kant says, because activity, being change, implies a permanent substratum as its subject. He even declares this criterion to be sufficient without the criterion of permanence.

Paralogisms, that, just as experience is needed to find the causes of events, so experience is held by Kant to be our only guide in discovering substance. " If I am to declare a thing to be a substance in the phenomenal world, perceptible predicates (*Prädicate seiner Anschauung*) must first be given me, so that I may distinguish the permanent from the transitory, and the substratum (the thing itself), from what is merely its attribute (*was ihm bloss anhängt,*)[1]"—," So far from being able to deduce these properties " (permanence etc.) " from the mere category of substance, we are bound rather to make the permanence of an object, as given in experience, our ground, if we are to apply to it the concept of a *substance*, for empirical use."[2]

Perhaps the main importance of the first Analogy for the general interpretation of Kant's philosophy lies in its relation to the issue between the subjectivist and the phenomenalist views of the physical world. The application of the category of substance to physical phenomena is in itself a repudiation of subjectivism, and the very arguments used to establish it are used elsewhere by Kant to refute (subjective) " idealism." But for our particular object, the discussion of Kant's treatment of causality, the chief points to note are :—

1. That the deduction of substance suggests a new proof of causality, and that the conception of substance includes that of necessary connection,

2. That substance is regarded by Kant as the presupposition of all change and so of all causality.[3] As intermediate and subaltern concepts connecting substance and cause Kant introduces activity (*Thätigkeit*), action (*Handlung*) and force (*Kraft*).[4] " *Handlung* " is there described as " the relation of the subject of causality to the effect," and is regarded as the ground of all change and for that very reason as an infallible[5] criterion of the presence of substance. Now, leaving aside the question of the possibility of the application of the category of substance to the empirical self, we shall pass on to reciprocity.

Kant's proof of reciprocity. In dealing with causality Kant had already noted that our distinction between objective succession and objective coexistence was based on the fact that the order of our perceptions was irreversible in the case of the former, reversible in the case of the

[1]*A.*, 399.   [2]*A.*,349   [3]*B.*, 230 ff.=*A.*, 187 ff.   [4]*B.*, 250=*A.*, 204-5.
[5]Because the subject of change, according to Kant, itself never changes, *v.* footnote to last page.

latter. But now, in dealing with reciprocity, he adds that reversibility alone would not give us knowledge of objective coexistence. (By itself it would merely give us an alternating succession of perceptions). As in the case of causality, objective order can only be reached if we presuppose a necessary law connecting the reversible perceptions. But a law connecting perceptions of coexistent states of different substances involves interaction between these substances, and interaction just when they coexist, *i.e.*, reciprocity. The argument is least obscurely expressed in the proof added in the second edition, which we shall proceed to quote.

" Things are coexistent, if in our observation of the empirical (*der empirischen Anschauung*) the perception (*Wahrnehmung*) of the one may follow the perception of the other *reciprocally* (*wechselseitig*) (which, as we have shown in dealing with the second Analogy, cannot occur in the case of phenomena succeeding each other in time).[1] Thus I can direct my perception first to the moon and then to the earth, or, reversing the order, first to the earth and then to the moon, and, just because the perceptions of these objects can follow each other reciprocally, I say that they coexist. Now coexistence is existence of the manifold at the same time. Yet we cannot perceive time by itself, so as to deduce, from the fact that things are placed at the same time, that the perceptions of them may follow each other reciprocally. The synthesis of imagination in apprehension would, therefore, only show that in each case one of these perceptions was in the subject when the other was not there, and *vice versa*, not that the objects are coexistent, *i.e.*, that if the one is, the other is also at the same time, and that this is necessary if it is to be possible for the perceptions to follow each other reciprocally. Hence there is needed a concept of the understanding (*Verstandesbegriff*) of the reciprocal sequence of the determinations (*Bestimmungen*) of these bodies coexisting outside[2] each other, to enable us to say that the reciprocal sequence of perceptions is based on the object, and thereby represent their coexistence as objective. But the relation of substances, where the one contains determinations, the ground of which is included in the other, is the relation of influence, and if, reciprocally, the former contains the ground of the determinations in the latter, the relation of intercourse (*Gemeinschaft*) or interaction (*Wechselwirkung*).

[1] B., 257–8.
[2] We should note the limitation to space implied in these words.

Consequently the coexistence of substances in space cannot be recognised in experience except under the presupposition of an interaction between them, so this is also the condition of the possibility of things themselves as objects of experience."

This line of argument is also used in the first edition version, but is backed by another, which we must class as empirical, not transcendental. " It is easy to notice in our experiences that it is only by continual action on us from all parts of space that our senses can be conducted from one object to another ; that the light, which plays between our eyes and the heavenly bodies, effects a mediate intercourse between them and us, and by means of this intercourse can show us the simultaneous existence of the latter ; that we can in experience change no place (perceive this change) without matter on all sides serving to make the perception of our position possible ; that it is only by means of its reciprocal influence that matter can prove its own simultaneous existence, and thereby the coexistence of the remotest objects (though only mediately)."[1] In the next sentence, Kant argues for reciprocity from the continuity and unity of space in general. " Without intercourse (*Gemeinschaft*) every perception (of phenomena in space) is separated from the others, and the chain of empirical representations, *i.e.*, experience, would with a new object start again right from the beginning ; the former experience would have no connection with it in the least and stand in no temporal relation to it." However, in a footnote to B.,265 Kant expresses the view that the unity of the world as a whole is not a proper ground to deduce reciprocity from, but rather a deduction, whether conscious or unconscious, from the principle of reciprocity itself.

The third proof contained in the first edition version argues from the necessity of an objective ground for the subjective unity involved in the possibility of experience. " In our mind all phenomena, as included in a single possible experience, must stand in a ' communio ' of apperception, and if objects are to be represented as related in coexistence they must determine the position of each other in a single time so as to make up a whole.[2] If this subjective communio is to rest on an objective ground or be referred to phenomena as substances, the perception of the one must, as ground,

[1] *B.*, 260 (fourth paragraph in first edition).
[2] *B.*, 261–2 (fifth paragraph in first edition).

render possible the perception of the other, and *vice versa*. Then only can we avoid attributing to objects the succession, which always occurs in our perceptions as apprehensions, then only may we represent these objects as coexistent. But this is a reciprocal influence, *i.e.*, a real ' commercium ' of substances. So, without such a commercium, the empirical relation of coexistence could not occur in experience." This argument is, of course, the same in principle as the main argument, *i.e.*, that first quoted.

This main line of argument is strictly analogous to that used to prove causality. Since our perceptions are declared by Kant to be always successive, the only criterion for coexistence he would admit was reversibility. But, just as we cannot say that succession in our perceptions represents objective succession unless it is determined by a necessary law, so we cannot say that reversibility in our perceptions represents objective coexistence unless it too is determined by a necessary law. We can say that A and B coexist only if our perceptions of them are subject to a law such that we can perceive either one or the other according to our movements in space. There must be a law such that, if we make certain movements in space, or shift our attention, we *necessarily* perceive A, while if we make other movements, we *necessarily* perceive B, just as, for a succession in our perceptions to represent an objective succession, there must be a law such that under certain conditions of position in space, etc., the succession of perceptions in question will necessarily follow. The assumption that A and B coexist is, or, at any rate, implies the assumption that, if I had, instead of turning my attention in the direction of A, turned it in another given direction, I should have necessarily perceived B. The main argument for reciprocity, as for causality, may be summarised as follows :—

We are conscious of objective $\left\{ \begin{array}{l}\text{succession.}\\ \text{coexistence.}\end{array} \right\}$ Objectivity implies a principle of necessary connection (*Verstandesbegriff*).[1]

The principle of necessary connection for the $\left\{ \begin{array}{l}\text{successive}\\ \text{coexistent}\end{array} \right\}$ is the principle of $\left\{ \begin{array}{l}\text{causality.}\\ \text{reciprocity.}\end{array} \right\}$ Therefore the principle of $\left\{ \begin{array}{l}\text{causality}\\ \text{reciprocity}\end{array} \right\}$ is proved for all $\left\{ \begin{array}{l}\text{successive}\\ \text{coexistent}\end{array} \right\}$ states of objects.

[1] Because the understanding was the faculty of the *a priori*.

The same cautions must be added to our inter-
Criticism of pretation of the argument as with causality.
Kant's In the first place, we must regard reciprocity as
argument. a logical implication of objective coexistence, not
as the law governing a psychical process by which
we somehow cross the gulf between the subjective and the
objective. In the second place the argument must not be
supposed to depend on the extraordinary assumption that our
apprehension is merely successive, for Kant has really shown
that once we admit objective coexistence at all we must admit
reciprocity. This we must hold to be represented in our
perceptions either by subjective coexistence or by subjective
reversibility (though Kant does not admit the former),
but it seems clear that neither can give us *objective* coexistence
unless it is determined by laws in the object.

But reciprocity, as proved by this argument, does not seem
to be quite reciprocity as understood by Kant. Reciprocity is
established in the sense that coexistent states of different
objects, or any perceptible states of coexistent objects, must
be regarded as *necessarily* coexisting with or succeeding
each other alternately, but this is not the same as saying
that these states determine each other. Even if we, like
Kant, reduce causality to necessary uniformity and exclude
anything implying the view of it as activity or as involving
any sort of intrinsic logical connection between cause and
effect, as opposed to mere necessary regularity of sequence,
yet we cannot say that any event determines or helps to
determine another unless the first is necessary to explain[1]
that other causally. But two events might coexist necessarily
and yet have no causal, or determining, connection with
each other, but might be severally capable of full causal
explanation without introducing the other. Similarly two
perceived events in different substances might be necessarily
connected in the sense that the perception of the one followed
by certain movements in space would necessarily be succeeded
by the perception of the other, and yet either might, as in
the former instance, be capable of full causal explanation
without introducing the other. The fact that A and B
necessarily coexist is quite compatible with the present

[1]It might be objected that " explanation " already presupposes a
view of causality as something more than mere necessary uniformity.
But I am only using " causal explanation " in the sense of reference
to laws connecting an event with other events, adequate to predict
that event from the other events in question.

state of A being deducible according to causal laws from a set of events not including the state of B coexisting with this state of A, nor any other state of B either. Just as in the second Analogy Kant does not claim to prove that, whenever B succeeds A, A causally determines B, so in the third Analogy he should not have claimed to prove that, if A coexists with B, A must help to determine B and *vice versa*. All he can prove is that there are some conditions necessarily determining the coexistence or succession of A and B.

Nor does the argument from the continuity and unity of experience seem to prove reciprocity in the sense of universal interaction. All that is needed to give the bare minimum of unity in physical phenomena that is necessary if they are to become objects of experience seems to be (1) causal continuity between the earlier and later stages of the world-process such that every stage is necessarily connected with the precedent part of the process, (2) a connection between coexistent states either as attributes of the same substance or as standing in some spatial relation to each other. That spatial relation in itself implies reciprocal interaction I can see no means of proving. It has been suggested that Kant was moving towards an argument from space analogous to the fourth first edition argument for causality from time.[1] Just as it had been argued there that precedent times determine subsequent, and that, therefore, because time is a mere form of phenomena, precedent must likewise determine subsequent phenomena, so Kant might have argued here that. as the different parts of space presuppose and determine each other, the different phenomena in space must presuppose and determine each other likewise. But such an argument, it seems, would be liable to the objection which we raised against the similar argument for causality.[2] The different parts of space, taken in the abstract, as of time, determine each other, no doubt ; they do so in the sense that by exclusion they fix the limits of each other. But this kind of determination is quite different from causal interaction of phenomena, or from any determination, whether causal or logical, of their content by each other. We cannot pass from one kind to the other and simply say that, because the different parts of space (or time) determine each other in the former sense, phenomena determine each other in the latter, without justifying the transition by a further argument

---

[1] Prof. Kemp Smith, *Commentary*, p. 385.   [2] Pp. 74 ff.

which is not forthcoming.   In *The Metaphysical Rudiments of Natural Science* Kant himself asserts that what is true of space need not be true of the contents of space, but this principle he sometimes seems to forget.

Our conclusion is that reciprocity in the sense of universal interaction cannot be proved by reference to the possibility of experience, as causality can.   It must be regarded as (1) for the physical world, a scientific hypothesis, backed by special arguments (like that from the physical conditions of perception used here by Kant and that from the relativity of motion, applied in the *Metaphysical Rudiments of Natural Science*), and, in fact, involved in doctrines of physics like the law of gravitation.   (2) An Idea of Reason.   Then it becomes closely allied to the coherence theory of reality, the view of the universe as a systematic whole, such that every part affects and conditions every other part and that the full knowledge of any part would be impossible without knowledge of the whole.

We may add the further remark that, if we do not hold to the view that all apprehension is merely successive, reversibility according to necessary laws need not be regarded as the only criterion of objective coexistence, for subjective coexistence, when that coexistence is necessarily determined by a law regarded as inhering in the object or objects, may serve as a proof of objective coexistence just as subjective succession, when necessarily determined in like fashion, proves objective succession.

Reciprocity, understood as a causal relation between the coexistent, is severely criticised by Schopenhauer, who describes causality as " the true, but only form of understanding," and the other eleven categories as windows that look nowhere (*blinde Fenster*).[1]   He complained that according to Kant's view of reciprocity a phenomenon stood in the relation both of cause and effect to other coexistent phenomena and so at once preceded and followed the latter. This criticism, of course, involves the assumption that simultaneous causation is impossible, which is here backed by the argument that, if cause and effect were simultaneous, they would constitute one unchanging state, while the category of causality implies change and is therefore inapplicable under such conditions.   Cause and effect, Schopenhauer says, are not things, but states, and each of these states

[1] *Die Welt als Wille und Vorstellung*, Leipzig edition, (Brockhaus), pp. 5,44-8.

includes in itself the states of both interacting bodies. The proposition that there can be no action without reaction does not express a reaction of the effect on the cause. If it did, it would be self-contradictory, because the future (the effect) cannot react on the past (the cause). All the principle can mean is that there is always a division of the effect between the two interacting bodies. But this involves no new category beyond causality. The supposed instances of reciprocity may be reduced to either (1) two causal series in each of which the successive stages belong to two different substances alternately, or (2) a state[1] of rest, action and reaction, or rather counteraction, being equal. In the first case, there is no category involved but causality ; in the second case, we have only an unchanging state, which, as such, leaves no scope for either causality or reciprocity, both of which could only be realised as determining change. Such is Schopenhauer's criticism of reciprocity.

But, while Schopenhauer is probably right in holding that reciprocity, as usually conceived by Kant, cannot legitimately be treated as a separate category from causality, it does not seem to us that the category involves a direct contradiction, as Schopenhauer holds. For (1) Kant thinks of reciprocity not so much as a relation between coexistent states of different substances, but rather as a relation between successive states of coexistent substances, at any rate when he thinks of it as specifically causal in character. It is of the alternate *sequence (Folge)* of determinations that a concept of understanding (*Verstandesbegriff*) is needed, and, since our perceptions of coexistent objects are regarded as successive, the necessary laws which condition them must be regarded as connecting successive perceived states of different objects. (2) Schopenhauer's main contention is, as we have seen, based on the argument that simultaneous causation is impossible because in simultaneous causation cause and effect would constitute one unchanging state while all causation implies change, but, where we had a series of causal laws connecting the simultaneous stages of two different processes of change, there we should have simultaneous causation, hence simultaneous causation need not imply an unchanging state, but may be a relation between two parallel and simultaneous processes of change.[2] The question of the actuality of

[1] As when equal weights are put on the two scales of the balance.
[2] *V.* Prof. Broad, *Perception, Physics and Reality*, p. 125 circ.

I

simultaneous causation this remark, of course, leaves untouched.[1]

But does Kant really mean by reciprocity only causal interaction ? In the earlier version of the argument Kant identifies the two explicitly,[2] and in a letter written in 1783 he says that reciprocity is the reciprocal causality of substances as regards their determinations.[3] In the second edition version, however, Kant uses the more general terms " ground " and " influence " (*Grund* and *Einfluss*) instead of terms implying causality,[4] and, as the second edition was published some time after the letter referred to had been written, it is possible that Kant may have changed his mind on the subject.   But we should note that the same terms " ground " and " influence " are also used in what Professor Kemp Smith holds to be probably the earliest version of the argument.[5]   Further, the tendency of Kant to regard the laws involved in reciprocity as laws connecting not *coexistent* states but *successive* states of coexistent objects brings the category closer still to causality.

If by reciprocity is simply meant causal interaction between different substances, the third Analogy is certainly not sufficiently distinct from the second to justify Kant in making a separate category of it, especially in view of the fact that boundaries between different " substances " are far too fluid to permit any rigid distinction between events in the same substance and events in two different substances.

On the other hand, if causal interaction is not meant, it is still difficult to distinguish a separate category of reciprocity in addition to and apart from (1) dual causality ; (2) merely spatial relations ;   (3) the relation of different coexistent attributes of the same substance, which was not what Kant meant by reciprocity but might have provided scope for the application of a third category ; (4) an Idea of Reason, giving us the coherence-view of the universe.   No doubt reciprocity was thought by Kant chiefly as the minimum amount of determination and interrelation needed to make order in space possible, but when we come to specify it more exactly we are at once involved in difficulties of the kind pointed out above.

Kant himself admits that the third category is always a

[1]Kant explicitly admits the actuality and frequency of simultaneous causation.

[2]*B.*, 259 (2nd paragraph of first edition). [3]*Berl*, I., 344. [4]*B.*, 257.
[5]*B.*, 261 (=A 214–5).

combination of the first and second,[1] but he denies that this admission makes it superfluous.[2] " The third category indeed springs from the union of the first and second, however, not from a mere external combination of them, but through *a union, the possibility*[3] *of which itself constitutes a concept,* and this concept is a special category. So the third category is sometimes not applicable where the first two are valid, *e.g.,* one year—many future years—are true concepts, but the *totality* of future years, that is, the collective unity of a future eternity, capable of being thought as *a whole* (as though it were completed) is inconceivable. But, even where the third category is applicable, it always includes something more than the first and the second taken both in themselves and together, *i.e.,* the *deduction* of the second from the first, which is not always possible. For example, necessity is nothing but existence in so far as it can be deduced from possibility ; reciprocity is the reciprocal causality of substances as regards their determinations. But, that determinations of one substance can be produced by another substance, is something which we cannot just assume, but which belongs to the unifying connections without which there could be no reciprocal relations of things in space[4] and so no external experience." So, he concludes, the third category adds an original determination of its own to the first and second combined, just as in a syllogism the conclusion contains, besides the combination of the two premises, an addition contributed by Reason, namely that whatever is conditioned in the way expressed by the middle term will be conditioned in the way expressed by the predicate of the major premise.

That a proof of the first and second categories is not the same thing as a proof of the third, although the third may be regarded as equivalent to the first plus the second, is of course, clear. As Kant contends, it does not follow directly that, where we can apply the first and second, there we can also apply the third, and it is also true that, where we apply the third, the combination of the first and second transforms both. A substance conceived as standing in a relation of thorough-going reciprocity with other substances is not the

---

[1]*Berl,* I., 329, and *Prolegomena,* 325 (footnote).   [2]*Berl.,* I., 344.
[3]This presumably means that the possibility of applying the third category to objects does not follow directly from the possibility of applying the other two.
[4]Note reference to space.

same as a substance conceived as an independent permanent, just as, to take Kant's example, the conclusion in Logic is not a mere combination of the premises, because the premises conceived as leading logically to the conclusion are different from the premises taken in isolation. The question whether the third is to be regarded as a category separate from the first and the second is one of degree, but the chief criterion is whether the proofs are different in principle, and it is clear that the main proof of reciprocity is simply the main proof of causality remodelled to suit coexistent objects.

Note on Simultaneous Causation.

The consideration of reciprocity suggests the question of simultaneous causation. As we have seen, Kant seems more inclined to think of reciprocity as a relation between states of different coexistent objects than between actually simultaneous states of these objects, but in the discussion following the proof of the second Analogy he admits the possibility of simultaneous causation, and even says,[1] " The greater part of the efficient causes[2] in nature are simultaneous with their effects, and the sequence in time of the latter is only due to the fact that the cause cannot produce its whole effect in a single moment. But, at the moment in which the effect first arises, it is always simultaneous with the causality of its cause, since, if the cause had ceased a moment before, the effect would not have occurred at all."

Kant, however, seems to confuse simultaneity and continuity here. It does seem evident *a priori* that causation cannot operate after a blank time during which *no part* of the cause has changed, but this does not debar *continuity* of causation. Continuity involves neither simultaneity between the last stage of the cause and the first stage of the effect, nor the lapse of a blank time between cause and effect. Kant himself insists strongly that all causation is continuous, so it is likely that the argument for simultaneity just quoted is really a mistaken way of stating continuity. A proof of continuity is given in the very same section, where Kant argues that the continuity of all causation follows from the

---

[1]B., 248 (=A., 202–3).
[2]The original reading, " cause," harmonises better with the next sentence, where Kant regards the first moment of the effect as always, not only mostly, simultaneous with the cause, but is less easy to reconcile with the piural *Wirkungen*.

continuity of time.[1] It is true that by this " continuity " he seems to mean here rather that any change produced by causation must be continuous than that the cause must be continuous with the effect, but the two involve each other, for (1) all changes are produced by causation and so on that view continuous, (2) in any continuous change each state of the change must be at once continuous with the next stage and the cause, or part of the cause, of the next stage, so it would follow that in all change at least part of the cause is continuous with the effect.[2]

The supposed occurrence of simultaneous causation raises the difficulty that the second Analogy as formulated only applies to successive events, but Kant meets this difficulty by distinguishing between dynamic and temporal sequence. In the case of simultaneous causation, he points out, the cause may be distinguished from the effect by the fact that given the cause the effect follows but not *vice versa*. But the only empirical criterion, he says, is still temporal sequence.[3] By this Kant seems to mean that in such cases, while cause and effect are simultaneous, the *beginning* of the cause precedes the *beginning* of the effect. In the previous paragraph, however, he seems to be thinking [4]rather of the effect being deducible from the cause but not *vice versa*. But the question seems to be one rather of definition than of principle, and Kant fails to prove the necessity of admitting simultaneous causation at all.

[1]*B.*, 253 ff.(=*A.*, 207ff).
[2]I do not mean to indicate that I agree with Kant's proof of the " continuity " of causation. As we have seen in another instance, it is not legitimate to make all attributes of abstract time attributes of its contents without a special justification of the procedure in each case.
[3]*B.*, 249 (=*A* 204).
[4]A very questionable distinction. However, it is not necessary to draw a sharp distinction between cause and effect.

CHAPTER VI

The Application of the Categories to the Empirical Self

THIS chapter we shall devote to considering the question of the application of the categories to the empirical self. Kant gives an explicit proof of the analogies only for the physical, and does not say whether this proof is intended to apply to the psychical also or not. He proceeds, in fact, as if there were either no such thing as psychological knowledge at all, or it involved no problem of objectivity corresponding to the problem solved for the physical by the help of the categories. Yet, so far from expressly limiting the category of cause, at any rate, to the physical, he assumes, especially in his discussion of freedom, that the empirical self is as completely determined by causality as any physical object. Hence the double question arises :—(1) Does Kant mean to apply the categories to the psychical as well as to the physical ? (2) Ought they, on critical principles, to be so applied ?

For most people of the present day there is a strong flavour of mysticism and unreality about the word, " psychical." Yet it is obvious on the least reflection that not only physical objects but also thoughts, feelings, desires are real facts of which we must take account, though they might perhaps be said to have a different genus of reality. I mean by judgments about the psychical nothing more recondite or mystical than such assertions as—I enjoyed myself very much yesterday. He has a very selfish character. I feel very hot. They are *intending* to organise a university here. All these statements refer to psychical facts—pleasure, character, feeling, intention. A good half of the statements of every-day life are of this kind, and a critique which claims to test all the main types of knowledge or supposed knowledge must fail in its duty if it ignores them. If the principles of Kant's critique are universal and based on the consideration of all experience as such and not only of a selected part of it, if they are not to be only the foundations of a special science or special scientific method, but to be coextensive with the whole realm of experience, they must be brought into relation with the psychical. As a matter of fact, Kant does, of course, deal with the psychical pretty extensively, though he does not set himself the question : How is psychology possible ? in the same way as he sets himself the questions : How is mathematics possible ? How is physics possible ? The omission can only be described as very unfortunate (though it might be said that the discussion on inner sense in the second edition version of the transcendental deduction provides the main outlines of the answer to that question.)[1] But to unravel the confused threads of Kant's argument on the subject of the relation of the categories to the empirical self is a matter of great difficulty.

Does Kant mean to apply the categories to the

Kant's general views on the application of the categories to the empirical self : two conflicting tendencies. psychical as well as to the physical ? Unfortunately it is quite impossible to give a plain " Yes " or " No " to this question, owing to the presence of two conflicting and unreconciled lines of thought in the author. All we can do is to point out and illustrate these two tendencies and give some estimate of their relative importance in the Kantian philosophy.

As we have pointed out, Kant deduces the analogies only for the physical world, and his phraseology often seems to imply that he did not regard judgments about our feelings as involving the categories. In the first Analogy he without apology simply identifies substance and quantity of matter. In the second Analogy his examples refer to the physical, and the problem, to solve which causality is invoked, is the problem of distinguishing a physical from a psychical event. As long as the sequence is a sequence of representations only, causality is not called in ; it is only because some sequences are sequences of physical events that causality is invoked in order to enable us to distinguish between this order of physical events, as determined, and the psychical order of " mere perceptions " as undetermined. Since the point that is held to distinguish a physical from a psychical sequence of events is just that the former is causally determined, the implication would seem to be that the latter is not thus causally determined. Throughout, the objective is identified with the physical. Kant says, " If I supposed that nothing precedes an event on which it follows according to a rule, . . . then I could not say that two states follow each other in the phenomenon, but only that one apprehension follows the other ; which is merely something *subjective* and determines no object, so cannot count as knowledge of any object whatever (not even of something purely phenomenal.) "[1] This apparently implies that the statement that one apprehension follows another does not presuppose the categories and cannot count as cognition. This implication is explicitly stated in the *Prolegomena*, where Kant distinguishes between " judgments of perception," which do not require pure concepts of understanding (*i.e.*, the categories), and judgments objectively valid, which are produced by the subsumption of " judgments of perception " under the categories.[2] Thus judgments about psychical events are there held to be possible without the categories. With the third Analogy it is still clearer that Kant is only thinking of the physical—in fact he expressly limits its application to objects in space.[3]

Here we have one tendency of Kant's thought, which we may describe thus. He concentrates his attention on the physical sciences only and finds genuine knowledge only in these. Psychology is denied the title of a science. Space is held to be just as essential a condition of the application of the categories as time is, and hence of all cognition and judgment. The empirical self is made so dependent on the physical objects with which it comes into contact, that, if we subject it even to that very relative isolation to which we habitually subject separate physical objects in judging *e.g.* " This table is of wood," we are held to have passed beyond the sphere in which judgment is possible. It would follow that the very large class of statements about the psychical, referred to above, are not judgments[4] at all—what they are, it is more difficult to see. The second Analogy may be easily interpreted on these lines as proving the universality of causal determination by showing that we must distinguish the objective from the subjective, if we are to have physical

---

[1]*B.*, 239–40(=*A.*, 194–5).   [2]Sections 18, 22.
[3]*V.* second edition, statement of principle to be proved (*B.*, 256), also *B.*, 258, 260 (=*A.*, 213–14).
[4]Kant's treatment of them as " judgments of perception " in the *Prolegomena* (section 18) is equivalent to a denial that they are really judgments at all, since all judgments are held to imply the objective unity of apperception, and this unity is not involved in so-called " judgments of perception."

science at all, and without physical science there is no knowledge worth the name,[1] and that it is only possible to make the distinction in question if the order of our perceptions which is said to represent the real physical order of events is causally determined, the proof thus seeming to imply that any other order of experience is undetermined. (Whether it really does imply this we shall try to find out later.) The psychical is regarded as determined only in so far as it consists in perceptions of the physical; there are, strictly speaking, then, no psychical, only physical laws of causation. And, because the categories cannot be applied in the psychical sphere, in that sphere there can be no judgment and no knowledge.

This line of thought also appears in the transcendental deduction. The doctrine of the dependence of the self on objects, elaborated there, is, of course, of the greatest importance for Kant's system and of the greatest philosophical value, but, when Kant insists that the transcendental unity of apperception is only realised in knowledge of objects and that all knowledge is of objects, this must not be taken as necessarily excluding knowledge of the psychical, for the empirical self may after all be counted by Kant as an " object" in such passages. But there can be little doubt that here, as throughout his philosophy, he was *mainly* thinking of physical objects. On the other hand, it is our opinion that the transcendental deduction, as a whole, supports the other line of thought which makes " judgments of perception " real judgments involving the same transcendental synthesis as judgments about physical objects, and hence likewise subject to the categories. This we have already (in Chapter III) tried to show, and we shall return to it later. But, for the present, we are confining ourselves to the anti-psychological side of Kant's thought. We may note that in one passage, at any rate, in the transcendental deduction he denies the title of judgment to any statements about the relation of my perceptions. A judgment, he says, is a relation that is *objectively valid*.[2] Such a relation is sufficiently distinct from the relation of these very same representations, in so far as it has merely subjective validity, *e.g.*, according to laws of association of ideas. The laws of association only entitle me to say : " If I carry a body, I feel weight "—not, " It, the body, is heavy." The latter statement means :—

[1] This sentence does not represent our own view, needless to say
[2] *B.*, 142.

"these two representations are combined in the object, *i.e.*, regardless of the particular state of the subject, and are not merely together in perception, (however often the perception be repeated)." As elsewhere, too, Kant couples space and time together as the conditions under which every manifold must stand in order to be an object of cognition to us.[1]

Later in the Critique Kant introduces the important doctrine that the categories can only be rendered intelligible by the help of outer sense. " It is still more noteworthy, however, that in order to understand the possibility of things in conformity with the categories and so exhibit (*darzutun*) the *objective reality* of the latter, we need not only perceptions, but, in all cases, *external* perceptions.[2] If we take, for example, the pure concepts of *relation* we find that (I) in order to provide something permanent in perception corresponding to the concept of substance (and thereby exhibit the objective reality of this concept), we need a perception *in space* (of matter), since space alone is determined as permanent, while time, with all the contents of inner sense, is in a perpetual state of flux. (2) In order to exhibit *change*, as the perception corresponding to the concept of *causality*, we must take as example motion, or change in space, indeed it is through motion alone that we can picture to ourselves changes (*uns Veränderungen anschaulich machen*), the possibility of which changes can never be comprehended by pure understanding. Change is a combination of contradictorily opposed determinations in the being of one and the same thing. But, how there can out of any given state issue a state of the same object contradictorily opposed to the first state, is something which reason cannot make intelligible without an example or indeed comprehensible without a perception. This perception is the perception of the motion of a point in space. It is the existence of such a point in different places (as a sequence of contradictorily opposed determinations), that can alone first enable us to picture change ; for, in order afterwards to make even inner changes thinkable, we must first represent time, as the form of inner sense, under the image of a line, and the inner change under the image of the production of the line (motion), and so by the help of external perception make intelligible the successive existence of ourselves in different states. The real reason of all this is that all change presupposes something permanent in perception for it to be observed at all as change, and in inner sense no permanent perception can be found."

We must note that Kant does not here deny the possibility of applying the categories to the object of inner sense, but only asserts that their application cannot be understood without the help of outer sense. Further ; the objections advanced by Kant in the two cases[1] of substance and cause are of quite a different character from each other. In the case of causality Kant objects that, in order to think causality at all, we need images drawn from space. But that causality cannot be thought without the help of these images, even if psychologically true, certainly does not prove that causality is applicable only to objects of outer sense, any more than the fact that we can only judge by using words or images of some sort proves that our judgments are valid only of words or the other images we may use, nor need we suppose that Kant intended to prove anything of the kind about causality by this remark. His argument against substance seems, however, a direct attack on the possibility of its application to the empirical self, at any rate as a " constitutive " principle. He argues that there is nothing permanent in the empirical self, and, since substance must in his view be absolutely permanent, it follows that there can be no substance there at all. It further raises a difficulty not only against the application of substance, but against the application of causality, for, as Kant points out in the last sentence quoted, change, which is presupposed by causality, itself presupposes substance. We shall return to this important point later, at present we shall just remark that his inability to discover a permanent element in the empirical self was the chief reason which hindered Kant from applying the categories in this sphere.

In the *Nachträge*, published by Benno Erdmann, Kant maintains that space is needed to make a determinate concept *a priori* possible, and that inner perception, because it alone could not provide the element of sensation, would not by itself give us any knowledge of objects *a priori*.[2] In the *Reflexionen zur Kritik der reinen Vernunft* Kant says that,[3] when anything can be known *a priori*, it means that " it has an object, and is not merely a subjective modification,"

[1] We might say that in the case of each of the three categories the objection proceeds on quite a different principle—the cases of substance and reciprocity we shall discuss later.
[2] XVIII.   [3] 971.

and again,[1] " The mere consciousness of perceptions, however, refers all representations only to ourselves as modifications of our state ; they are then separated from each other and, in particular, are not cognitions of anything and refer to no object. They therefore do not yet constitute experience,which must indeed include empirical representation, but include such representation only as at the same time cognition of the objects of sense." In these *Reflexionen* he also makes a curious distinction between representations given in experience which need a necessary law to be cognisable, and representations made by us, of the reality of which we are immediately conscious, so that " a state in us, which we ourselves make, can be known as a true state even without a ground " (*i.e.*, apparently, without the category of causality).[2]

Again, in a letter to Beck, Kant says that, if the individual representation " is merely referred to the subject, its employment is aesthetic (feeling), and the representation cannot become a known fact."[3]   In another letter[4] Kant remarks that objects of sense can only be given in *space* and time, and in another he says,[5] " One is not really entitled to say that a representation is connected with a thing other than itself, but only that, if it is to become a known fact, it must be referred to something else, (other than the subject in which it inheres), by which reference it becomes communicable to others.   For apart from this it would belong merely to feeling (pleasure or pain), which in itself is not communicable." These last passages, especially, support an interpretation of Kant which makes him hold objective judgments and real knowledge to be impossible in the psychical sphere, but, in view of Kant's sharp distinction between subject-self and object-self, even these last paragraphs do not seem absolutely to exclude the possibility of such judgments about the object-self, since even here what is perceived is different from the perceiving subject *i.e.*, the subject-self, and feeling as feeling, *i.e.*, till referred to external objects or to the object-self, is " incommunicable " in any case.   However, this seems a forced and unnatural interpretation of the passages in question, and it is better to suppose that, if Kant was indeed thinking of this implication of his remarks at all, he meant, at the time of writing, to exclude altogether the possibility of objective judgments about the empirical self.   That this was not his consistent view we shall soon see.

[1]983.   [2]946.   [3]*Berl.*, II., 467.   [4]*Ib.*, 468.   [5]*Ib.*, 599.

Similarly the passages from the *Reflexionen*, quoted above, seem to imply that awareness of feeling as a state of the self (subjective modification) is not to be ranked as knowledge at all. There is, however, always the possibility that he may, while his mind was occupied with the undoubted importance of physical objects for knowledge, have unguardedly let fall certain expressions, which implied an identification of " objects " with physical objects, just because it was that class of objects which he was thinking of, and not because he had formed the considered opinion that the empirical self ought not to be treated as an object of knowledge at all.

But let us now have a glance at the other side of Kant's thought on the topic. This is well expressed in the discussion[1] of inner sense in the transcendental deduction. In this passage outer and inner sense are regarded as strictly parallel, and knowledge of the empirical self as possible under similar conditions to those required for the knowledge of external objects. The form of outer sense, space, is indeed not present in introspection, but this is not taken as vitally changing the conditions of self-knowledge, and certainly not as banishing this " self-knowledge " from the sphere of knowledge altogether. In the case of cognition by introspection, as in the case of the cognition of physical objects by external perception, there are required two elements—(1) the given element, the manifold ; (2) the element of order contributed by a synthesis of the mind. From this the corollary is drawn that the empirical self is, like physical objects, part of the phenomenal world.

That self-knowledge is possible is, in fact, the primary assumption of the argument here. The passage gives the answer to the question how it is possible that the self should only know itself as a phenomenon, but the question clearly assumes that the self knows itself at any rate as a phenomenon. Without the assumption of this self-knowledge the whole argument would be purposeless. When an inquiry is made as to how such and such an occurrence is possible, we must take it as assumed that the occurrence is real, unless the purpose of the inquiry was merely to disprove its reality by a *reductio ad absurdum*, which is of course, not the case here. In fact, in this passage Kant, starting from the actuality of self-

---

[1] *B.*, 152–9. I do not see how it is possible to combine the two lines of thought by saying that the self (empirical) is on Kant's view *wholly* determined but determined *only* by physical and physiological causation, but *v.* note at end of chapter, pp. 167–8.

knowledge, draws certain further metaphysical conclusions about the nature of the self, especially its division into subject and object self, these conclusions being based on a consideration of the conditions in the absence of which our self-knowledge, known to be actual, would not be possible. That the basis of the argument is the assumption of the actuality of self-knowledge is clear all through, but especially in B 157–8 where Kant repeatedly uses the term "*Erkenntnis*" as applied to the self in discussing the question under what conditions that "*Erkenntnis*" is possible.

So it is clear that in this passage Kant holds introspection, as taken apart from the observation of physical objects, to give us real knowledge. Further, this kind of knowledge is held to imply the categories as much as knowledge of physical objects. For Kant states definitely that this inner sense yields no determinate knowledge without a synthesis. It might be held that, even if the categories were not applicable to inner sense, there would be required a kind of synthesis by which the mind gave its manifold some sort of " subjective " order in time without employing the categories, but that the synthesis in question here is meant to involve the application of the categories is clear. For (1) it is assigned[1] to the understanding and the understanding is essentially the faculty of the categories : understanding has no meaning for Kant apart from the application of the categories. (2) It is said of apperception that " so far from being identical with the inner sense, it, as the source of all combination, is applied to the manifold *of perceptions in general*, under the name of the categories, and to objects in general prior to all sensible perception ; while inner sense, on the other hand, involves the mere form of perception, but no combination of the manifold in the latter and so no *determinate* perception.[2] Determinate perception is only possible through the consciousness of the determination of perception by means of the transcendental activity of imagination (synthetic influence of

[1]*B.*, 153. " What determines the inner sense is the understanding and its original (*ursprüngliches*) faculty of combining the manifold of perception, *i.e.*, bringing it under one apperception (as that on which its very possibility depends)."   Lower down (*B.*, 154) Kant speaks of this synthesis as a " transcendental activity of imagination " which he, however, equates with "a synthetic influence of understanding" in the last line of the paragraph.   That this " activity of imagination " is held to be ultimately the work of understanding is also clear from the last sentence of *B.*, 153.   [2]*B.*, 154.

understanding on inner sense) which I have called the imaging (*figürliche*) synthesis." Now, " perceptions in general," it seems, must include perceptions of the empirical self, since Kant expressly says in this section that we are capable of such " perceptions." But the action of apperception on perceptions in general is here expressly said to involve the categories. Further it seems impossible[1] to avoid identifying the combining influence of apperception on the manifold of perceptions in general, just referred to, with the synthesis said both in 153 and 154 to be the condition of determinate perception of the manifold of inner sense, and, if so, the remark that the former synthesis involves the categories must, of course, apply to the latter.

The strict parallelism between inner and outer sense, on which Kant insists, cannot be maintained without such a synthesis for inner sense, involving the categories. In B50 Kant actually goes to the length of saying that we can conclude from the attributes of a line that time, as strictly analogous to a line in space, will possess the same attributes with the one exception that its states are successive and not coexistent. In the passage under discussion (B156) he argues from the parallelism of inner and outer sense that, because outer sense can only enable us to know what is phenomenal, inner sense can likewise only reveal to ourselves our phenomenal self and not ourselves as we really are. But he might have argued from their parallelism in just the same way that, because outer sense and inner sense are parallel, and outer sense requires a synthesis according to *a priori* categories to produce determinate perception, inner sense does likewise. Or, rather, that inner sense requires such a synthesis is assumed and included in his very statement of their parallelism, because, if inner and outer sense are not parallel in such a fundamental point, they can not be regarded as strictly parallel at all. The doctrine of their parallelism

---

[1](1) In 153 Kant makes the synthesis which determines inner sense consist in bringing the manifold under a single apperception, in 154 the faculty of apperception is said to involve the categories ; (2) The synthesis of 153 is itself a process of combination, but in 154 all combination is ascribed to apperception working through the categories ; (3) In 154 it is pointed out that the inner sense by itself has the defect of not being able to supply combination, which defect prevents it yielding a determinate perception, yet in the same sentence the working of apperception through the categories is declared to be the only source of combination · it therefore must be needed to make inner perception determinate.

is founded on analysis of the general character of knowledge typified both in self-knowledge and in knowledge of external objects. Its chief value lies in the recognition of the given, empirical element in self-knowledge. Introspection must not in itself be regarded as in any higher degree a creative activity than cognition of the external world ; the content of knowledge is in introspection, too, given to us empirically and not created by our act of knowing. We may, of course, change our experience by activity on our part, but we do not by our act of knowing change our experience as it was at the moment known, e.g., when I cognise my experience of a moment ago it is evident that I do not by my act of cognition change my experience of a moment ago. This point is of the greatest importance when considering subjective idealism.

Without recapitulating what we said in the chapter on the transcendental deduction, we must note that the line of interpretation we there supported made the proof start with the validity of " judgments of perception " and then proceed from these to the transcendental unity of apperception and the unity of objects.[1] If our arguments there carry weight—(and this is, at any rate, an important line of thought in the deduction)—Kant obviously then regarded "judgments of perception " as real judgments involving the transcendental synthesis and the categories. And the importance for Kant's philosophy of a doctrine which is made a main basis of the transcendental deduction can hardly be overestimated. We may, therefore, refer the reader back to our third chapter for confirmation of the importance of this tendency in Kant's thought.

That real knowledge of the empirical self, as taken in abstraction from physical objects, is possible, seems to be assumed throughout the *Anthropology*. That this knowledge is possible on lines parallel to the knowledge given by outer sense, and that it involves the categories is expressly asserted in at least one passage.[2] Kant there declares (1) that we *know* ourselves as we appear, (2) that inner experience gives appearance (*Erscheinung*), not illusion (*Schein*) ; (3) that this " appearance," though not itself a judgment, can be converted into " *innere Erfahrung*,"—" *Erfahrung* " being clearly meant there in the sense of " empirical judgment," (4) that such " *innere Erfahrung* " involves *a priori* categories

(*Verstandesbegriffe*). Not that there is a total absence of passages which express the other side of Kant's thought in the *Anthropology*. Kant held it necessary to insert strong cautions regarding the dangers of excessive introspection, and objects to " psychology " as involving the assumption that we can perceive an immaterial soul-substance, thus explaining his preference for the term " anthropology," as not presupposing the existence of a soul.[1] In the same passage he speaks of the mental disease which takes what is really only " the play of representations of inner sense" for " *Erfahrungserkenntnis*," thus seeming to imply that inner sense does not give " *Erfahrungserkenntnis*."[2] But that " *Erfahrungserkenntnis* " is possible by inner sense seems to be an assumption on which depends the very possibility of the *Anthropology*, as a system of observed psychical data involving general laws.

It is also important to note that, while in the introduction to the *Metaphysical Rudiments of Natural Science* Kant seriously[3] disparages psychology and denies it the title of a science, he does not give as one of his grounds either that objective judgments are impossible about the empirical self or that the categories in general are inapplicable here.

In Prolegomena Section 49 Kant says that the combination (*Verknüpfung*) of physical phenomena according to laws of experience (*Erfahrungsgesetze*) proves their objective reality " just as much as the combination (*Verknüpfung*) of phenomena of inner sense proves the reality of my soul (as an object of inner sense)." But " *Verknüpfung* " according to " *Erfahrungsgesetze* "[4] must surely involve the categories. In

[1]*H*., 444, 474–5.   [2]*Ib*., VII., 474–5.

[3]Kant there says that psychology can never be a *Seelenwissenschaft* nor even a *psychologische Experimentallehre* analogous to chemistry, but only *eine Naturbeschreibung der Seele, i.e.*, a historical account made as systematic as is possible with history as opposed to science. The reasons he gives are (1) That, because time has only one dimension, the application of mathematics in psychology is limited to one single principle, the law of continuity ; (2) that we can only mentally abstract, not really separate and put together different elements in a mental state, and thus are debarred from using the experimental method of chemistry ; (3) that we cannot observe the mental state of other people, and if we observe our own, we alter it in the process, thus vitiating our conclusions from introspection (*H*., IV., p. 361).

[4] It can hardly but be meant here that the *Verknüpfung* for inner sense involves the *Erfahrungsgesetze* like that of the outer sense to which it is here made parallel.

K

B 50 ff. of the *Critique*, time (like space) is declared to be objective and to give objectivity to its contents. In the second edition Paralogisms (B406–7) Kant definitely asserts self-knowledge as a fact. The self is declared to be known as object " in so far as its manifold can be combined according to the universal condition of the unity of apperception in thought," by which latter Kant presumably means the synthesis through the categories.

An important passage which makes clear these views of Kant may be found in the first of *Sieben kleine Aufsätze* written by Kant for Prof. Kiesewetter in 1788–91.[1] It is an answer to the question—Is our thinking an experience ? " Experience " (*Erfahrung*) is defined as the judgment expressing an empirical cognition (*empirische Erkenntnis des Objekts*), so the question goes to the root of the problem. Are empirical judgments on inner sense, taken apart from external objects, possible ? Kant's answer is in the affirmative, and the passage was written after the insertion of those second edition amendments which tended to enhance the importance of outer relatively to inner sense. Kant proceeds : " If I think a square *a priori*, I cannot say ; this *thought* is experience ; but I can say this well enough if I grasp in perception a figure that is already *drawn* and by means of imagination think the combination of the manifold of the same under the concept of square. In and through experience I am instructed (*belehrt*) by means of the senses ; but if I think an object of sense merely capriciously, then I am not instructed by it and in my representation do not depend at all on the object, but am its sole creator."

In the next paragraph Kant makes a further distinction, " But the consciousness, too, of having such a thought is no experience, just because the thought is no experience and consciousness in itself is nothing empirical." From this it would seem at first sight that he is denying the possibility of knowledge by introspection, but it is quite clear from what comes next that this is not the case and that the sentence just quoted must be interpreted in a different way. " All the same," he says next, " this thought produces an object of experience or a determination of the mind, which can be observed, namely, in so far as it is affected by the faculty of thought. I can therefore say : I have experienced what is involved in comprehending in thought a figure with four

[1] *H.*, IV., 499.

equal sides and right angles in such a way that I can demonstrate its properties.   This is the empirical consciousness of the determination of my state in time by thought ; thought itself, though it happens in time, has no reference to time in thinking the properties of a figure." This means clearly that the self as changed by the act of thinking is an object of empirical knowledge (*Erfahrung*).   Therefore the consciousness referred to in the last line quoted must be different from the consciousness referred to in the first line of the paragraph.   Now below (at the end of the next paragraph) we see the words : " But the consciousness of originating an experience or of thinking in general is a *transcendental consciousness, not experience*."   Hence we must, clearly, identify " the consciousness of having such a thought " cited above with the transcendental consciousness, which at once distinguishes it clearly enough from the consciousness stated to involve empirical judgment. The activity of thinking obviously must involve some kind of consciousness, and this consciousness must involve some awareness of our activity, we must somehow know what we are doing.   Yet we are not engaged in introspection, we are concentrating our energies on quite other objects than the self, we do not know what we are doing in the same sense as if we were making explicit judgments about our own activity.   Hence this consciousness cannot be identified with the empirical cognition which makes the phenomenal self its object.

The terms " thought " (*Gedanke*) and " experience " (*Erfahrung*) are both somewhat ambiguous. *Gedanke* may mean either the content or the act of thought, and, because the content is not empirical, it does not follow that the act of thinking is not an experience in the usual sense of the term, *i.e.*, a conscious state of the self.   It does, however, follow that the act of thinking is not an " experience " in the sense in which Kant defined " experience " at the beginning of the *Aufsatz*, *i.e.*, an empirical judgment.   An empirical judgment cannot be derived from this thought till the latter has become for us something *given*, so, as Kant says, the mere addition of consciousness cannot make it an object of knowledge till it is given for consciousness, in which case it must be synthesised, and we then have quite a new kind of consciousness of it.   This is called the " empirical consciousness of the determination of my state in time through thought," and Kant adds that without this determination in time " experience " would be impossible.   Yet it is Kant's doctrine that time-determination is impossible without the categories—hence judgments of inner sense, it seems, must also imply the categories. So Kant here both explicitly states that we can have an " *Erfahrung* " of the state of the self, *Erfahrung* having been just defined as empirical judgment, and implies that such an " *Erfahrung* " like an " *Erfahrung* " of outer sense involves the categories. In the second and third of these *Aufsätze* there are also remarks of value for our subject. The third *Aufsatz*, like the first, assumes empirical cognition and distinguishes the empirical from the transcendental consciousness of the self on the ground that transcendental consciousness does not involve giving the self a determinate place in time, while the empirical consciousness does. In the second *Aufsatz* Kant, in denying the possibility of miracles, tries to give a separate proof of their impossibility for inner and outer sense. That for inner sense is based on the ground that every psychical event in the phenomenal world must have a cause which is itself phenomenal. It thus assumes the validity of the principle of causality in the psychical sphere. It is worth noting that the proof for outer sense is, on the contrary, based on the principle of reciprocity. The latter is, as elsewhere, treated as the essentially spatial category.

[1]The view we are discussing is also expressed in certain passages of the *Transition from the Metaphysical Rudiments of Natural Science to Physics* published posthumously in the *Altpreussische Monatsschriften* (Hefte 19–21). There Kant distinguishes (1) the consciousness of myself as subject (*i.e.*, the transcendental self-consciousness), (2) the cognition of myself through perception and concept, (3) the position (*Setzung*) of myself in space and time. Even the third, let alone the second, is said to occur according to *a priori* principles, *i.e.*, presumably, the categories.[2] He more than once describes perceptions as members of the unitary physical system in which everything is interconnected by laws of motion :—" Perceptions are effects of moving forces of matter working on the subject in one system of these forces and in one single possible experience."[3] " All moving forces of matter through their unity and common relation (*Gesamtver-hältnis*) in space and time constitute a whole under the laws of motion in matter and also those of the affection of the

---

[1]For a general account of subject *v.* Adicke's *Kant's opus postumum* especially chapter on " *Selbstsetzung* " (*Teil IV*, Abschnitt I, Kap. 2)
[2]Heft 19, p. 576.   [3]*Ib.*, p. 125.

senses."[1] " The universe as object of sense is a system of forces of one matter, which affect each other externally and objectively in space through motion, and internally and subjectively through the sensation of substances with consciousness, *i.e.*, as objects of perception."[2] In one passage he sets the two systems of perceptions and physical objects in opposition to each other, but still regards them both as " systems." " On one side are perceptions (empirical representations produced by external influence), combined in a systematic whole, on the other side experience itself, according to the form of thought, a system of the manifold of empirical perception."[3] Here both lines of thought reveal themselves—the name of experience is assigned to the physical only, but a psychical " system " is set in opposition to it. The latter admission is diametrically opposed to the view expressed elsewhere that perceptions, taken apart from the physical objects to which they refer, are not objects of real knowledge and do not come under the categories. Other passages apply not only the category of cause but also the category of reciprocity to psychical events. We may note also that Kant very[4] frequently speaks of perceptions as the effects of the forces of matter on the self, thus applying causality to the latter. The phrases, " appearance of appearance " or " appearances of the second grade " are frequently used to stand for our representations of physical objects (*i.e.*, representations of " *Erscheinungen* ").

But the most decisive consideration is that in every discussion about freedom in the *Critique of Pure Reason*, the *Critique of Practical Reason*, the *Foundations of the Metaphysic of Ethics* and the *Critique of Judgment* alike, Kant assumes the entire determination of the empirical self by laws of causality. That freedom has to be reconciled with universal psychical causation, and that desires as such cause actions in a purely mechanical way, is the view of Kant whenever he discusses freedom. In fact, the whole discussion loses its sense if the empirical self is not subject to causality. For then there is no antinomy between causality and freedom. And, further, this subjection to causality is asserted as the proved result of the *Critique of Pure Reason*. When we consider the enormous influence that ethical questions generally and the problem of freedom in particular had on

[1] *Heft* 19, p. 268. [2] *Ib.*, p. 594. [3] *Ib.*, p. 453.
[4] Prof. Kemp Smith says at least 26 times. One or two of the quotations already made provide examples of this.

Kant's thought, it becomes quite impossible to regard a doctrine that lies at the basis of his whole discussion of freedom, so that without it the latter would lose all its meaning, as a mere, hastily-assumed and incompatible by-product, and not as a fundamental principle of his philosophy. It would be a strange inconsequence on the part of Kant to assume as the basis of his whole ethical work and of an important part of the *Critique of Pure Reason* itself (*i.e.*, the third and fourth antinomies) a principle which the central discussion of the *Critique of Pure Reason* had shattered. Does not Kant in the introductory part of the latter expressly make it one of the main objects of his philosophy to reconcile universal causality with freedom ? And nowhere does he ever suggest that this reconciliation may be effected by showing the category of causality to be inapplicable to the self as phenomenal !

Thus we see that the view of self-knowledge as parallel to knowledge of the external world and of the categories as applicable not only to physical objects but also to the empirical self is of the utmost importance in Kant's philosophy, and that, without the assumption of the validity of the categories as proved to be universal for psychical as well as for physical events, important parts of Kant's philosophy become inconsequent or even meaningless. This may drive us to reconsider the points that we cited against the view. We must remember especially that, where Kant uses the term " object," he may mean to include the object-self and not only physical objects ; thus, as we have already pointed out, when he says that all knowledge is of objects, he does not necessarily mean to exclude self-knowledge. This point should always be remembered in citing passages in favour of the anti-psychological line of thought in Kant. But all the same we must admit that there are numerous passages which definitely oppose the application of the categories to the empirical self. This is simply one of the most striking cases of inconsistency to be found in Kant. We may note that in the second edition of the *Critique of Pure Reason* both tendencies find clearer expression than in the first. In the second edition Kant insists far[1] more on the importance of physical objects for knowledge, but on

---

[1] *e.g.*, *Refutation of Idealism* added in the 2nd edition (*B* 275 ff.), estatement of principle of reciprocity limiting this category to space *B* 256), suggestion that the categories must be schematised in reference to space as well as time (*B* 291 ff). A difference may also be noted in the first and second edition statements of the general principle of the Analogies (*B*., 218).

the other hand in the second edition discussion of inner sense in the transcendental deduction he provides us with one of his clearest statements of the possibility and requisite conditions of empirical self-knowledge.

Perhaps the greatest difficulty is that, while the application of the categories to the psychical is assumed later, they are only proved of the physical, and the wording of the proof, as we have seen, sometimes even seems positively to exclude their application to the psychical. But it seems to us that, with causality at any rate, the proof is in principle a proof not of the validity of causality for physical objects only, but for all possible objects of knowledge, the principle on which it rests being that cognition always involves objectivity and that objectivity always involves necessity—that the very possibility of cognising something objective implies that our representation of it is determined, and further that, whatever else the objective world is, it must be at least a system of laws connecting and determining the immediate objects of experience (percepta). But the empirical self is objective, the state known in it is distinguishable from our consciousness of that state and therefore it must determine the consciousness of it ; the empirical self also involves a system of laws connecting and determining our immediate percepta. Therefore causality seems to be proved to be valid of it. But to this point we shall return later.

In the second Analogy Kant was interested only in establishing those *a priori* principles which are required as an indispensable basis for physical science, and consequently limited himself to the consideration of causality as necessarily implied in the cognition of physical objects and ignored the question of its application to the self. But in the cognition of physical objects we abstract and reject as subjective that part of our experience which we do not regard as determined by the object perceived, and, till we have done this, our experience cannot be called cognition of a physical object. One apprehension follows another in our mind, but as yet the apprehensions are not referred to any object by us. This we may accept as true on either view of inner sense, but this is not the same as saying that the judgment that one apprehension follows another does not involve a cognitive act which refers the apprehensions to the self as object. Yet Kant passed imperceptibly from the first point of view which is quite right to the second, the justifiability of which is much more doubtful. He was led to do so by the fact that in cognition of the physical world we treat our psychical state as irrelevant in so far as it is not determined by the object cognised. In themselves my psychical states may be objects of genuine knowledge, but, when I am seeking knowledge of the physical world, the psychical state through which I acquire this knowledge is a mere means to the cognition of something beyond itself, and any variations in the psychical state, not ascribed to the physical object, are treated as purely subjective from the point of view of the knowledge I am seeking. They are nothing for my present purpose, and must be regarded as merely incidental, and not allowed to modify my view of that object which I am seeking to cognise. But this only means that they are not data required for my present cognition ; if, on the other hand, I have adopted the psychologist's point of view towards them it is my psychical state that is alone relevant, and it is the physical object cognised that must as such be disregarded, if I am to attain the knowledge I desire. Now in all cognition, whether of the physical or of the psychical, my representation of the object cognised must be treated as subjective and hence irrelevant, except in so far as it is determined by the present object of cognition, but that does not mean that it is itself incapable of being the object of another judgment or cognition. The fact that I see a house first and then look away and see a tree must not be allowed to distort my judgment as to the relations of the two, so that I say, " the tree succeeds the house and is not coexistent with it," (ignoring the fact that I could just as well have seen the tree before I saw the house as *vice versa*), but this is not the same as saying that the order in which I perceive the two coexistent objects may not itself be an object of a genuine judgment—" I see the house before the tree and do not see them simultaneously." So Kant's proof of the second Analogy still leaves it open for him to establish and apply causality in the psychical sphere also.

Ought "substance" to be applied to the empirical self? Kant's view. We shall now pass on to substance and its application to the empirical self. The importance of this question for us lies in the fact that Kant declares substance[1] to be the presupposition of causality, so that, if substance is not applicable to the empirical self, it raises difficulties against the application of causality.

[1]This is perhaps most clearly shown by the remark at the beginning of the second Analogy, where Kant says that all succession has been

Because Kant was unwilling to surrender the view of substance as requiring an absolute permanence in change, other than the laws governing change, he encountered insuperable difficulties when he came to consider the application of this category to inner sense. For *absolute* permanence is, obviously, not to be found in the empirical self. Further, by Kant's hypothesis that all apprehension is merely successive, even *relative* permanence was excluded. It might be thought that the noumenal self could supply the requisite permanent element, but to this there were two fatal objections. First, the noumenal self was conceived as out of time and not as a phenomenal object in time, given in perception, yet it was only to such phenomenal objects that the category could be applied.[1] That the noumenal or subject self can never be perceived as such, because if it is once made an object of perception it becomes the object-self or empirical self and as such is in time and no longer the presupposition of all temporal experience, and that without a perception to which it can be applied substance is only a logical category and cannot be understood as involving real permanence, is the doctrine of the *Paralogisms*. Clearly the schema of substance, *i.e.*, permanence *in time*, cannot be applied to what is not in time. Secondly , the noumenal self is for us nothing apart from the form of unity which is realised in phenomena, but the category of substance was regarded as a necessary element in this form of unity. The noumenal self could not be identified with what was only an element in itself, (as far as known by us). The whole deduction of the separate categories is an analysis of that unity of experience which is for our knowledge the equivalent of the conception of the noumenal self, and to have gone back to the latter again in the way suggested would have been simply to repeat the statement that there is a synthetic unity, without showing under what conditions the objects of experience can conform to that unity. This failure to find a permanent element in the empirical self thus raises for Kant a special difficulty as to the application of substance to inner sense.

shown in the first Analogy to be change, *i.e.*, modification of the attributes of substances. But causality, of course, presupposes succession throughout and hence must presuppose substance. That all succession is succession of the determinations of a substance is clearly regarded as the central teaching of the first Analogy throughout.

[1]As a " constitutive " and significant principle.

We have already quoted the passage where Kant declares that, to make the categories intelligible, we need outer sense as well as inner sense, and pointed out that the objections here advanced in the cases of causality and substance are quite different in principle.[1] In the case of causality Kant objected that we cannot think time or succession without the image of a line, and hence, for us to understand causality, we need the help of images drawn from space. With substance he objects not only that we are bound to use spatial images in thinking of it, but that there is given in inner sense no permanent element, and hence nothing to which the category of substance can be applied. " In order to provide something permanent in perception corresponding to the concept of substance (and thereby exhibit (*darzutun*) the objective reality of this concept), we need a perception *in space* (of matter), since space alone is determined as permanent, while time, with all the contents of inner sense, is in a perpetual state of flux."[2] Similarly, in the *Paralogisms* Kant accounts for the absence of *a priori* knowledge in psychology as follows : " Although both are phenomena, the phenomenon of outer sense contains something stationary or enduring (*Stehendes oder Bleibendes*), which gives us a substratum underlying its transitory (*wandelbaren*) determinations, and so a synthetic concept, *i.e.*, that of space and a phenomenon in space, while time, the sole form of our inner perception, contains nothing enduring, and so enables us to recognise only the succession (*Wechsel*) of determinations, and not the object capable of determination by them (*den bestimmbaren Gegenstand*).[3] For in what we call the soul, everything is in continual flux and there is nothing enduring, except, perhaps, (if one insists) that Ego, which is so simple, just because this representation contains no content, and hence no manifold, for which reason it seems to represent, or, better, designate (*bezeichnen*), a simple object."

Kant is always uncompromising in his opposition to those thinkers who held it possible to prove the immortality of the soul " metaphysically " from its substantiality. In the *Paralogisms* which are devoted almost entirely to an attack on this view, he teaches that, while we must think of the knowing self as always a *subject*, never a predicate, we cannot from this conclude that the schema of *substance*, permanence in time, is applicable to it. For the knowing

----

[1]*V.*, above, pp. 128 ff.   [2]*B.*, 291.   [3]*A.*, 381.

self is not a perceptible object in time at all, it is always the object-self, not the subject-self or knowing self, that we *perceive* in introspection. Further substantiality could in no case be regarded as a possible premise from which to prove permanence, because we can only declare anything, to be a substance[1] if we already empirically know it to be permanent. In the *Nachträge* (published by Benno Erdmann) Kant clearly expresses his intention to limit the proof of the category of substance to outer sense. This is shown by the following remarks adjoined to the beginning of the first Analogy. " Here we must show that this proposition applies to no substances but those in which the whole process of change is effected through moving causes only, and itself consists in motion only, and so in change of relations."[2] " Here the proof must be so directed as only to fit substances as phenomena of outer sense, hence it must be based on space, which space and its determination therefore exist for all time."[3] " All that can be distinguished in experience from what passes away is quantity, and this can only be estimated in terms of the extent of the merely relative effect with similar external relations, hence only applies to physical bodies."[4]

In *The Metaphysical Rudiments of Natural Science* Kant makes some interesting remarks on the subject. Matter, he says, consists of parts external to each other and every part of matter, however small, must be regarded as itself a substance.[5] But the quantity of matter consists in the number of its parts, therefore it could only be diminished by the annihilation of some of its parts, and this, as we have seen, would involve the annihilation of substance. " On the other hand, what is regarded as object of inner sense can as substance have a quantity which does *not consist in parts outside each other*. Hence its parts are not fresh substances, and their origination or annihilation cannot be an annihilation of a substance ; and so its increase or decrease is possible without impairing the validity of the principle of the permanence of substance." Here Kant actually applies the category of substance to the psychical, and in the next sentence he speaks of " the substance of the soul," but the value of this admission is quietly taken away by the acknowledgment that " the substance of the soul " cannot be shown

[1]In the real, as opposed to the logical, sense of the term (*v.*, A.. 349, B., 406, 412). [2]*Nachträge*, 77. [3]*Nachträge*, 80. [4]*Id.*, 81 (*c.f.* also *Reflexionen on substance esp.* 1045). [5]*H.* iv., pp. 437-8 : cf. p. 449.

to be permanent, which must mean that it is not a substance in the "real" sense at all, for, according to Kant, that substance, in the "real" sense, is permanent, is an analytic proposition. It appears then that the self is here only treated as substance in the logical sense, as being always a subject and never a predicate. Kant declares, in fact, that the gradual evanescence to which it is subject may be conceived as leading to its absolute annihilation, without involving any contradiction of the principle of substance.[1]

Our general conclusion is then that Kant shrank from applying the category of substance to the self as object of knowledge, and shrank from it as a result of his failure to discover therein anything absolutely, or even relatively, permanent. Similarly, in the second edition *Refutation of Idealism*[2] he makes the absence of anything permanent in the self the basis of an argument for the reality of the external world. In the last-mentioned passage it would seem as though Kant had modified his view of the relation of succession in time and substance. In the first[3] Analogy he seems to hold that succession can only be known as determined in time and so be real as a phenomenon if it is a succession of states of a substance, in contrast to the permanence of which we can alone determine the succession in time. Here, however, he seems to hold that, for time-determination to be possible, it is enough that we should be conscious of *some* permanent substance by means of which we can measure the rate of the succession, and not necessary that the succession should itself be a succession of determinations of the substance in question. The substances, which Kant declares to be

---

[1] The formulation of the proof of the first and second laws of mechanics also seems to imply that the application of substance and cause is not limited to matter. In discussing the second law, Kant remarks that life is "the capacity in a *substance* of acting according to an internal principle," and that there is no such inner principle of change in a substance except desire, thus implying that beings moved by desire, a psychical factor, can be treated as substances. Again, on p. 440 it is said that, if we are to seek the cause for a material change in something living, we must seek it in another *substance* (*i.e.* the soul) distinct from, but combined with matter. Similarly, in his posthumous work (*Altpreussische Monatsschriften*, Heft 19, p. 594) Kant refers to minds affected by sensation as "substances with consciousness."

[2] *B.*, 275.

[3] *V.*, *B.*, 230-3 (including first paragraph of second Analogy).

necessary for us to determine in time the succession in the self, are clearly something other than the self ; the consciousness of my own being is, as a result of that proof, declared to be also an immediate consciousness of the being of *other things outside me*, the whole object of the proof is to establish the reality of *external*, physical bodies. And *external* bodies cannot be substances of which the changes in my empirical self are states ; whatever the empirical self is, it is not an attribute of the heavenly bodies or the clocks by which we measure time.

Now this point is of considerable importance for the question of causality. For, if succession, to be determined in time, must always be itself a succession of states of a substance, and the category of substance is inapplicable in the psychical sphere, only two alternatives are left open, both very difficult to hold. Either causality cannot be applied at all in the psychical sphere, or the empirical self is the attribute of its own physical body as a phenomenal substance. I can find little evidence that Kant inclined to the latter view ; the former view he repeatedly affirms and still more repeatedly contradicts. It is, however, I think, the case that he generally does not treat his doctrine of substance as implying either conclusion, and there is, of course, no need to do so once the view that the substance may be external is accepted. We may say that it seems to be Kant's general view that, as schematised, causality can and substance cannot be applied to the empirical self.

In the case of reciprocity Kant seems definitely **Ought reci-** to exclude the psychical from the field of this **procity to** category. We have already noted the limitation **be applied to** to objects in space asserted in several places in **the empiri-** the third Analogy.[1] In *The Metaphysical* **cal self?** **Kant's view.** *Rudiments of Natural Science* we may note that, after stating the metaphysical presuppositions of what he calls the second[2] and third laws of mechanics, *i.e.*, pointing out that they presuppose the universal validity of the categories of substance and cause respectively, he says that he will now show the further implications of these general principles in the special case of matter, thus implying that the application of substance and cause is not limited to matter. Yet in stating the presupposition of the proof of his fourth

[1]Second edition statement of principle to be proved (*B.*, 256), also *B.*, 258, 260.
[2]The law of conservation of matter and the law of inertia.

law[1] of mechanics, the law which depends on reciprocity, he implies that the proof of this mechanical law, though expressly intended only for physical action and reaction, is valid in all cases of reciprocity, just because reciprocity cannot be applied at all except to physical action and reaction. He does not, as with the second and third laws of mechanics, hint that his proof only affects a special case and not every application of the category involved.

The question of the application of reciprocity to the empirical self has not the same importance, for us at any rate, as the application of substance, since it is never made the presupposition of causality; further, since it is a relation between different substances, the question narrows itself down to a consideration of the relation between mind and body. In the first edition Paralogisms Kant says that, once transcendental idealism is accepted, the question whether the physical can cause changes in the psychical is seen to be absurd, because, if the body as phenomenon is meant, it is merely a representation, and so it is clear that it cannot be an external cause, but, if the noumenal ground of the body is meant, we are talking of what we know nothing, and it is quite impossible to say on the ground of similarity or dissimilarity in the phenomenon what the noumenon can or cannot cause.[2] Hence he declares the hypotheses of pre-established harmony and supernatural assistance to be unnecessary, because the alleged difficulty of supposing interaction between soul and body, of which difficulty the two hypotheses in question are advanced as solutions, is seen to be no real difficulty if transcendental idealism is adopted. This remark, however, refers to the relation between soul and body as noumena, not to the relation between phenomenal states of soul and body. It certainly does not imply a denial that such states may be connected by necessary laws ; no dissimilarity between two events need be incompatible with the necessary succession of one on the other, because the real ground of the succession need not be found in the events that succeed or precede each other. Yet Kant has only proved the universal validity among phenomena of causality and reciprocity in the sense of necessary succession and coexistence. However, he shrinks from admitting a causal relation between soul and body.

But, in his posthumously published work, Kant, as we have seen, clearly thinks of the empirical self as co-member

[1] The law that physical action and reaction are always equal. [2] A., 390

with physical objects in a connected system of interacting forces, involving reciprocity, and he applies the term *Gegenwirkung*, from which, of course, follows reciprocity (" *Wechselwirkung* "), to the relation between soul and matter.[1]   The soul is there conceived as reacting on matter in a way analogous to a physical force.   This is not, however, Kant's usual view.

We have seen Kant's varying views on the subject ; **Ought Kant** we shall now turn from the exegesis of Kant to an **to have** independent consideration of the question whether **applied the** Kant ought to have applied the categories to the **categories to** empirical self or not.   The remainder of the chap- **the empiri-** ter should be understood as containing only our own **cal self** views and not an interpretation or exposition, **throughout?** **Our own** though indirectly a criticism, of Kant.   Now it **view.** seems to us [2] that, if it is possible to make any " judgments of perception " at all, the order of feelings and perceptions must be objective in the same degree as the order of physical events perceived, and that if objectivity implies necessity in the one case, it must do so in the other.   If I judge on the evidence of introspection that I have a certain perception or feeling, my judgment and my cognition of the feeling can be no more identified with the feeling itself than my cognition of a physical object can be identified with the physical object cognised.   In both cases the judgment refers to something beyond itself as its object. It is certainly easier to express the proof of the second Analogy in terms of the physical than in terms of the psychical, because psychical events are not in the same sense events for all human experients, each such event can be perceived only by one subject.   Hence the characteristic of universality is not so prominent.   All the same it is not absent, for, if there is no universality in the sense that the experience is the same for different experients, there is universality in the sense that the experience must be the same for the same experient under the same conditions, and that any variation in the experience must be due to a corresponding variation in the conditions. Yet all that is proved in the second Analogy, even for the physical world, is that under the same conditions the same event must occur, and it is our contention that this proof can be applied to the psychical as well as to the physical.

For—and this is just Kant's proof of necessary connection applied to psychical events—we must distinguish between

---

[1] *Altpreussische Monatsschriften*, Heft 19, pp. 271, 290.
[2] Objections to our view will be considered shortly.

memory and imagination or mere association of ideas, and they can only be distinguished if ideas of memory follow a determinate, necessary order, independent of our caprice and not the fruit of chance, but throughout causally necessary. For, ideas of memory we must refer to an object, *i.e.*, the empirical self, and reference to an object has been seen to involve necessity. We cannot refer our percepta to the empirical self as known data unless they are determined independently of our act of perceiving, and the empirical self must be regarded as involving a system of laws that connect together our percepta of introspection.

The perception by introspection of a psychical event seems to involve the necessary determination of the content of our experience of introspective cognition by the event cognised, or, as Kant would say, of our " representation " of the event, such that, if under the given circumstances we carry out this act of apprehension by introspection, the experience could not be other than it is. If I hold my memory of having felt angry to represent a real event, then I must suppose that, if I recall my previous feelings of anger to my mind, the idea of them I get is not a mere matter of chance which might vary without any cause, but is, in so far as it is a correct and genuine remembrance, necessarily determined by that previous experience of anger which I now remember. Otherwise I could not possibly say that I remembered feeling angry, I could not possibly know that next time I tried to recall the event, I might not remember something totally different as occurring at the time when according to my earlier memory-experience I thought I remembered myself to have felt angry, and this without any psychological or physiological cause of the illusion, thus making it quite impossible to say which was right and which was wrong, further that this might not happen each time I tried to recall the experience. What possible justification could I have in ascribing the content of my mind in my present experience to my past experience of feeling angry if the two were not connected by a necessary law ? For otherwise the latter would have nothing to do with the former whatever. It is not itself my experience at the present moment—I am not feeling angry now, only remembering that I felt angry before —yet it must determine my experience at the present moment, otherwise I should be unable to hold that the content of my present memory in any sense represented the nature of the event remembered. In so far as my present experience of remembering of itself[1] gives me knowledge of a past experience, it must be regarded as necessarily determined in its nature by that experience, if the memory might vary without any cause, the experience remembered remaining the same, then it would be no more a memory of the particular experience I say I remember in it than of any other past experience. To know an object through a perceptum, the perceptum must obviously, in so far as it enables us to know the object, be determined by the nature of the object known. I obviously cannot remember any event without my idea of it being determined by the event remembered, and the more so, the more correct my idea of it.

Kant indeed holds that our knowledge is limited to percepta, ("representations") and that these cannot give us any knowledge of the subjective elements of feeling and thought as they really are, any more than they give us knowledge of the nature of the thing-in-itself behind physical phenomena. But this does not affect the validity of the argument. In any case (1) judgments about the psychical, just as much as judgments about the physical, refer the events or states judged about to an object, but reference to an object means inclusion in a system of necessary connection ; (2) it is quite as necessary to suppose that certain psychical judgments based immediately on perception are true as that certain physical judgments are, but for us to hold that our percepta give us real knowledge and to distinguish them from ideas of imagination, we are bound to suppose them to be necessarily determined independently of our will ; (3) judgments like " I felt angry an hour ago " must at any rate give us the appearance of a real state, but any appearance must, on this view, be determined by the noumenal reality of which it is an appearance. But if it be necessarily determined by a noumenal reality, the successive moments in the phenomena must obviously succeed each other with necessity. (The noumenal reality would, of course, have to be regarded as determining it, not as cause in time, but as logical ground ; of the inconsistency, real or apparent, of this with the unknowability of the noumenal we need not speak, as we are not attempting to defend Kant's theory of the thing-in-itself). (4) If all judgments[2] about the psychical, like all judgments about

---

[1] I.e., without any explicit process of inference.

[2] Points (1), (2) and (4) at any rate would, of course, apply to anyone who adopted the same position about the self as the subjective idealist about the physical world, if such a position be indeed possible at all.

L

the physical, are interpreted in terms of possible perception, the judgment that I felt angry an hour ago must mean that, if I had looked inwards an hour ago, I should have had a perception of myself as angry, which statement at once introduces necessary connection between the action of looking inwards and the perception in question.

But it seems a quite impossible position, even for an idealist, to hold, as Kant apparently does, that the empirical self is nothing but our " representations " in introspection and memory. And many would say that any " representative " theory of perception, such as Kant seems to hold, in regard to our perception of the self is absurd. So it may be urged (1) that determination of our experience in perceiving (or remembering) the self does not imply determination in the experience perceived, (2) that we cannot say that the possibility of memory and introspection proves even our " representations " of the self to be determined, for the simple reason that we have no such representations. But to these objections we can reply in the same way as we did to the corresponding objections about the physical world. If judgments about psychological events involve objectivity at all, it seems that this objectivity must involve reference to a necessarily connected system just as it did in regard to the physical world. Further, just as the conception of a physical object is primarily the conception of a link between our disparate experiences serving to harmonise and account for them, the self is primarily the conception of a link between the different states of the self that we happen to remember, but it cannot link them up at all unless the successive states intermediate between those we happen to remember are themselves causally connected. Again, we cannot remember, or discover in introspection, an experience as ours unless we perceive that experience as member of a causally connected process, as fixed determinately in a certain place in our life, as causally continuous with what comes before and after. Otherwise it would be absurd to say that we perceived it as *our* experience or as happening to us. But, if so, we have necessary connection, and so, in the case of what is changing in time, causality. The question at issue is not what we perceive " directly," but whether the act of cognition is to be distinguished from the act of imagining. If so, what is cognised in introspection, must be necessarily determined (independently of our act of cognising it) ; if not, there can be no knowledge of the self at all.

It does seem, however, that we must distinguish the content of our mind at the moment of remembering from the experience remembered, for the simple reason that the one is present and the other past, and that the past cannot be literally a part of my present experience, although my present experience in some sense *immediately* refers to it. But, if so, the experience remembered must determine the experience of remembering in so far as the latter gives us the truth about the former at all. So we have in memory a necessary connection between our present experience in remembering and the past remembered. Yet what experience does not involve some element of memory? Again, just as we have argued that necessary connection between actual and possible percepta of physical objects can hardly be separated from necessary connection between the perceived or perceivable states of the physical objects themselves, we might equally well argue that the necessary connection in our experiences of remembering could hardly be separated from necessary connection in the experiences remembered.

And in any case, we might argue that, whatever the self is, it must, at any rate, be or involve a system within which our conscious states are necessarily connected, otherwise all continuity and unity are gone. How can any state be a state of the self and yet not be necessarily connected with the other states of the same self?

Most of these remarks apply to views of the self very different from that held by Kant, but, as Kant's view on this point with its absolute separation between the noumenal and empirical self has been almost universally abandoned by philosophers, it is important to see whether the method of proof in the second Analogy can be applied to the self as commonly regarded. In my opinion it can be applied to establish the universality of necessary connection for all perceptible states of the self. This conclusion, it seems, could only be avoided by identifying my judgment about a psychical event attributed to my (empirical) self with the event judged to occur. In that case it may be maintained that so-called judgments about the psychical are not real judgments because they do not involve objectivity—no such judgment refers its content to anything other than itself—and hence " knowledge " of the psychical becomes impossible. We may be charged with begging the question by the very use of the term, judgment, on the ground that judgment implies objectivity and that objectivity must here be denied, but in the

absence of any other suitable term we shall continue to use
" psychical judgment " in inverted commas to signify the
act of awareness involved in recognising by introspection
a certain empirical state of the self as such.   We do not by
the use of the term intend to assume any objectivity whatever
in advance ;   our subject of inquiry is whether this act of
awareness does or does not involve objectivity.   If, and only
if it involves objectivity, may we call it judgment in the full
sense.

The criticism we have to face, namely that " psychical
judgments " about myself do not[1] involve objectivity, may
be supported by the argument that in such " judgments " a
mistake is impossible, that if I know nothing else I must, at
any rate, know my own state of mind.   It certainly seems
difficult to imagine that anyone can make a mistake in judging, e.g., " I have a perception of green (or feeling of pain),"
but the argument is useless unless it can be maintained not
only that some, but that all, of the class of " psychical
judgments " are infallible.   Now it seems quite impossible
to hold that mistakes never occur in " judgments " of
memory ;   if I cannot make a mistake in " judging " :
" I have a perception of green (feeling of pain) now," I
certainly could make a mistake in " judging " :   " I had a
perception of green (feeling of pain) an hour ago " ; still more
could I make a mistake in " judging " about other people's
perceptions and feelings.

Now it is doubtful whether all " psychical judgments "
are not judgments of memory, whether all introspection is
not really retrospection ;   but, leaving this point aside, it
seems impossible to maintain that we are infallible even in
cases of judgment based on present introspection.   Is it not
exceedingly difficult to observe accurately how one feels,
what one sees, etc. ?   Is it so easy to say, for example, what
the content of our mind (images, etc.) is exactly when we are
thinking of a complicated philosophical argument, what
images we use and especially what there is in our mind beyond
the images—and there must be something, because sensible

[1]The question whether a " psychical judgment " by myself about my
own state is distinguishable from that state must of course not be
confused with the question whether perception of my state in introspection or memory involves a " representation " (image) of the state
perceived distinct from that state itself.   Nobody who maintains the
direct theory of perception regarding the physical world would maintain
for that reason that a physical state and my judgment that it existed
were indistinguishable.

images or words cannot possibly be adequate to enable us to think about it intelligently without some consciousness of meaning ?   If no psychologist has ever been able to analyse this satisfactorily, is it not a proof that immediate judgments of introspection, so far from being infallible, are sometimes as difficult to make as any judgments ?   No doubt inner perception like outer, (in so far as it is merely perception and not yet judgment), cannot itself make mistakes, but this is only because perception is not judgment ; if we judge we proceed to analyse our percepta, and this must, it seems, always leave room for mistakes.   That certain " psychical judgments " must be regarded as practically infallible does not prove that the judgment and what is judged about are the same, only that in the particular case the data are so simple that we have perfect command of them.

The only reason why it seems almost a truism to say that one cannot make mistakes about one's feelings at the moment one has them, appears to me to be that the object judged about (the feeling) is already tacitly identified with the judgment that I have it.   If we do not already assume that the two are identical, there does not seem any reason to suppose absolute infallibility, in which case the argument would derive its only basis from the very conclusion of which it is itself adduced as the main support.   That we may treat many judgments, both of present introspection and memory, as *practically* infallible, is not disputed.

Even if infallibility were established in the case of " judgments " based on present introspection, I do not see that it would prove identity between " judgment " and object judged about even here, let alone in the case of all " psychical judgments." For " judgments of memory," at any rate, must, it seems, be distinguished from their object, *e.g.*, I cannot say that to remember a pain in the past is the same thing as to experience the pain, (on the contrary, I may experience[1] pleasure in the remembrance, because I am now free from the pain).   I cannot say that to remember the experience of eating my breakfast is the same as the experience of eating my breakfast, still more must " judgments " about the psychical states of other people be distinguished from their object.   Yet, if the " judgment " that I have a feeling of

[1]Or, since pleasure and pain may be combined in a single experience, perhaps we should rather say that pleasure may be predominant in the remembrance of the experience, while pain was predominant in the experience remembered.

pain is different from my feeling of pain when anyone else makes this judgment about me, and even when I make it about myself from memory in an hour's time, when the pain has ceased, and say that I had this particular feeling of pain at 11 a.m. to-day, then surely it must be different from the feeling of pain when I make it about myself at the time when I feel the pain. What is different surely cannot be made the same by the accident of who makes the judgment and the time at which it is made, even if this accident should, as is contended, ensure the accuracy of the judgment.

But whether infallibility, could it be established, would or would not prove identity between " judgment " and object judged about, the possibility of error does prove a distinction between judgment and object judged about. If the judgment and what is judged about are identical, the judgment cannot possibly be false. If the judgment, " I am in state X," and state X in me were identical, then the judgment, " I am in state X," could never be wrong, because, if it were wrong, I should not be in state X and therefore could not make the judgment, " I am in state X," the judgment and state X being *ex hypothesi* identical. But the possibility of error we claim to have shown in some, if not in all, " psychical judgments," and if one single case of error can be established, this seems enough to shatter the view that " psychical judgments " differ from judgments about the physical in not possessing objectivity and hence necessity. If it were held that judgments of memory were fallible and objective, but judgments of immediate present introspection infallible and so not objective, the admission as to judgments of memory would be enough for us, because all perceptible psychical states may be made the object of a judgment of memory by the subject of whom they are the states, hence an admission that judgments of memory involve objectivity and so necessity would be equivalent to an admission that the category of necessary connection was valid of all perceptible psychical states.

It might still, I suppose, be contended that even if such " psychical judgments " are not always identical with the psychical event judged about, they are identical when they are what we normally call " true," but there seems to be no generic difference in psychological character between true and false judgments about our own perceptions, etc., to justify such a radical distinction as would be involved in maintaining that in the one case the judgment is the same as the psychical event judged about and in the other case quite distinct. If we are bound to distinguish them in the case of error, there seems no reason whatever to make them identical in the case of truth. Besides, if it is once admitted that error is possible in such judgments, truth must be possible, and truth always implies objectivity, or a distinction between the judgment and the object judged about. Otherwise the judgment, being identical with what is judged about, would not be true ; it would be simply itself. So much is implied in the contention of the critic that we are trying to answer, namely, the contention that these so-called psychical judgments are not judgments at all because there is no distinction in them between judgment and object judged about.

If mistakes[1] ever occur, either in judgments of present introspection or judgments of memory, then it seems that the contention that " psychical judgments " do not involve objectivity and so are not real judgments at all, falls to the ground. But that there has never been, and could never be, such a mistake, it seems impossible to maintain, at any rate in the case of judgments of memory, and, in view of the difficulties of psychological observation, I do not see how it can be contended that even judgments of present introspection are free from error. Perhaps indeed we should say that all " psychical judgments " are judgments of memory, for they can hardly be absolutely contemporaneous with the experience judged about, as the process of judgment must take time, and introspection at the moment when I was having the experience would[2] itself alter my experience, i.e., the object of perception in introspection, and so vitiate my conclusions from it. Now in the case of " judgments " of memory it would seem that the act of judging cannot be identified with the object judged about, for the very simple reason that the judgment is in the present and the object (event) judged about in the past. But this, truism though it may seem, appears to us quite enough by itself to settle the whole point at issue. Judgments of memory cannot be identical with their object, because the judgment and the object belong to different times, therefore judgments of memory have objectivity. Objectivity carries with it necessity, therefore any psychical state that can be cognised

---

[1]Excluding, of course, merely grammatical or verbal mistakes.

[2]That all introspection is really retrospection seems the best answer to Kant's objection in *The Metaphysical Rudiments of Natural Science* to the possibility of a real science of psychology based on introspection.

by memory is subject to principles of necessary connection. But any psychical state, if perceptible at all, must be capable of being cognised by memory; therefore all perceptible psychical states are subject to principles of necessary connection. Non-perceptible psychical states, (other than systems of perceptible psychical states and laws connecting such states), we may abandon to our adversary and wait till he can give us a clear idea of any such state.

However, we hold that it must be admitted that not only judgments of memory, but also judgments of present introspection, (if these are not indeed really themselves also judgments of memory and therefore *a fortiori* objective), involve objectivity. It may at first sight seem over-subtle to distinguish between a feeling in myself and the cognition of the feeling at the moment I have it, but, after all, what is this but the popular distinction between the self-conscious man and the man who is not self-conscious? We are no doubt always in some degree implicitly conscious of any feeling at the time we have it, but this is different from turning to it and explicitly recognising it as such ; if it were not, we should all be expert psychologists incessantly psychologising with ourselves as objects, and psychologising with such accuracy that we never by any possible chance made a mistake. For, if the feeling is the same as our judgment about it, then, each time we have the feeling, we make the judgment, and the judgment can never be wrong, for, if it were wrong, the feeling described and therefore the judgment itself, which is *ex hypothesi* the same as the feeling, would not occur. When engaged in a vigorous activity, we must be conscious of what we are doing, but this consciousness must be distinguished from that analysis of our state of mind which can alone give rise to " psychical judgments." So far from a feeling being the same as the explicit cognition of itself, such cognition tends to check the feeling by diverting our attention from the object which excites it. It seems, then, that even in judgments of immediate perception we must distinguish the judgment from its object, on general grounds, quite apart from our argument that the possibility of error must[1] be admitted in such judgments, an argument which, if right, would by itself at once establish objectivity. In the case of judgments of memory both points seem, if anything,

[1] It seems to us that all " psychical judgments " are rendered theoretically liable to error by the mere fact that they are bound to make use of universals and hence presuppose analysis of the particulars observed.

clearer, and, as we have tried to show, the objectivity of judgments of memory alone seems quite a sufficient basis to prove necessity of all psychical states. Once objectivity is admitted, the argument from objectivity to necessity can proceed in the same way as in regard to the physical world. But we need not try the reader's patience further, we need only refer him to the general argument from objectivity to necessity for the physical world, now confident that it will also hold good for the empirical self, if we have succeeded in showing that judgments about the empirical self also imply objectivity and that the cases are therefore analogous. To one who has grasped the main principle of Kant's proof of causality in the case of the physical world, the sketch of the argument in its application to the psychical that we have given earlier[1] is perhaps superfluous.

But besides the argument of the second Analogy there is the further line of argument that an object can only be thought as a necessarily connected system of attributes, and can only be regarded as maintaining its continuity and identity in change, if there is a thoroughgoing necessary connection between the earlier and the later stages of the process. But this clearly establishes necessary connection for the empirical self, perhaps even more convincingly than for the external world, because it is still more imperative to regard even the empirical self as in some degree a unity and as maintaining its continuity in change than it is thus to regard the external world.

It may be asked how on our view we can distinguish those percepta which we refer to the physical object perceived from other percepta which we do not so refer, and objected that it was just the purpose of Kant's proof of causality to show that the physical can only be distinguished from the psychical by the presence of necessary connection in the former and the absence of it in the latter. The question of the interpretation of Kant we have already discussed ; about the difficulty involved in this vital distinction and its bearing on our theory we shall say just a few words. The difficulty cannot, it seems to us, however acute in itself, be an adequate ground for the rejection of the view that necessary connection is a category universally valid of the empirical self. For, if it is difficult on our view to distinguish those of our percepta which refer to physical objects from other percepta, it is impossible, on any view which denies necessary connection to the self, to distinguish between cognition by introspection or memory and mere imagination or association of ideas, for this cannot be done unless cognition in perception involves the necessary determination of our percepta by the object, whether physical or psychical, that is perceived. Now, while a view which denies necessary connection to the empirical self would still enable us to make this distinction with regard to physical objects, it would deprive us of the power to distinguish between imagination and perception by memory or introspection. This distinction, just as much as the distinction between the physical and the psychical, is bound up with the very foundations of our knowledge. But our view is not grounded merely on the need for finding means of making a certain distinction, it is based on the analysis of cognition in perception, and this, we claim, has shown that, while our way of distinguishing between cognition and imagination follows necessarily from such an analysis of the nature of cognition, the suggested way of distinguishing between the physical and the psychical is rendered impossible by it, because the analysis has established necessity not only for physical but also for psychical states. That we can find no other way of making the distinction would not justify us in seeking a way that we know to be impossible.

If it is asked how we are to meet the difficulty on our own view, we may reply that, on our view, while the psychical and the physical are alike necessarily determined, percepta of physical objects are distinguished from other percepta by being members of a different causal system, which has the especial characteristic of uniting and determining in a uniform fashion the percepta of different percipients. Where we mistakenly regard sense-illusions as representing the real nature of the physical object we perceive, the mistake consists in referring our percepta to a wrong causal system, for, though all percepta are given from the beginning as members of some necessary causal system, this will not help us in the perception of a particular object unless they are members of that causal system which constitutes the object we are looking at. There is no royal road to the distinction between percepta of the physical object and irrelevant percepta ; in particular cases we can only establish to which causal system the percepta belong by special, empirical reasoning. That such special causal reasoning is necessary is surely borne out by all experience as to sense-illusion.

Further, even if the view that all causation is physical is accepted, this will not dispense us from the necessity of appealing to special causal laws in cases of illusion. For, even supposing causation to be only physical, we still cannot refer all percepta determined by causation to the physical object perceived, for sense-illusions too may be quite as much determined by physical causation, yet they[1] cannot be so referred ; we have still to make the distinction between the percepta we refer to the physical object perceived and those which we do not so refer rest on membership in different orders of causation, not on the presence of causation in one case and its absence in the other. It consequently seems very doubtful whether the assumption that all causation is physical would lessen the difficulty at all.

The application of substance. Our own view. We must now say something about the question of the application of substance to the empirical self. The importance of this question for us lies in the fact that substance may be regarded as presupposed by causality, in the sense that causality is only a connection between successive states of one substance ; and hence the difficulty in discovering a permanent element in the empirical self, which generally held back Kant from applying the category of substance in this sphere, may be thought also to hinder the application of causality.

But we have tried to show in our discussion of substance that Kant did not succeed in proving the principle of substance in any sense which involved the presence of an absolutely permanent substratum in all change. His arguments, if valid, establish substance in no less than four different senses, none of which involve absolute permanence :

1. The independence of the physical as against subjective idealism.

2. The uniformity of purely temporal (and perhaps spatial) relations.

3. A regularity of physical changes sufficient to serve the purposes of measurement.

4. An identity in change involving causal connection.

In none of these senses does the principle of substance seem in the slightest degree inconsistent with the application of

[1] If the " Neo-Realist " theory as to so-called sense-illusions be accepted and these be held to be just as much real physical entities as any, then the argument that causality ought to be denied of the psychical, in order to make the distinction possible, cannot be used.

causality to the empirical self. Of course, we must admit that our psychological changes are not sufficiently regular to measure time with the requisite accuracy, but the same applies to many physical objects, and it certainly cannot be shown that all causality is a connection between the changing states of those substances which move with sufficient regularity to help us to measure time, *i.e.*, presumably, clocks and certain heavenly bodies ! Yet it is only if all causality is held to be a connection between the changing states of a substance that the failure to apply substance to the empirical self can be said to be inconsistent with the application of causality.

There is a sense in which the category of substance is the presupposition of all knowledge. All empirical judgments must be referred to a system of some sort, and this is the usual sense of the term " substance." Substance in this sense is essentially an assertion of unity in the object known, and its importance lies not in the presence of an unchanging substratum—a barren and unintelligible conception—but in the presence of necessary connection. This reduces itself to (*a*) thorough causal connection between past, present and future, (*b*) the union in a system of what we call different attributes of the same substance (or qualities of the same object), whether they coexist or succeed each other. This necessary connection we have already tried to establish for all perceptible psychical as well as physical events.

We must now turn to reciprocity.[1] Can that too **The appli-** be applied to the psychical? We can put the **cation of** matter quite briefly. We undoubtedly can **reciprocity.** **Our own** observe states of our empirical self as coexistent **view.** with states of external objects, (if we cannot observe them simultaneously, we can at any rate observe their coexistence in that way in which, according to Kant, we can alone observe any coexistence, by observing first one of the coexistent objects, here the empirical self, then the other, and *vice versa*). But we can only observe them as objectively coexistent if our percepta of them are conditioned by a necessary law determining the coexistence or alternate sequence of these percepta. That objective coexistence or succession implies necessary coexistence or succession, we have already concluded. That one of the objects is psychical can hardly make any difference, unless the psychical is denied objectivity altogether, a view that we have already considered

[1]*V*. above, pp. 147-9.

and, rightly or wrongly, rejected. If perception of the inner as well as of the outer is held to be necessarily determined in so far as it is real cognition, reciprocity is but one case of this general principle and presents no special difficulties. It does not seem possible to base a satisfactory proof of the category on the nature of space alone. We must, however, refer the reader to our general account of the category and point out that we there argued that what Kant really has succeeded in proving in the third Analogy is not universal interaction, but necessary coexistence.[1] If so, the proof would not itself exclude a doctrine of psycho-physical parallelism, which regarded the states of body and soul as determined, but determined independently of each other, nor would it necessarily imply the causal determination of the empirical self by what is outside it.

In the passage in the Analytic, already referred to, where Kant maintains that the categories can only be rendered intelligible by the help of outer sense, he brings forward as his reason for this contention in the case of reciprocity the difficulty as to how we can " represent to ourselves the possibility that in several existent substances the existence of the one should be affected causally by the existence of the other, and *vice versa*, so that from the existence of something in the first substance there follows the existence of something in the others, which cannot be understood from their existence alone.[2] This is what is demanded by the principle of reciprocity, and this is quite incomprehensible among things each of which is completely isolated by its own substantiality. . . .We can, however, well enough understand the possibility of reciprocity (of substances as phenomena), if we represent them to ourselves as in space and so as given in external perception. For space includes in its own *a priori* idea formal outer relations, as conditions of the possibility of real relations (in action and reaction and so reciprocity)." We may compare Kant's first work, where he reduced the conception of space to that of the interaction of substances, so that he then held reciprocity to be already involved in the mere conception of existence in space. Here, however, Kant appears to be only contending that, if substances already stand in certain relations to each other, *i.e.*, spatial, it is easy to see that they may also stand in other relations, *i.e.*, those expressed by the categories of causality and reciprocity. The argument against

<hr>

[1] *V.* above pp. 116, ff.   [2] *B.*, 292, ff.

the intelligibility of interaction apart from space is based on the old view of substance as an absolute, not a relative, conception, involving complete independence. The attributes of a substance, it was thought, must be deducible from its " notion," a view which barred interaction between substances, since, if interaction were a fact, some of the determinations in one substance would be caused, or, rather, partly caused, by determinations in another substance and would, therefore, not be deducible from the notion of that substance to which they belonged, but would have to be explained by reference to other substances. Hence the pre-established harmony of Leibniz. Kant was very interested in the problem in the early part of his career and tried to avoid the difficulty by a *via media* between the doctrine of a " physical influence " and the occasionalist view. (In the latter part of his life he, of course, regarded speculations of that kind as " dogmatic.") Nowhere does he answer the objection of Spinoza that, if all substances are independent, there can only be one substance in the world. In any case reciprocity would seem to be irreconcilable with the absolute independence of substances, and it does not seem possible to avoid the contradiction by the mediation of spatial relations. Whether substances are in space or not, they cannot be absolutely independent if they interact ; therefore either the old view of the world as a plurality of independent substances must be modified, in which case the difficulty disappears without invoking space, or the antinomy is insoluble even with the aid of spatial relations. Even if space were shown to presuppose universal interaction, it would not remove the difficulty, but only prove that objects in space are not substances in the old sense of the term. So much for reciprocity.

Two limitations of the application of the categories to the psychical.
We have tried to establish the universality of necessary connection in the psychical as well as in the physical sphere, but two limitations must be added—(1) Kant of course, rightly or wrongly, never meant to apply any proof of necessary connection to the noumenal self. Whether he was right or not in doing so is a question which we do not propose to discuss now. What the meaning of the distinction between the noumenal self as free and the phenomenal self as determined really is, whether it represents a tenable point of view, and how far it helps us towards the solution of the problem of freedom, are points that we shall have to say a little about in a later chapter.

(2.) In saying that we hold the category of causality to have been proved to be universally applicable in the case of psychical, as in the case of physical events, we do not mean by causality mechanical causality, but are using the term in the wide sense of necessary succcession, as Kant does in the second Analogy and elsewhere. Causality, as generally applied empirically, involves an atomism which aims at reducing all complex wholes to aggregates of simpler elements in such a way that the necessary connection between two such wholes may be completely reduced to a series of laws linking each element in the one with each element in the other. But all that the second Analogy proves is that, if B follows A, the succession A–B is necessary. It does not prove that this necessity is of a type which can be reduced wholly to causal laws connecting single elements in the process, it does not prove that all wholes are mere aggregates and does not involve the denial of a causation by which the whole determines the parts as well as a causation by which the parts determine the whole. This point was not realised by Kant at first; in the *Critique of Practical Reason* and the *Foundation of the Metaphysic of Ethics* he assumed that all causality was mechanical and that the *Critique of Pure Reason* had proved the universal validity, not only of causality, but of mechanical causality, in the psychical sphere. But in the *Critique of Judgement* he comes to recognize the distinction between the two kinds of causation.

We have indeed contended that the categories are applicable to the empirical self in the general sense of necessary connection, but if causality is understood as this atomistic, mechanical causality, we can still say with Professor Caird, " Even the action of the environment on a living being cannot be truly conceived according to such categories as those of causality and reciprocity, taken in their ordinary sense.[1] Still less can we treat in that way the relation of the objects known to the self that knows them. In so far as the objects with which we start are essentially objects related to feeling and knowledge, we cannot separate the determinations they have as objects in space from the further determination which comes to them from such relation. And this further determination, with the application of higher categories which it involves, is not an *external* addition to our knowledge of objects as in space, but a step towards the

[1] *The Critical Philosophy of Kant*, vol. I., pp. 595–6.

discovery of the ultimate meaning or reality of that knowledge. In this point of view, therefore, it is evident that to contemplate our experience as *inner* experience is simply to enrich our outer experience by bringing in the thought of its relation to feeling in ourselves as sensitive subjects." For causality and reciprocity, as generally understood at any rate, involve an atomism which renders them quite inadequate for the self, but this does not rule out as inapplicable to the self the more general category of necessary connection, which is, in fact, all that Kant succeeded in proving. That Professor Caird still held cognition of the empirical self by perception to imply a synthesis according to principles of understanding involving necessary connection is quite clear, especially from his discussion of the transcendental deduction, where he insists that " judgments of perception," and even consciousness of images of perception as such, involve this synthesis.[1]

The distinction we have touched upon is of the utmost importance, for many shrink from the universal application of causality to the self as incompatible with any moral action, but to us the real foe seems to be not necessity but mechanical causality. By causality or necessary connection as proved in the second Analogy we do not mean a causality which makes of the self an automaton absolutely determined in all its acts by the laws of motion, or even by its own past acts, or a mere aggregate of interacting motives and presentations, but a causality which leaves room for action by the whole man, action not completely to be accounted for by any combination of motives or desires as isolable factors, action not wholly determined by any past events, but only by the man's character as a principle running through past, present and future, and not exhausted in any congeries of conflicting motives, in any series of conscious experiences, a necessity which may be at least as reconcilable with morality as an indeterminism which asserts that moral actions occur without an adequate cause in the character of the agent. In this chapter we have tried to show that necessary connection is a principle universally valid of the empirical self, but we can only accept a necessity which we may hope to reconcile with that freedom which is an indispensable condition of moral action. Whether this is a reasonable hope we must consider later.

3. In our discussion of freedom in chapter VIII it must,

---

[1] *The Critical Philosophy of Kant*, vol. i., p. 350 ff.

however, be remembered that we have not attempted to prove the necessary determination of the self[1] as a whole by what is external to it. For we have only applied the argument to events in time, and the self is not merely a series of events or a process in time. We have argued that there must be necessary connection within each self, because otherwise there would be neither unity nor continuity nor objectivity in the psychological sphere, but we have made no attempt to establish the doctrine that each self as a whole is determined by the rest of the Absolute. Whether an argument like Kant's, if logically developed, would lead to metaphysical monism we do not propose to consider. So we are not arguing against the view that each individual mind constitutes a " new beginning," in the sense of something not in any way wholly determined by or deducible from either what has gone before or a timeless Absolute. The arguments we have used are all arguments for necessary connection *within* the self, not arguments for the determination of the self by what is external or temporally prior to it. This remark must not, of course, be taken as a declaration in favour of the doctrine that each self is a " new beginning " in this sense, but only as an assertion that the arguments we have used here do not seem to us, at any rate as they stand, to put any serious difficulty in the way of anybody who wishes to maintain that doctrine. Whether they could be developed in such a way as to refute the doctrine is another and more difficult question, but of one thing there can be no doubt—in his ethical works Kant, rightly or wrongly, maintained that everything phenomenal in the self was deducible from antecedent and external phenomena.

Note on another possible interpretation of Kant.

It may be said that Kant meant not that the self was undetermined, but that it was wholly determined by physical and physiological, and not at all by psychical causes. But this view would still make the psychical subject to some kind of causality in time and so would agree little better with the various passages we have cited against the application of the categories to the self, and would involve Kant in a material-

---

[1]The application of the proof of reciprocity in the psychological sphere would at most only show that coexistent states of different selves were necessarily determined, not that they were causally determined by each other or by external substances (*v.* above, pp. 116 ff.).

M

ism as regards phenomena which, as far as I can find, is never asserted, still less proved, in the *Critique of Pure Reason* and is quite inconsistent with the ethical works, where he recognises psychological (phenomenal) causation throughout. And this view would need a proof that all states of the empirical self are causally determined just as much as the view we are defending, and would have to be defended against more or less the same objections as that view in addition to other objections peculiar to itself. So, even if it were Kant's view, at any rate the greater part of our argument in this chapter would be needed to support it and could remain unchanged, and it certainly does not seem to us either a view ever explicitly held by Kant or a logical consequence of his principles.

Note on the Relation of the Æsthetic to the Analytic.

We may be criticised for not having introduced a discussion of the Æsthetic, as the stepping-stone to the position of the Analytic, but we claim to have shown ambulando that an independent discussion of the Analytic is quite practicable. To our mind the importance of the Æsthetic for the Analytic consists in two points :—(1) Its idealism. But it is better to base idealism on the general argument from the relativity[1] of an object to a subject of experience than on the special arguments which Kant uses to show the ideality of space and time. Further, as we have tried to show, it seems that the main principle of Kant's proof of causality may be accepted even by a realist. (2) As Kuno Fischer has insisted, it is important for the argument of the Analytic that time should not be regarded as a " thing," by which we can date any event without the help of other events. But this fairly obvious point is not one that is likely to meet with much opposition at the present day, and is rather obscured than made clear in the Æsthetic.

---

[1] In the transcendental deduction this takes the (inadequate) form of the contention that all relation is contributed by the understanding.

CHAPTER VII

Cause and Ground.—The First Cause Antinomy

WITH the discussion of Kant's proof of causality completed, we may regard the main part of our task as done. But the last words of the preceding chapter have brought us face to face with the problem of freedom, and owing to the age-long opposition between causality and freedom, a discussion of the former cannot be complete without some treatment of its relation to the latter. This treatment is expressly given by Kant in his *Critique of Practical Reason* and his *Foundation of the Metaphysic of Ethics,* but requires to be supplemented by a consideration of the *Critique of Judgment.* However, before touching on this problem, we shall first discuss another point of considerable interest and importance, with which we have not yet dealt, namely, the relation between cause and ground. Perhaps we shall find it to be not altogether unconnected with the question of freedom, and in any case it deserves discussion in its own right.

In considering both points it is essential that we should realise exactly in just what sense Kant has succeeded in proving causality. Now, as far as we can see, the argument outlined in the foregoing chapters only proves causality in the sense of necessary succession. Neither does it prove the necessity to be " mechanical " (a point to which we shall return in considering freedom) ; nor does it make the cause the logical ground of the effect (which concerns the point at issue now). Causality, as meaning necessary succession in time, is undoubtedly regarded by Kant as the temporal schema of the logical category of ground and consequence, but that there is any connection of the logical sort between particular causes and effects as phenomena such that the one could ever be deduced from the other *a priori,* he not only never attempts to prove, but emphatically repudiates. As applied to phenomena the " activity " and logical views of causality were alike abhorrent to him. On this point

Kant gives no sign of having changed from his position in the sixties, when he declared that it was no more intelligible *a priori* that my will should move my body than that it should move the moon. It is one of his favourite arguments against those who condemn freedom as unintelligible that the causal nexus between physical phenomena is also unintelligible. He always insists that " the possibility of change does not admit of being recognised *a priori*."[1] " For as to a cause being possible, which changes the state of the things, *i.e.*, determines them to the opposite of a certain given state, on this subject understanding gives us no information whatever *a priori*, not only because it does not comprehend the possibility of it at all, (for we are without this comprehension in several instances of *a priori* knowledge), but because the liability to change only affects certain determinations of phenomena, the identity of which can be taught by experience alone, while their cause is to be found in the unchangeable."[2] The last few words express Kant's conviction that the rationale, the real ground of the causal connection always belongs to the noumenal sphere and is for this very reason unknowable. He did not hold, (like a number of present-day philosophers), that there was no logical connection involved in the causal sequence, but he ascribed this logical connection not to the causally connected appearances themselves but to their noumenal conditions.

This explains, too, his application of causality to the " thing-in-itself," which has often been attacked as a gross absurdity, on the ground that it was quite incompatible both with his general view as to the unknowability of what is not phenomenal and his denial of the validity of the categories beyond the limits of possible experience. But, whatever may be thought of the general account of noumena, the application of causality in the sense of the logical category of ground to such noumenal entities is not incompatible with the denial that the schema of the category—*i.e.*, necessary succession in time—can be so applied.[3] However, since no proof has been given that every phenomenon requires a logical ground to account for it, it is difficult to see how Kant could justify his argument to the " thing-in-itself " as a ground necessary to account for phenomena, much less reconcile this with its absolute unknowability. For it is only

---

[1]*E.g.*, Erdmann, *Reflexionen*, 753.
[2]*B.*, 213 = *A* 171 ; *cf. Kant's Letters*, Berl., II, 337.
[3]*V.* Riehl, *Geschichte des Kritizismus*, pp. 569 ff.

as unknown ground of the content of perception that the thing-in-itself as generally treated in connection with physical phenomena has any meaning. (The view that the possibility of moral action implies free causation on the part of a noumenal self is another matter). It certainly seems as though Kant were moving towards the more tenable view of the noumenal world as the whole of which phenomena are parts, but it can hardly be said that he ever arrived there.

But, putting this aside, his philosophy inevitably tended to relegate causality in the sense of dynamical agency to the noumenal sphere, so that, as in the passage last quoted where Kant says that the cause of the changes in phenomena " is to be found in the unchangeable," it sometimes seems as though, so far from real causality being excluded from the noumenal sphere, it is only found there and not in phenomena at all. Especially when phenomena are regarded in Berkeleian style as only representations in individual minds, does it appear incorrect to say that they exercise a causal influence on each other, something like saying that my perception of a match lights my perception of wood. But, if we remain true to the definition of causality as necessary succession and do not look for anything beyond it, there is clearly nothing inappropriate in calling phenomena causes and effects, and it is, of course, only in this sense that Kant has proved the universal validity of the principle of causality for phenomena. This sense of causality represents that one of its characteristics, or supposed characteristics, which is least disputable, and so there seems no reason to hesitate to apply the term to phenomena, once it is correctly defined. For the sense of intrinsic logical connection we already have another term at our disposal, " ground." From the subjective idealist point of view,[1] it is only because it is simpler to make use of causal laws connecting common elements in percepta of different individuals than causal laws connecting individual perceptions, that causal laws in regard to what we call the physical world are always stated in the former way, the common element in different perceptions being for the sake of simplicity treated as a self-subsistent thing and its complete dependence on these individual perceptions ignored. Hence the application of the causal laws in question to our perceptions of the physical instead of to physical objects themselves seems strange and inappropriate, though the causal necessity

[1]We do not, of course, commit ourselves to this view.

is present all the same even as regards our individual perceptions.

It is clear that, the more Kant verges towards the subjectivist view, the more difficult it would be for him to ascribe to the phenomenal causes anything of the nature of dynamical agency. The antithesis between a subjectivist and a phenomenalist view on the question of causality is well stated by Prof. Kemp Smith.[1] " From the one point of view appearances are representations merely, and accordingly are entirely devoid of causal efficacy. They are not causes and effects of one another. They have not the independence or self-persistence necessary for the exercise of dynamical energy or even for the reception of modifications. Being ' states of the identical self,' all causal relation, dynamically conceived, must lie solely in their noumenal conditions. Causality reduces to the thought of necessitated (not necessitating) sequence. It is, as Kant has suggested in A 181— B 224, a mere ' analogy ' in terms of which we apply the logical relation of ground and consequence to the interpretation of our subjective representations, and so view them as grounded not in one another but exclusively in the thing in itself... The corresponding phenomenalist view of the causal relation receives no quite definite formulation either in this section or elsewhere in the *Critique*, but may be gathered from the general trend of Kant's phenomenalist teaching. It is somewhat as follows : The term ' analogy ' is viewed as having a meaning very different from that above suggested. The causal relation is not a mere analogy from the logical relation of ground and consequence, it is the representation of genuinely dynamical activities in the objects apprehended. These objects are not mere states of the self, subjective representations. They are part of an independent order which in the form known to us is a phenomenalist transcript of a deeper reality. If the causal relation is the analogy of anything distinguishable from itself, it is an analogon or interpretation of dynamical powers exercised by things in themselves,[2] not of the merely logical relation between premises and conclusion. The objects of representation may exercise powers which representations as such can never be conceived as possessing. Between the individual's subjective states

---

[1] *Commentary*, pp. 373–4.
[2] Prof. Kemp Smith adds the following footnote, " Kant, of course, recognises that we cannot make any such positive assertion ; to do so would be to transcend the limits imposed by Critical principles."

·and things in themselves stands the phenomenal world of the natural sciences. Its function, whether as directly experienced through sense-perception or as conceptually reconstructed through scientific hypothesis, is to stand as the representative in human consciousness of that noumenal realm in which all existence is ultimately rooted. The causal interactions of material bodies in space are as essentially constitutive of those bodies as are any of their quantitative properties. Causal relation, even in the phenomenal sphere, must not be identified with mere conformity to law. The true and complete purpose of the natural sciences is not to be found in the Berkeleian or sceptical ideal of simplification, but in the older and sounder conception of causal explanation."

However, it seems that the phenomenalist view of causality outlined above must be regarded rather as a possible development of the Kantian philosophy than as a view ever held by Kant himself. Nowhere can I find any evidence of him abandoning his view that causality does not involve any dynamical activity, or *a priori* intelligible connection, as binding together the phenomenal cause and effect. The most that can be said is that in his posthumously published work, *The Transition from the Metaphysical Rudiments of Natural Science to Physics*, with its more realistic view of matter, there is a certain tendency to be discovered in that direction. The importance of the " phenomenalist " tendency generally in Kant's work is very great—but on this particular point it does not seem to find clear expression.

Now, regarding causality as proved in the sense that all sequence is necessary, and in that sense alone, we may ask the further question whether this is enough and whether we are not justified in also assuming the presence of what might be called " intrinsic connection " between cause and effect. By " intrinsic connection " I mean such a connection between particular causes and effects that the former even taken apart from their causal relation to the latter are logically incoherent without the latter and *vice versa*. Then a particular causal law is not only a statement that a certain event or kind of events must always under given conditions be followed by a certain other event or kind of events, but the expression of the fact that the nature of one event is bound up with the occurrence of another in a way analogous to that in which the existence of a triangle is bound up with its possession of angles the sum of which is equal to two right angles.

Then such laws do not merely answer the question—How? but help us a little nearer towards seeing the answer to the question—Why? One view of causality, while recognising that the principle possesses necessity, so that, if A is the cause of B, B must always occur if A occurs, does not recognise any intrinsic connection between A and B. It recognises causal laws as statements that certain uniformities hold good under all circumstances, but denies the possibility of a rational understanding of the connection involved in these uniformities. The object of causal laws is held to be never to explain but always only to simplify and predict; they do not reveal to us an intelligible, rational connection, but only brute fact. The causal relation is regarded as purely external and not dependent on qualities in the cause and effect, other than this relation itself, in such a way that it could be deduced *a priori*, even theoretically, from them. Not only does this view, like the Kantian, relegate the rational connection involved in necessary succession to a non-phenomenal sphere, but, going further, it denies the need of supposing such a connection at all. According to it there would be no more real, intrinsic connection between the striking of a match and the flame it causes than between the striking of the match and an earthquake at the other end of the world which occurred immediately afterwards; the only difference would be that the striking of a match and the appearance of a flame could be correlated conveniently in the form of a law sufficiently general for rough practical needs, because they were always (with certain exceptions that could be easily accounted for) found to accompany each other in experience, while the striking of a match and the earthquake could not; but apart from experience it would still be just as reasonable to suppose that the striking of a match would cause an earthquake at the other end of the world as that it would cause the match to burst into flame. The burning of a match could hardly, on that view, be said to be *due* to the striking of it, but only to follow uniformly on the latter. This uniformity would be necessary because we could not conceive the same set of causes not to be followed by the same effects, but its necessity would not be due to anything in the match, but be further inexplicable. Surely this paradoxical conclusion is sufficient to make us pause before accepting the view in question. One thing is quite certain, that necessary, uniform succession is not all we usually mean by causality. By causality is popularly understood a dynamical force which enables one thing to produce changes in another, the effect is held not merely to succeed the cause but to be determined by some intrinsic quality in the latter. This common-sense view at least deserves consideration.

However, the opposing view that reduces causality to mere necessary uniformity must be considered to be, in the main at any rate, true as regards present human knowledge. We can give no reason for any law of nature, except by making it a case of another, wider law, likewise empirically discovered. We know the law of gravitation, but this law does not enable us to see why material bodies should attract each other according to their mass and distance, it is only a generalised statement of the fact that they do. We know that certain substances, when absorbed by eating, will nourish and others destroy our tissues, but we cannot see why they should do so. We can no doubt analyse them further and discover that, for example, meat is nourishing because it contains a large proportion of nitrogenous substance, but we could not tell *a priori* whether this nitrogenous substance would be likely to nourish or poison us. Only where mathematics can be applied do we see necessity in such a way that any alternative becomes inconceivable to us, but, because mathematics alone can never establish what quantity there will be at a later time or in another part of space from the quantity there is here and now, (only *e.g.*, that, if there is 2 + 2 here and now, there must be 4 here and now, not that, if there is 2 + 2 here and now, there will be 4 here in an hour's time or now a mile away), mathematics cannot be made the sole basis of any causal law whatever.

But this is not the same as saying that causality is a merely external relation, and that it is ultimately and essentially unintelligible. We may remark, in the first place, that such a view is quite irreconcilable with the view of the universe as a truly coherent whole such that every fact about anything ultimately implies every other fact and would involve self-contradiction if it stood alone, and with the postulate of the ultimate rationality of the real. Now this view, and still more this postulate, deserve at any rate careful consideration, backed as they are by weighty convictions, and it is at least a *prima facie* objection to any view that it conflicts with them.

But, passing on, when we turn from the physical to the psychological sphere, this view is harder to maintain and still more paradoxical in its results. For, while we cannot see the intrinsic connection between different physical events, it seems that we can see the intrinsic connection between the receipt of an insult and subsequent resentment, between success and joy when we subsequently become aware of it, between love and grief at the death of the object of one's love. But these are all cases of intrinsic connection between a prior state of mind and a subsequent event or between a prior event and a subsequent state of mind, that is, they are cases of causality. No doubt the reaction to an event is modified by the self as a whole, and this self cannot be altogether reduced to isolable data connected by causal laws, but we seem to see the intrinsic connection between different characteristics or purposes of the self and a given reaction. We see that it is natural that, for example, an insult should tend to arouse anger, though not inevitable, because the law may be prevented from taking effect by the intervention of other factors ; we see that love on the loss of its object must in itself give rise to grief, we have a sense that this is due to the intrinsic nature of love as known apart from this characteristic, that it is a fully intelligible fact and needs no further accounting for. We feel that there is no further room for the question—Why ? while in the case of a physical event we have always to leave the question—Why ? unsatisfied, and can only answer the question—How ? that is—How must the process which led to this result have gone on ?—not—" What was there in the preceding event that explains and makes intelligible the necessity for such a result to occur ?   But, if we can detect intrinsic[1] connection between cause and effect in the psychological sphere, it is a very strong argument for there being such connection also in the physical sphere.

It may be objected that, while these connections are intelligible *a priori*, they are not cases of causal connection at all, but only applications of the law of non-contradiction, *e.g.*, desire for an object may be said already to include pain, in so far as the desire is frustrated, so that this pain may be discerned by mere analysis of the desire, as A may be discovered by mere analysis of A, B, C. But this is an impossible view unless they are not different events at all. If they are really different events, the connection is not analytic, but synthetic, and we have discovered an instance of an intelligible, necessary, synthetic connection between

[1]If our consciousness of intrinsic, intelligible connection between psychical states be an illusion due to constant experience, why do we not have it with regard to physical events ?

different events, which is just what we are looking for. A synthetic, necessary connection between different events is just causality. To take a simple instance, joy in the presence of an object implies pain at its loss, and we contend that this is not a case of merely empirical knowledge but that the connection has *a priori* intelligibility. Now the objector cannot ascribe this *a priori* intelligibility to a merely analytic connection. For, in the first place, the law of non-contradiction, in its analytic sense, can only be applied to what is strictly contemporary ; if X is included in Y, X must be present at the very moment in which Y is, for otherwise Y itself could not be present either. But it is obvious that pain at the loss of an object is not contemporary with joy at its presence. Further, secondly, for any analytic argument from joy to pain to be possible at all, pain would have to be included in the very concept of joy *qua* joy, which is absurd. If joy implies pain, it is an implication by opposites of each other, and of all implications this surely can put in least claim to be merely analytic. Similarly, the anger called forth by an insult cannot be itself part of the cognition of the meaning of the insult, the joy of success cannot be itself part either of the physical achievement of success or of the pre-existent desire for success, yet in both cases they seem to follow by a sort of rational connection.[1] Unless the judgment, " I feel joy at the presence of an object," is the same as or includes the judgment, " I feel pain at its loss or partial loss," the connection[2] between the judgments must be synthetic, and the connection between the emotions as events must be of the nature of causality. But, as we have already said, it is difficult for us to see how in cases like this the admission of an intelligible *a priori* connection can be avoided.

[1]We might also object that, if the connection were analytic, the sequence of one emotion or event on the other would be, not only probable, but inevitable, for it would be actually included in the other. If A is actually included in B, it must be present whenever B is, whatever other factors intervene. Yet, *e.g.*, the pain that tends to arise on the loss of an object that gave pleasure, the anger that tends to follow an insult, etc., are certainly not inevitable, but may be checked or prevented by other factors, *e.g.*, a feeling of pleasure at something else or a strong diversion of interest. For our description of the connection as necessary was not meant to imply that the one event must always produce the other, only that it must produce it in the absence of special counteracting conditions. It cannot be said that the two might be analytically connected in the sense that one does not actually include the other, but only a tendency towards it, for this would simply be another way of saying that the connection was synthetic.

[2]As is mostly admitted now, no real judgment can be merely analytic.

But, even in modern physical science, we have the principles that the effect must be "contained[1] in the cause," and that any process must be "continuous," *i.e.*, that there must be no breaks in it of such a character that there is at any point of it a hopeless disparity between cause and effect.   This shows that scientists are not satisfied till they can find a certain degree of homogeneity between cause and effect, and, although this cannot always be achieved by us, the mere fact that, when we fail to find it, as in the case of the relation between mental and physical events, we are perplexed and at a loss, proves that we expect homogeneity, that some types of causation actually found in the world, because homogeneous, present themselves as more intelligible to us than others, and that we will not rest till we can find this intelligibility. That like should cause like is regarded, not only as more in accordance with experience—(whether such[2] a principle is supported by experience is very doubtful indeed)—but as more intelligible than that cause and effect should be unlike.

Or, to go to the other extreme, if we adopted Berkeley's

---

[1] This seems a very unsuitable metaphor (*v.*, below, pp. 182-3), but at any rate it well illustrates the demand for some intelligible connection between cause and effect.

[2] Can there be anything much more unlike than water and oxygen and hydrogen together just before their combination into water, than a coloured image and certain wave-lengths, than an act of will and a movement in my body, than a wound and a sensation of pain, than an engine and the noise it makes ?   It may be objected that the dissimilarity is avoided by the denial of the physical reality of secondary qualities combined with the adoption of the hypothesis of psycho-physical parallelism, but it is at any rate clear that, of the events which we find in constant conjunction by experience, many, if not the majority, appear quite unlike each other.   Yet, for the general principle that like causes like to be adequately founded on experience, almost all cases of constant conjunction (the only or main empirical criterion of causality) would have to be cases of conjunction of like with like.   The adoption of the principle that like causes like is obviously not subsequent to the hypothesis of psycho-physical parallelism, without the adoption of which cause and effect must in experience be constantly dissimilar, but on the contrary constituted the most powerful motive for the adoption of this very hypothesis itself.   There is no conjunction of events which we have experienced more frequently than the conjunction of a feeling and a physical change, yet of all conjunctions this seems the least intelligible. What we have said must not, however, be interpreted as an argument for psycho-physical parallelism, for, if it is difficult to suppose that a physical change can produce such a different kind of event as a feeling, it is equally difficult to suppose that they can be states of the same substance, unless the substance is made totally unknowable, in which case it would be just as easy to maintain interaction between two unknowables.

view and regarded every physical event as due to the will
of God operating without the mediation of any other event or
object, yet we should be bound to suppose that there was
something in the apparent cause which made God think it
suitable that it should be followed by the apparent effect,
for otherwise the act of God in connecting the two would be
unmotived and irrational—so we should have even then to
suppose a connection between cause and effect in theory
deducible *a priori* from their intrinsic nature.

But can we really maintain at once that causality involves
necessity and that it is merely an external relation? From
the standpoint put forward—apparently the usual one of a
naturalistic philosophy—the necessity is admitted,[1] because
the premiss that " E has always followed A B C D in the
past " cannot justify the conclusion that " E will follow
A B C D in this new instance," unless it is taken to indicate
a necessary connection between A B C D and the sequence of
E. Only the necessary connection means from that point of
view just the brute fact, further unintelligible, that E must
follow A B C D. But can we talk about what involves
" must " as a brute, unintelligible fact? Necessity is not an
actuality, it is an implication. And it is in fact universally
or almost universally admitted that a causal law involves the
relation of implication between cause and effect. Now if
Kant has succeeded in establishing the universal validity of
causality in the sense of necessity or implication, the question
remains whether this also involves what we have called "intrinsic connection " between cause and effect. If it does not, we
must hold, on the one hand, that the judgment that " A (the
chief efficient cause) occurs under conditions B C D " implies
the judgment that " E follows," and, on the other, that
A B C D is *not* so connected with E that it is logically impossible
for the former judgment to be true without the latter being
true also. That seems to be the usual position of the naturalistic school (besides other philosophers). Implication is
admitted because we can deduce the effect from the cause,
but it is not admitted that the effect is so dependent on the
cause as to make the implication logically (as opposed to
actually) necessary, given the cause alone, *i.e.*, it is held
both that the effect and the cause are so interconnected that
one cannot occur without the other also occurring, and also
that a judgment as to the occurrence of either is self-sufficient

[1] Even those who deny it in words admit it in fact by allowing that
argument from cause to effect and *vice versa* is possible.

without a reference to the occurrence of the other, has no logical connection with the judgment as to the occurrence of the other apart from the accident that owing to the conjunction of the events in experience it is possible for us to make one judgment an inference from the other. But to say that a judgment implies another judgment and yet is logically possible without that judgment being true, and so is not logically dependent on that judgment, to say that the events are so interconnected that one follows with necessity from the other and yet that the judgments as to their occurrence are not intrinsically connected at all, seems to come perilously near self-contradiction. No doubt we infer causal connection from the observation of constant conjunction without insight into intrinsic connection, but it seems also right to say that we only infer the repetition of this conjunction because we suppose the constant conjunction in the past to be due to a connection intelligible in principle, though not by us. This may all seem hopelessly academic and quite out of touch with the practical discovery of causal laws, but is the demand for greater intelligibility of connection between cause and effect altogether without influence on physical science, (where it takes the form of a demand for homogeneity and continuity), and, especially, on psychological inference ?

We thus seem to have some ground for admitting that causality (necessary succession) involves intrinsic connection.[1] Kant, after all, does not really deny this conclusion, for he insists only that intrinsic connection cannot be found by analysis of the causally connected phenomena, and yet supposes the real ground of this necessary connection to lie in the noumenal sphere. There can be no doubt that he regards noumena as the ground of phenomena generally, and the differing content of particular causal laws as due to noumenal characteristics ; and, as " ground " for him certainly means " logical ground," this is equivalent to placing the intrinsic, intelligible connection behind causality in the noumenal world, except that this opposition could be regarded by him only as of the nature of a faith of reason, not as a " dogmatic " tenet of philosophy. He declares " dogmatically " for the existence of a something, humanly unknowable, other than phenomena, but its ultimate intelligibility,

[1]As we shall see later (pp. 189 ff.) this view of causality does seem to make the problem of the infinite regress of causes slightly more difficult, but this does not seem to me a fatal objection.

as opposed to its mere existence, is for him a matter of faith, not of knowledge. Kant then is inclined to ground the relation of necessary succession (phenomenal causality) on an ultimately intelligible connection in the noumenal sphere. But, if we abandon the view of the noumenal as simply the unknowable ground of our sensations regarded as outside all phenomena, and substitute for it the view of the noumenal world as the whole of which phenomena are parts, we could accept this belief. We need not suppose that either we or any other type of intelligence could possibly predict the effect with *a priori* certainty from the cause[1] taken alone, but only that the cause constitutes *part* of a ground that would ultimately explain the effect ; and we certainly do not mean to debar the view that particulars can only be fully intelligible in reference to the whole, a whole conceived as more than a mere sum of its parts, as more than a mere aggregate. If reality be truly a coherent whole then full knowledge of the cause would carry with it full knowledge of the whole universe and so of the effect, this not only in the sense that the cause is *externally* related to everything else, but in the sense that no fact about it can be perfectly understood in isolation but is so implicated with other facts that no internal quality can be found the knowledge of which does not ultimately imply its external relations and so the whole of reality. Be that as it may, we are certainly not contending that the effect is wholly explicable from the cause, or any set of causes, but only that it is so connected with its causes that part, at any rate, of the logical ground for its occurrence is to be found in their intrinsic internal, or relatively internal, qualities.

In an earlier chapter we emphasised the importance of Kant's discovery of the distinction between cause and logical ground,[2] and we can still maintain this distinction quite consistently with what we have just said about intrinsic connection. What we mean by the distinction is, in the first place, that we must not take the cause as constituting the *whole* logical ground of the effect (or even the whole past as constituting a sufficient logical ground for the whole future). Nothing that we have said need exclude the determination of phenomena by a supra-temporal principle as ground. Intrinsic connection between cause and effect does

---

[1]Cause is used here in its popular sense of principal or immediately efficient cause.

[2]*V.*, above pp. 32 ff.

not suffice to make the cause the whole ground of the effect, and so would not be incompatible with what Kant calls noumenal causality (*i.e.*, determination of the necessary succession of phenomena by a noumenal ground). Indeed, so far from intrinsic connection between cause and effect being incompatible with Kant's " noumenal causality," the latter presupposes some such intrinsic connection between phenomenal cause and effect. For it is always a particular causal connection that it has to explain, and no particular connection could possibly be explained without taking into account the particular (*i.e.*, phenomenal) characteristics of the objects connected. Any reason for the connection of A and B must include a reason, derived from the particular qualities of B, why it, rather than any other particular, is connected with A. As we have seen, even a Berkeleian must admit that the particular qualities of his " ideas of God " must influence God's selection of their order as apparent physical causes and effects, *i.e.*, their particular character must be such that it is wise for God to choose that *this* effect should follow *this* cause rather than any other. The cause may perfectly well be " intrinsically connected " with the effect without constituting its *whole* ground, and, I should think, must be, for otherwise the cause would be identical with the Absolute.

Secondly, in distinguishing cause and logical ground, Kant and Hume meant to insist that the causal nexus was not analytic. Now, if logical connection is regarded as purely analytic, as it was generally up to Kant's time and by Kant himself, causality cannot possibly be identified with any type of logical connection whatever. For, if the effect could be discovered by mere analysis of the cause taken by itself, it would be an element in the cause such that without it the cause could not occur, but, since the cause generally or always precedes the effect, it must have occurred prior to the effect and so without the effect. Yet, since the cause *ex hypothesi* includes the effect in its nature, it could not be said to occur apart from the effect without a flagrant self-contradiction. If A is B and C, etc., then to deny B is to deny A, and A cannot occur without B occurring at the same time. If we could prove that the effect must be contained in the cause[1] in the

---

[1]To say that the cause must contain the effect is only a metaphorical way of expressing likeness or quantitative correspondence between cause and effect. The relation cannot possibly be one of inclusion in

sense that it was discoverable by mere analysis of the cause taken alone, then the effect would be simultaneous with the cause. So all causation would on that view have to be simultaneous, an obviously impossible position, since the world-process would then not occupy any time at all. Or, we might say, whether simultaneous or successive, the cause and effect must be different events and so one cannot be included in the other.

If there is any intrinsic connection in causation, this connection must be synthetic, not analytic. This, of course, involves the abandonment of the analytic view of thought, a view which may, however, now be regarded as moribund, condemned because merely analytic judgments could only yield tautologies and never real knowledge.[1] Because Kant was unwilling to relinquish this analytic view, he was unable to conceive phenomena as possessing any true organic unity. Though he would probably have held the causal connection to be logically explicable from the noumenal point of view, he regards it as a merely external form of unity imposed by our understanding on a heterogeneous and, in itself, quite unconnected diversity. As Prof. Caird has so well shown, the ineradicable dualism between form and content, which replaced for Kant the Cartesian dualism between mind and matter, prevented him ever admitting that intrinsic unity between phenomena to which causation points, just because for him the manifold was diversity without unity and thought unity without diversity.

As everything in the physical world is, according to the view of science, held to act on everything else, so it would seem that, if intelligible at all, causality can hardly be fully intelligible except in the light of the whole. But, at the same time, some elements in the whole may be isolated from the rest more easily than others, and in proportion to the ease of this isolation we can get a better idea of their connection. This would account for the fact, if I am right in my contention and it is a fact, that we can see the intrinsic rationale of the causal connection better in psychological than in physical studies, for it is clear that a human, individual mind is more

the normal sense of the term, it can only be one of implication, and so any metaphor seeming to involve inclusion is misleading.

[1] As Prof. Caird has pointed out, it may be noted that the very use of the category of logical ground to connect the phenomena with the noumena as ground of the former is impossible unless this category be synthetic and not merely analytic, as Kant declared it to be.

N

of a self-sustaining unity, more of a real whole than a physical object is.

It must not be supposed that what we have said either excludes or commits us to the so-called " activity " view of causation. By this I mean the view which[1] assimilates the causal relation to psychical effort or volition. It is no doubt true that the idea of causation is psychologically derived, in part at any rate, from the experience of volition. Kant himself admits in his posthumous[2] work : " We should not recognise the moving forces of matter, not even through experience, if we were not conscious of our own activity in ourselves exerting acts of repulsion, approximation, etc." However, as Kant does not develop the topic, we may be likewise excused from doing so, especially as it involves far-reaching speculations of an idealistic or quasi-idealistic type. If all causation could be assimilated to volition, it would still involve intrinsic connection, *i.e.*, between the will to achieve a change and the change achieved. The attempts to assimilate all causation to volition are in fact based on the argument that volition provides that instance of causal connection which comes nearest to being intelligible to us *a priori*. This may be so, and the connection between the act of will and the thought[3] willed may certainly be adduced as another instance of the superior intelligibility of causal connection in the psychical sphere. But we do not assume that the type of causal connection involved in volition is the only one ultimately intelligible.

Now enough of a problem that is not dealt with **The first** at length by Kant. We shall pass on to quite a **cause** different subject, the first cause antinomy. A **antinomy.** consideration of this at once closes Kant's treatment of causality in the *Critique of Pure Reason*

---

[1] *V*. Prof. Broad, *Perception, Physics, and Reality*, pp. 78–90.
There seem to be four alternatives with regard to this " activity," considered as the supposed ground of the causal relation. (1) It may mean simply a power of production, in which case to say that it belongs to the cause is to explain nothing, but only to repeat that a cause can produce an effect. (2) It may mean an unknown quality which would account for causation if we knew it, in which case it explains nothing. (3) It may mean a quality analogous to what is felt in the conscious psychical state of effort or volition. (4) It may mean a quality analogous to the state of the willing subject itself.

[2] Quoted by Prof. Ward in his *Naturalism and Agnosticism*, fourth edition., p. 483.

[3] Not, of course, the physical motion. The causal connection between mind and matter, assuming there is such a connection, is certainly far

and paves the way for the discussion of freedom given in his ethical works. Perhaps an apology is due for treating two such heterogeneous topics in the same chapter, but we may find that they are after all not quite so unconnected as appears at first sight. So we shall plunge straight *in medias res* and proceed to quote the proof of the thesis of the third antinomy itself.

" Suppose there is no causality but that according to laws of nature.[1] Then everything *which happens* presupposes a precedent state on which it follows inevitably according to a rule. But the precedent state itself must be something which has happened (come into existence in time, not having existed before), since, if it had always been in existence, its consequence would have also not originated then for the first time, but would have always been in existence. Therefore the causality of the cause through which something happens is itself something *that has happened,* and as such again presupposes according to natural law a precedent state and the causality of this state, but that state in turn presupposes a still earlier one and so on. Consequently, if everything happens according to merely natural laws, there is always only a dependent (subaltern), never a first beginning, and so the series of causes determined by each other is never complete. Now natural law just consists in nothing happening without a cause sufficiently determined *a priori.* So the proposition that all causality is possible only through natural laws contradicts itself if taken as absolutely and universally valid (*in seiner unbeschränkten Allgemeinheit*), and this can therefore not be regarded as the only kind of causality.

We must therefore accept a causality through which something happens without its cause being again determined by another precedent cause according to necessary laws, *i.e.,* an *absolute spontaneity* of causes, so that they can begin *of their own accord* a series of phenomena, which follows natural laws, thus involving transcendental freedom. Without this the series (*Reihenfolge*) of phenomena on the side of the causes is never complete, even in the course of nature."

In the appended note Kant argues that the thesis, if it proves the necessity of a free first cause also proves the possibility of human freedom, since, if one event occurs without an antecedent cause, others may do so likewise. But, he

from being a specially intelligible one, but rather of all the most unintelligible.

[1]*B.*, 473–4.

says, while it would, if established, justify us in accepting human freedom as a fact, provided an independent reason for its acceptance could be found, *e.g.*, in the fact of morality, it does not prove this freedom, but only the freedom of God. The third[1] and fourth antinomies are indeed identical in principle, in both cases the thesis aims at proving the existence of God by an appeal to the category of causality, in both cases the antithesis refutes the thesis by pointing out that the category of causality involves the dependence of every state on a previous state and so leaves no state that is in itself necessary and does not owe its existence to determination by other events.   In the fourth antinomy, however, both thesis and antithesis are complicated by the addition of arguments to show that an appeal to the category of causality cannot prove the existence of a necessary being outside, but only, if at all, within the world of phenomena, but, as both thesis and antithesis agree on this point, it forms no inherent part of the antinomy. It is important to realise that in both antinomies the argument puts God in the rank of a phenomenon ; it is not Kant's object here to discuss the strictly " metaphysical " arguments for the existence of God, but only that line of argument which seeks to prove God's existence by the use of the category of causality as schematised in time.   This is just what for Kant constitutes the defect of both thesis and antithesis, they seek to prove or disprove the existence of what is not phenomenal by a method of argument which, because based on a category as schematised in time, can only be used to find new phenomena.

The third and fourth antinomies have the peculiarity that both thesis and antithesis are based on the same principle, the principle of causality.   The thesis argues that causality implies a first cause, or necessary being, the antithesis that causality is inconsistent with either.   " Every beginning of action presupposes a state of the cause in which it does not yet act, and a dynamically first beginning of action presupposes a state, which has no causal connection (*keinen Zusammenhang der Causalität*) with the precedent state of the very cause that acts, *i.e.*, does not in any way follow from it (*auf keine Weise daraus erfolgt*)."[2]   So freedom is here

---

[1] In the actual statement of the thesis of the third no reference is made to human freedom (though this subject is raised in the appended note and bulks large in the solution).   We shall, however, reserve the discussion of the problem of human freedom for our next chapter.

[2] *B.*, 474.

declared to be quite irreconcilable with the universality of
causation, while in the thesis the causal principle is itself
declared to lead to self-contradiction unless freedom is
admitted.

Now one principle cannot, in one and the same sense, both
demand and exclude a free first cause and a necessary being.
The antinomies, to be real antinomies, must have a thesis
and antithesis which start from different and apparently
non-contradictory premises, not a thesis and antithesis which
are founded on the same premiss and so explicitly contradict
each other from the beginning of the argument. However,
Kant says in B 487[1] that, while both thesis and antithesis
follow from the same premiss, namely," that[2] the whole
past time includes the series of all conditions," the thesis
only considers the series of conditions from the aspect of
totality, the antithesis only from the aspect of the contingency[3] of its members. Kant says in criticising the argument
of all four antinomies in general terms, that the error consists
in the use of a syllogism in which the term, " conditioned,"
(das Bedingte) bears a different sense in the major premiss,
from what it does in the minor.[4] The major premiss is,
" if the conditioned is given, then the whole series of all[5]
conditions of this conditioned is also given," but this premiss
is said to be only correct if the conditions are things-in-
themselves and the term " the conditioned " is used " in the
transcendental sense of a pure category."[6] That by this, as
applied to the third and fourth antinomies, is meant the sense
of logical ground, is clear from Kant's general doctrine that
causality, when not schematised in time, is reducible to the
logical relation of ground and consequence.

Further, he explicitly declares the mistaken argument of
both thesis and antithesis to be due to the following fallacy.
" If something is given as conditioned, we, owing to this[7]
illusion, presuppose (in the major premiss) its conditions and
their series, as it were, *unseen*, because this is nothing but the
logical requirement that in order to make a given conclusion
we must have completely adequate premises, and there is in
this case no temporal sequence to be found in the combination
of the conditioned with its condition, they are presupposed

[1] = *A.*, 459.
[2] *Die ganze verflossene Zeit die Reihe aller Bedingungen in sich fasst.*
[3] *I.e.*, presumably their dependence on each other.
[4] *B.*, 527–8 (=A, *circ.* 500).   [5] *B.*, 525 = *A* 497.
[6] *B.*, 527, *ad fin.*   [7] *B.*, 528, beginning.

in themselves as given *simultaneously.*" But in the minor premiss that "objects of the senses are given to us as conditioned,"[1] the term "conditioned" is used, he says, "in the empirical sense of a concept-of-understanding (*Verstandesbegriff*) applied to mere phenomena,"[2] and hence does not warrant the conclusion that the whole series of conditions conditioning a phenomenal event is given, provided that event itself is given. The difference in the sense of the term "conditioned" as used in the minor premiss is declared to consist in the addition of time :—" The synthesis of the conditioned with its condition and the whole series of the conditions (in the major premiss) involved no limitation through time at all and no concept of succession.[3] On the other hand, the empirical synthesis and the series of conditions in the phenomenal world (which is subsumed in the minor premiss) is necessarily successive and they are only given as following each other in time, consequently I was not able to presuppose the absolute *totality* of the synthesis and of the series represented thereby in the minor premiss just as well as in the major. For, while in the major all members of the series are given in themselves (without the condition of time), in the minor they are only possible through the successive regress which is only given in its actual fulfilment."

We shall now briefly go through the proof of the thesis of the third antinomy in the light of these passages. It is based on the principle of causality interpreted as meaning that "nothing happens without a cause sufficiently determined *a priori.*"[4] This[5] definition assimilates it to the principle of sufficient reason, involving, as it does, no reference to time. From this standpoint Kant criticises the view which regards the cause of an event as always to be found in a precedent state, and adopts the antagonistic view that in one case at least (*i.e.*, that of the first cause) the cause is to be found, not in another precedent event, but in itself. The argument is as follows. For an effect to occur, all the causes necessary for its existence must have already come into being, but, if each cause requires a precedent cause to account for it and so on *ad infinitum*, any event presupposes for its occurrence the completion of an infinite series of events

---

[1]*B.*, 525.   [2]*B.*, 527, *ad fin.*   [3]*B.*, 528.
[4]*B.*, 474 (end of first paragraph of thesis).
[5]What we say about the third antinomy applies to the fourth *mutatis mutandis*, in so far as the latter appeals only to causality and does not use "metaphysical" arguments.

in time. But the infinite can from its very nature never be completed. Hence, unless we suppose a first event which does not again need a precedent cause to account for itself, and so deny the truth of the doctrine that no event can occur without a precedent cause, we are involved in a contradiction.

The difficulty to which the thesis owes its plausi-
Criticism of bility is then the difficulty of regarding an infinite
Kant's series as completed. The desire to avoid this
doctrine of same[1] difficulty gives rise to the thesis of all four
antinomy. antinomies. It is perhaps expressed most clearly in the first antinomy, where it is argued that if we suppose the series of events to have had no beginning in time, *i.e.*, to be infinite in the direction of the past, we must suppose an infinite series of events to have elapsed and therefore to have been completed before the events of the present moment, but any series that is capable of completion must be not infinite, but finite.   It is not therefore a difficulty peculiar to causality and should not be adduced as a special argument against that principle.

It does, however, appear more acute if " cause " is identified with " logical ground," and causality is regarded as a principle of explanation and not only of necessary connection. If causality is interpreted as the principle that no event can occur without a sufficient logical ground to account for it, then it[2] is difficult to see how the whole of this logical ground can ever be found in the series of causes if the cause always lies in precedent events, because to refer an event to another cause as its ground is then simply to put the problem further back by referring for the explanation of its occurrence to something which itself needs explanation as the result of a preceding event.   The impasse to which we are brought if we seek to explain events as logically deducible from precedent causes is well expressed by Mr. Bradley.[3]   " We are fastened to a chain, and we wish to know if we are really secure. What ought one to do ? Is it much use to say, 'this link we are tied to is essentially solid, and it is fast to the next, which seems very strong and holds firmly to the next ; beyond this we cannot see more than a moderate distance, but, so far

[1]Hence Kant's insistence on the demand for " totality " as in each case the ground of the thesis.
[2]The difficulty is mitigated if the cause is made *part* only of the logical ground of the effect, but not wholly overcome.
[3]*Principle of Logic,* p. 100.

as we know, it all holds together ? ' The practical man would first of all ask, ' Where can I find the last link of my chain ? When I know that is fast, and not hung in the air, it is time enough to inspect the connection.' But the chain is such that every link begets, as soon as we come to it, a new one ; and, ascending in our search, at each remove we are still no nearer the last link of all, on which everything depends . . . A last fact, a final link, is not merely a thing which we cannot know, but a thing which could not possibly be real. Our chain by its nature cannot have a support. Its essence excludes a fastening at the end. We do not merely fear that it hangs in the air, but we know it must do so. And, when the end is unsupported, all the rest is unsupported.''

But, if the cause is not the ground of the effect, the difficulty involved in the infinite regress is not the difficulty of explaining the effect, but the difficulty of supposing an infinite series of events to be past and completed before any effect is produced, *i.e.*, just the same difficulty as had troubled Kant in the first antinomy. This difficulty of an infinite whole may or may not be soluble—many now claim to have solved it—but it is not a difficulty peculiar to causality, and so, we repeat, cannot stand as a special argument against the proposition that every event is determined by a precedent cause. What the thesis aims at showing is that the demand of reason for the explanation of phenomena cannot be satisfied by pointing to a precedent event as cause and so on *ad infinitum*, because we can never in this way reach the totality of conditions which is needed if we are really to understand the conditioned.

We shall now pass to the antithesis. This assumes[1] the view of causality which the thesis has criticised, *i.e.*, that every event must have an *antecedent* cause, and denies the conclusion of the thesis on the ground that it contradicts the principle of causality as interpreted in this way. But the ground used to back the universal validity of the principle of causality, as thus interpreted, is the argument that otherwise there would be no unity of experience. This is, however,

---

[1]The antithesis, however, Kant holds, like the thesis, errs in confusing both phenomena with things-in-themselves, and cause with ground, for it is only because of this double confusion that the antithesis seems to disprove the possibility of a first cause in the sense of a noumenal ground of phenomena ; the antithesis sacrifices the idea of ground to the idea of cause, while the thesis sacrifices the idea of cause to the idea of ground.

a conclusion of his critical philosophy and should not, therefore, be inserted in an antinomy which is supposed to occur
only at the pre-critical stage of thought.

In the thesis causality is treated as implying that every
phenomenon must have a sufficient cause,[1] not necessarily
an antecedent cause, and, for it to provide a separate argument for a first cause not dependent on the argument of the
first antinomy, " cause " must be interpreted in the sense of
logical ground. In the antithesis, however, the principle
of causality does not mean that every event must have a
sufficient ground, but that it must be connected by necessary
laws with a preceding event so that you can *infer* the one
from the other, but not, necessarily, so that you can *explain*
the one from the other. If causality is taken in this sense,
the infinite regress presents no difficulty beyond that already
pointed out in the thesis of the first antinomy, and causality
seems also to provide a separate argument for the infinity
of the series of past events beyond that provided by the
antithesis of the first antinomy. However, the argument
of the Analytic only proves that every event is necessarily
connected with a precedent event if it be already assumed
that there is no first event ; without that assumption it would
have only proved that any sequence that occurs must be
necessary. The objection from the side of causality alone
would be not to a first[2] event but to a cleavage of the whole
series of events into two (or more) separate parts neither of
which implied the other. The principle of causality, as thus
interpreted, cannot be used to prove that the world has no
beginning in time, but only involves an infinite regress if
we have already accepted the view that the world has no
beginning. So it seems that it is only if taken as an explana-
tory principle that causality involves a fresh difficulty as
to infinity beyond that already involved in the mere notion
that the series of events has no beginning, and that in any

---

[1]We have retained Kant's mode of statement throughout as regards
the words "a cause," although it does not seem altogether satisfactory
in its atomism as though the occurrence of an event could ever be traced
to a single other event as its whole cause.

[2]The occurrence of an absolute beginning of the whole temporal
series of events would not split the unity of the latter, which unity is
the argument urged on behalf of universal causality in the antithesis
itself.

case the difficulty as to an infinite whole is not peculiar to causality.

The thesis and antithesis of the fourth antinomy, in so far as they argue for or against the existence of a necessary being in the world, express in different words just the same line of thought as the thesis and antithesis of the third antinomy. For by an absolutely necessary being is meant just a being that is not an effect but only a cause, and is self-explanatory in a way that will not drive us to seek to explain it by a further precedent cause. (Kant expressly excludes " metaphysical " arguments based on the idea of the contingent in general from consideration here.) So, as in the third antinomy, the thesis uses the argument that every event presupposes the complete series of its conditions, the antithesis the argument that the existence of a necessary and so uncaused being would contradict the law of causality.

Summary of Kant's solution. Having tried to show the difference between the thesis and the antithesis in their way of interpreting causality, we shall touch briefly on Kant's solution of the antinomies. We have already noticed the dictum that the major premiss of the thesis is always, " if the conditioned is given, then the whole series of all conditions of this conditioned is also given."[1] Kant says that this premiss would be valid if for " given " (*gegeben*) were substituted " *aufgegeben* " (set as a task). It would further be valid even in its original form if the conditioned and the conditions were things-in-themselves, but, since they are phenomena, we cannot say that, if the conditioned is given, its conditions are also given. For, when we speak of the existence of a phenomenon not perceived at this moment, we only mean that if we made a certain regress we should perceive it, and we cannot suppose it to exist apart from this regress. Hence for the original premiss we must substitute the premiss, " that a *regress* to the conditions, *i.e.*, the continuation of an empirical synthesis on this side is commanded or *set as a task* (*aufgegeben*), and that there can never be a lack of conditions given through this regress."[2] All we have is " a *rule*, which commands a regress in the series of the conditions of given phenomena, which regress we are never allowed to bring to a stop with something absolutely unconditioned " (*bei einem Schlechthinunbedingten*). But this premiss does not contradict the infinitude of the

[1]*B*., 525 (= *A*., 497). [2]*B*., 527 (= A, *circ*. 500). [3]*B*., 536 (= *A*., 508).

series of conditions, for it does not assert that the series can be given as a whole. Thus the doctrine of the infinite divisibility of matter, rightly understood, does not mean that there are in existence an infinite number of minute portions of matter, but that, however much we divided matter, we should never reach a point where we could ideally divide no further. This is the general solution of the problem of infinity, which is applied to all four antinomies,—that we must neither assert the actual existence of an infinite series nor admit the possibility of any final stop to the infinite regress in phenomena. The subjectivism of the solution seems very unsatisfactory, but it is not our business to discuss the problem of infinity itself, which, as we have seen, is by no means peculiar to causality.

Kant treats the first and second pairs of antinomies differently ; in the first two antinomies he declares both thesis and antithesis to be wrong, in the third and fourth pairs he declares that they may be both right, the thesis of things-in-themselves and the antithesis of phenomena. The reason given is that in the first two antinomies there is a synthesis of the homogeneous, in the last two a synthesis of the heterogeneous.[1] Hence the thesis of the third and fourth antinomies can express a connection between such heterogeneous entities as phenomena and noumena. The solution of the third antinomy is largely occupied with the consideration of human freedom, a topic which is less unsatisfactorily, because less negatively, treated in the ethical works and which we shall have to postpone to the next chapter. What the thesis really claims to prove is (1) the existence of God as a free cause and creator of the world, (2) the possibility[2] of human freedom, and as regards the former it seems to us just another version of the thesis of the fourth antinomy. Without keeping too close to Kant's actual words, we may briefly summarise the solution of the third and fourth antinomies, in so far as it affects this point, as follows. (Human freedom we shall discuss later.)

The antithesis is right in asserting that there is no uncaused first cause and no absolutely necessary being to be found in the phenomenal world. This does not, however, mean that there is an actual infinite series of causes, but that, however far we go back in the series of events, we can never reach an

[1]B., 557 = A., 528 ff.
[2]Which is established by showing that the principle of causality itself implies at least one case of freedom.

event which does not presuppose a still earlier event or events to cause it. The law of causality, as proved in the Analytic, must be accepted as valid for all phenomena. But phenomena may, or even must, be regarded as having grounds in the things-in-themselves. These grounds cannot be regarded as themselves phenomenal, they do not appear in time and are consequently not subject to the category of causality as schematised in time, they are not determined by phenomena. But they may have an " intelligible "[1] causality of their own which will supply what is involved in the concept of freedom. This " intelligible " causality we can represent by the purely logical category of ground, but must not identify with that causality by which one event determines another in time. And there may[2] exist in the noumenal world something possessing the characteristics of what metaphysics calls the absolutely necessary being and theology calls God. The existence of such a being cannot be proved by an appeal to the category of causality, for this category has only been shown to be valid of phenomena. But neither can it be disproved by showing that everything in the world must be determined by antecedent causes, for such a being cannot be regarded as a part of the world or as something that comes into existence in time. That everything noumenal must be determined by antecedent causes is not only incapable of proof, but a quite meaningless proposition, since " antecedent cause" presupposes time, and time is not noumenal, but phenomenal. Both thesis and antithesis are infected with the same superstition, they both treat God as an object of sense and creation as an event in time ; the thesis recognises the demand of reason for an intelligible ground, but tries to find it where it cannot possibly be found, namely in the world of phenomena ; the antithesis recognises that it cannot be found there and therefore dogmatically denies its existence altogether. Yet any attempted proof or disproof of the existence of God, if based on the category of causality in the sense of necessary succession in time, must assume that God is an object of sense, for, as thus schematised, causality is valid only of objects of sense. There is another meaning which causality may bear, the meaning of logical ground, and God may still be the ground of phenomena causally interconnected, but we cannot prove this by an appeal to causality, nor can

---

[1] *I.e.*, non-sensible and so non-temporal.
[2] Kant makes the idea of an infinite series of causes and the idea of God as ground both " regulative." (*B.*, 592, 698, 700.)

we by any possibility make such a relation between the phenomenal and the noumenal intelligible to ourselves. The question whether there is or is not a first cause or an absolutely necessary being in the world of phenomena may be settled once for all in favour of the antithesis, but this question, rightly understood, has nothing to do with religion whatever. God may, for all we can tell, be the ground of the whole world-process without ever acting in time, so that God's causality is intelligible and not sensible at all. The way is left open for a proof of, or rather a well-grounded faith in, God, based not on metaphysical but on moral arguments.

Further, the belief in God is, even[1] theoretically, of value as inspiring us to look for a greater intelligibility and unity in the world than is at first sight visible to us. Reason calls us to seek such a unity and intelligibility and will not be satisfied without it, but this demand can never be realised wholly in any possible experience but only partially and progressively ; it is not a proof but a policy in research, a hope and an ideal. We must not attempt to satisfy it by positing an uncaused first cause or a necessary being in the phenomenal world in flat contradiction of these principles which alone make experience possible.

Such is the answer advanced by Kant. To discuss its theological bearings and its attempted solution of the antinomy of the infinite in general would carry us too far afield. Perhaps the most important point for us to observe here is that the demand of reason for a first cause is essentially a demand for an intelligible ground for the explanation of phenomena, not for an uncaused event at the beginning of the series of phenomena. We shall now pass on to the problem of human freedom, and the opposition of organic, or purposive, and mechanical causality.

[1]For statement of this view *v.* Appendix on Regulative Use of Ideas of Pure Reason, *B.,* 670-730 (= *A.*, 642–702).

CHAPTER VIII

The Problem of Freedom, or Mechanical versus Purposive Causality

THE problem of freedom was, of course, one of great importance for Kant, so great in fact that he regards all metaphysical reasoning as of value only in so far as it helps us to acquire a right idea of God, freedom and immortality. Its connection with the question of causality makes it impossible for us to avoid saying something on this subject too, but it is only with great diffidence that we embark upon it, and we do not propose to treat it with anything like the fullness that we have tried to attain in discussing the proof of causality. We are, in fact, in the difficult position of being obliged, because of its importance for the conception of causality, to deal cursorily in a single chapter with a subject which could only be treated with the least approach to adequacy by writing a whole book on it, a fact which must inevitably lead to serious defects in our treatment, because it is discussed not so much for its own sake as for its connection with Kant's thought on causality.

We may sum up the contribution of the *Critique of Pure Reason* to the problem as follows. First, it had in Kant's eyes proved the universal validity of the causal principle, as schematised in time, among phenomena, *i.e.*, it had proved that all phenomenal succession was necessary. Secondly, it had shown that this proof was not applicable to the non-phenomenal, and so not inconsistent with phenomena being determined by a supra-temporal, and itself uncaused, ground. These two principles constitute the structure on which Kant's solution of the problem is wholly based. On the one hand he insists that freedom must on no account break the chain of causality, or even of " mechanical " causality, connecting all phenomena. On the other hand he declares that freedom is not inconsistent with causality, because the same being may be at once free, as a noumenon, and necessarily determined by natural causation in all its acts, as a phenomenon. The *Critique of Pure Reason* thus claims to leave the way open for the acceptance of freedom, if required on ethical grounds ; and to do so just because it removes the *prima facie* contradiction between freedom and causality. Now it is the function of the ethical[1] works of Kant in dealing with freedom to show that freedom is a necessary postulate if the moral law is to be admitted as valid, and then to point out how it may be reconciled with universal causality on the lines suggested in the first Critique.

Now, if one thing in Kant's treatment of the problem is clear, it is that he holds freedom and natural causality to be irreconcilable if applied to the same being as existing in time. He again and again emphatically asserts that freedom and natural causality cannot be reconciled if phenomena are things-in-themselves, because then they must both be applied to the same being as temporal. This is plain enough, but we must not be content with it. If we wish to understand the solution of the problem as it presented itself to Kant, we must first try to see exactly what conception he had formed of each of the two irreconcilable terms and what grounds he gives for their absolute incompatibility. Then, when we have his statement of the problem clear, we may hope to discuss his solution.

Now we may trace two distinct reasons that made Kant regard the antinomy as insoluble so long as we do not go beyond the temporal or sensible.[2]   In the first place we have the antinomy between freedom as causation by reason on the one side, and causation by desire on the other. Desire Kant treated as wholly the result of external causes operating mechanically, as in essentially the same category as the physical movement of a billiard-ball as a result of impact. Now natural necessity (*Naturnotwendigkeit*) is defined in the *Foundation of the Metaphysic of Morals* as " the property of causality in all beings without reason, to be determined to activity through the influence of external causes."[3]   But little reflection is needed to show that moral action involves a

---

[1]In citing these works in the present chapter the reference is always to the numbers of the pages of the Akademie Ausgabe. In citing the *Critique of Judgment* the reference is to the sections and pages of the original (2nd and 3rd editions). These are the pages given in the three books in the ordinary Vorländer edition.

[2]For Kant the temporal seems to be just as much merely " sensible " as the spatial.   [3]446.

certain independence of external causes. To act as moral beings, we must obviously not be entirely under the sway of circumstances. This does not mean only that we must not be absoutely dependent on merely physical causation, but also that we must not be dominated by sense and desire, as determined by external objects ; and, as has just been remarked, Kant assimilated all desire to a merely mechanical reaction to a stimulus from without. So, will having been just defined as " a mode of causality of living beings, in so far as they are rational "[1] (vernünftig), freedom is defined as that property[2] of this causality by which it can work effects independently of foreign causes determining it." Freedom, in the " positive " sense, and autonomy (as opposed to heteronomy) are regarded as equivalent terms. For example, in the Foundation to the Metaphysic of Morals (446–7) it says, " Natural necessity was a heteronomy of efficient causes ; for every effect was only possible according to the law that something else determined the efficient cause to exercise its causality ; so what else can the freedom of the will be but autonomy, i.e., the property of the will by which it is a law to itself ? " A little later in the same work, Kant gives as the ground for belief in freedom, that, if there is no freedom, reason is not practical, i.e., does not control phenomena, but is controlled by something else external to it.[3] In still another place in the same work he says that the claim even of common sense to freedom is based on a consciousness that reason is independent of feeling and sensibility in determining action, and this power of determination by reason is contrasted immediately afterwards with the subjection of men's causality to " external determination according to laws of nature."[4]

Autonomy means that the self as free is directed by a law determined by reason, as the essential part of the self, and not by desires of particular objects. And we may trace in Kant's insistence on the autonomy of the self the double conviction that moral action cannot be determined merely by desire of sensible objects, and that the grounds[5] of moral action

[1] 446 (Abbott's translation in Kant's Theory of Ethics, p. 94).
[2] 446. [3] Ib., 448 (Abbott, p. 97). [4] 457 (Abbott, p. 103).
[5] The first point does not really involve the second, although Kant speaks as if it did, owing to his confusion between desire and purpose, a confusion which was the chief cause of the formalism of his ethics. That moral action cannot be determined by particular desires without the action of reason is not, as Kant sometimes seems to assume, equivalent to saying that it cannot involve a purpose to realise particular values as particular, even though value judgments may not be capable of derivation from experience.

cannot be empirical, but only *a priori*, and hence must lie, not in sensible objects, but in the self as reason. A self determined by desire would be determined not internally but externally, not by universally, and so objectively, valid grounds, but by subjective inclination, not rationally, that is *a priori*, but empirically.

But that freedom is to be identified with causation by internal or psychological, as opposed to external, causes, is certainly not a solution which commended itself to Kant. In the *Critique of Practical Reason* he emphatically asserts that freedom cannot consist in determination by internal grounds. Such psychological freedom, he declares, " would be, at bottom, no better than the freedom of a turnspit ; that, too, if once wound up, performs its movements of its own accord."[1] The opposition of freedom to natural causality is then not only, for Kant, the opposition of internal to external causality. We get a second antinomy equally prominent in his mind, the antinomy between moral responsibility and natural causation as determination by prior events.

Kant insists with much force that responsibility is incompatible with absolute causal determination of the present by the past. Replying to those who try to give a "psychological" explanation of freedom, Kant declares natural necessity to be absolutely irreconcilable with freedom because " it follows from the former that every event, and so also every action which occurs at a point of time is necessary under the condition of what existed in the preceding time.[2] But as the past time is no longer in my power, every action which I perform must be necessary through determining grounds, *which are not in my power*, *i.e.*, I am, at the moment of time at which I act, never free. Yes, even if I take my whole being to be independent of any and every external cause, (as God, for example), so that the determining grounds of my causality, and even of my whole existence, would not be outside me at all, yet this fact would not do anything at all to change that natural necessity into freedom. For, at every point of time, I still stand under the necessity of being determined to action by *what is not in my power*, and the *a parte priori* infinite series of events, which I should then always only continue according to an already predetermined order but never begin of my own accord, would be an unbroken chain of natural

[1]*Critique of Practical Reason*, 97 (Akademie Ausgabe).   [2]*Ib.*, 94.
O

causes (*eine stetige Naturkette*), and my causality therefore would never be freedom." A little later Kant declares that it does not matter whether an act is determined by internal or by external, by instinctive or by reasoned grounds, in no case is there freedom if the ground is only to be discovered in a temporally prior state, and so a state which is no longer in our power to determine.[1] So, he says, we may call all such natural causality, whether psychological or physical, mechanism.[2] In the *Critique of Pure Reason* and the *Foundation to the Metaphysic of Morals* he argues that morality implies that, although something did not happen, it ought to have happened (and therefore could have happened).[3] But in the attempt at solution the emphasis is always laid on the fact that, if there be anything such as a noumenal act at all, it cannot be determined by a precedent state in time, because, as noumenal, it is *ex hypothesi* not in time.

Kant is equally clear that the solution must not come through any breach in the chain of natural causation. That the principle of natural causality is universally[4] valid among phenomena was regarded as a proved result of the first Critique, and on that result Kant would not go back. Whatever Kant's views on the subject were elsewhere, there can be no doubt that in discussing the question of freedom he always assumes the universal validity of the principle of causality for the empirical self. Otherwise whence the antinomy? And, in detailing the solution, he always insists that the freedom of the noumenal self is not to be conceived as involving any breach in or contradiction of natural causality. His position seems to be that, if freedom and natural causality cannot be reconciled, freedom must go. "If the thought[5] of freedom actually contradicts itself or nature, which is just as necessary, then it must be abandoned altogether for natural necessity."

But a way of escape seems to be provided by the possibility that one and the same being may from different aspects be considered as at once necessarily determined and free. This way is secured by the distinction between phenomena

---

[1] *Ib.*, 96.   [2] 97.   [3] *B.*, 562 (=*A.*, 534–5), *cf.*, *B.*, 578 (=*A.*, 550).
[4] *e.g.*, *Critique of Pure Reason*, *B.*, 564, "the correctness of that principle of the thorough-going connection of all events of the sensible world according to unchangeable laws of Nature stands fast already as a principle of the Transcendental Analytic and cannot be broken (*leidet keinen Abbruch*)," *v.* also *Ib.* 568, 570, 574, 577–578, *Critique of Practical Reason*, 95, *Foundation to the Metaphysic of Morals* 455 (Abbott, p. 109).
[5] *Foundation to the Metaphysic of Morals*, 456 (Abbott, p. 110).

and things-in-themselves. What is easier to say than that the self as thing-in-itself or noumenon is free, and as phenomenon determined by natural causality in all its actions. At first sight, at any rate, this solution seems to come perilously near to being what Mr. Sidgwick described the solution of the third antinomy as tending to become, that is, an explanation by saying that " we may also suppose an unknown relation to an unknown entity, which is not a phenomenon, which *might* afford the required explanation if we only knew it."[1] " Surely," as this critic of Kant adds, " having got so far towards Agnosticism, it would be simpler to say that we might be able to give a satisfactory answer to the question of Reason, if we only knew more, but that is an attitude towards the unsolved problems and unreconciled contradictions of thought which it does not require the elaborate apparatus of the Critical Philosophy to adopt." This, as Mr. Sidgwick says, is what the solution comes to if we persistently hold to the absolute unknowableness of things-in-themselves and so deny the possibility of applying the category of causality with any real significance to the thing-in-itself. As we have remarked already, there is nothing inconsistent with the rest of the Kantian philosophy in supposing that causality, or rather " ground " as a merely logical category, *might* be applicable to the thing-in-itself ; but to suppose that we can have any justification for thus applying it is to abandon the view that things-in-themselves are absolutely inaccessible to human intelligence, though we may if we choose, of course, like Kant, technically retain the doctrine of their unknowable character by distinguishing between knowledge and " faith." But, in any case, the solution of the problem of freedom by an appeal to the distinction between the phenomenal and the noumenal self certainly strikes one *prima facie* as a cumbersome, meaningless, almost puerile attempt to pretend that the problem is answered when it has merely been shelved. But this should rather urge us forward than deter us from examining this solution further.

Now it seems clear that the freedom posited by Kant is not regarded as mere indeterminism. " In that the concept of a causality carries with it the concept of *laws*, according to which on account of something, which we call cause, something else, namely the consequence, must be posited, freedom,

[1] *Lectures on Kant*, pp. 177-8.

although not a property of the will according to natural laws, is not on that account lawless, but must on the contrary be a causality according to unchangeable laws, but one of a peculiar kind ; for otherwise a free will would be an absurdity (*Unding*)."[1] But what is the difference between natural necessity and the necessity of freedom ? The answer, as given here, is that, while natural necessity is a heteronomy of efficient causes, freedom is an autonomy, which means that the free will is " a law to itself."[2] The term " necessity " or " law " always occurs whenever Kant attempts to give a clearer description of the nature of our noumenal freedom. [3]He admits that free will must have a determining ground (*Bestimmungsgrund*) ; [4]he connects freedom closely with the idea of a " supersensible nature " and declares that by " nature " is meant " the existence of things under laws," and that the difference between a sensible and a supersensible order of nature is that in the former things exist under empirically conditioned laws, in the latter under laws [5] independent of all empirical determination. It is in this independence of *empirical* laws and in being a law for oneself by reason that autonomy, as opposed to heteronomy, is said to consist. He expressly repudiates the view that freedom consists in the power of choosing to act for or against the law (*libertas indifferentiae*), though admitting that a certain freedom qua defective may be empirically manifested in that way. The mere fact that Kant repeatedly and explicitly identifies freedom with determination by the moral law is sufficient to show his opposition to the interpretation of freedom as indeterminism or motiveless action. Such indeterminism Kant will not admit either in noumenal freedom or in the world of phenomena.

The noumenal causality of the self is closely connected with the logical category of ground. As we pointed out in the last chapter, Kant held that the cause cannot be identified with the ground of an effect hence it was quite open to him, as indeed it is for anybody who does not maintain that the cause must be the *whole* ground of the effect, to posit in the

---

[1]*Foundation to the Metaphysic of Morals*, 446 (Abbott, p. 94 ff.).
[2]*Ib.*, 446–7.
[3]*Critique of Practical Reason*, 29, cf. *Critique of Pure Reason*, B., 573, where free action is described as action on grounds of "understanding," (here used loosely to cover " reason ").
[4]*Critique of Practical Reason*, 43.
[5]These laws of freedom are always identified with moral laws; *v*. below. pp. 207—10.

noumenal world an intelligible ground[1] of particular phenomenal causal connections. This was rendered still easier
for him both by the difficulty of seeing any intelligible or
logical connection between causally connected events as
phenomena, and the occurrence of an antinomy between the
infinite regress in phenomena and the totality of conditions
required by reason. Both the difficulties suggested, or even
commanded, a search for an intelligible ground in the noumenal sphere. Further, as long as Kant clung to the subjectivist view of phenomena as mere representations, he felt
unable to regard them as in any degree self-subsistent and
was compelled to seek real dynamic causality elsewhere, *i.e.*,
in the thing-in-itself. Hence this conception of a noumenon
as ground, not cause, of phenomena was open to him to
develop, now that a consideration of the problem of freedom,
as the presupposition of morality, had given him at once a
more pressing and definite need for and a less negative idea
of this noumenal ground.

The conception of freedom, we have pointed out, stood for
Kant in absolute opposition both to causality by desire,
which he regarded as a merely mechanical reaction to external
sensible causes, and also to the one-sided determination of the
present by the past. Now it is clear that, once granted a
timeless self, there is no difficulty in supposing it to be free
from both these kinds of causation. To suggest that the
acts of the self as noumenal can be determined by sensible
objects as causes is absurd, because the noumenal self is the
ground of the existence of these very objects, qua sensible.
It is equally absurd to suggest that the self as noumenal can
in its present acts be causally determined by its past acts, for
to say this is to put in time what is *ex hypothesi* timeless.
Yet, if my present acts as noumenal are not determined by my
past acts, then the main difficulty vanishes, for the inconsistency of universal natural causation with responsibility
we have seen to be due to the apparent determination of the
present by the past in such a way that my present acts,
because determined by the irrevocable past, are not in my
power to do or not do at the moment of action. That free
acts are not undetermined but determined makes no difference
provided they are not determined either by external or by

---

[1]What we called the " intrinsic connection " of cause and effect
would not debar such a distinction unless it were held that the cause
must be the *whole* ground of the effect.

temporally prior causes.[1] But the conditions which determine them cannot be temporally prior. The noumenal acts cannot be causally determined by phenomenal conditions any more than a consequence can be the cause of its own ground —for the noumenal is the ground of the phenomenal—and of noumenal conditions none can be prior in time to any other.

" Of reason we cannot say that that state in which it determines the will is preceded by another, in which this state is itself determined.[2] For, since reason is itself no phenomenon and not subject to any conditions of sensibility, there occurs no time sequence in reason, even as regards its causality, and so the dynamical law of nature, which determines the time sequence according to rules, cannot be applied to it."—" The natural necessity which is incompatible with the freedom of the subject only belongs to the determinations of what stands under temporal conditions, and so only to the determinations of the acting subject as phenomenon. Therefore so far the determining grounds of every action lie in what belongs to the past time and is *no longer in the agent's power* (in this class must be also placed the acts he has already performed and the character thereby determinable in his own eyes as phenomenon[3]). But the very same subject, who is from another point of view conscious of himself as thing-in-itself, also considers his existence, *in so far as he does not stand under conditions of time,* and regards himself as determinable only by laws which he himself prescribes for himself through reason, and in this mode of his existence there is nothing to precede the determination of his will, but every act and, more generally, every determination of his being which changes according to inner sense, and even the whole succession (*Reihenfolge*) of his existence as sensible being (*Sinnenwesen*) is in the consciousness of his intelligible existence to be regarded as nothing but a consequence ; never as determining ground of his causality as *Noumens.* Now from this point of view the rational being is justified in saying of every act which he performs contrary to the law, (although it is sufficiently determined in the past as phenomenon and in so far is inevitably necessary), that he could have abstained from doing it. For the act with all

---

[1]*Cf. Religion within Bounds of Mere Reason, H.,* VI, p. 144 (footnote).
[2]*Critique of Pure Reason, B.,* 581 (=*A.,* 553).
[3]*Critique of Practical Reason,* 97–8.

the past which determines it belongs to a single phenomenon, his character, which he makes for himself, and according to which he ascribes to himself, as a cause independent of all sensibility, the causality of those phenomena."

All the same, according to Kant, all free acts as phenomena follow on each other and on other phenomena according to laws of natural causality. That means that their succession is necessary according to causal laws, *i.e.*, laws of invariable succession, it does not mean that the logical ground of the effect is to be found in the phenomenal cause, and so it leaves room for a determination by the noumenon as ground as well as a determination by the phenomenal causes. Phenomena follow on each other necessarily, just because they are determined by a noumenal ground. For determination by a ground of any sort obviously implies that any sequence in what is determined must be fixed and necessary, to deny this would be to say that what is determined by a ground might at the same time not be determined. "Every cause presupposes a rule according to which certain phenomena follow as effects ; and every rule requires a uniformity of effects, which establishes the concept of the cause (as a faculty).[1] This, in so far as it must be revealed through mere phenomena, we may call its empirical character. The empirical character is durable, while the effects appear in varying forms according to the diversity of the accompanying and, to a certain extent, limiting conditions." It seems best to interpret this passage as meaning that the intelligible cause (noumenon), if it is to exercise its causality at all, presupposes a rule according to which it produces one phenomenal effect rather than another, and that such rules involve observable uniformities of sequence in phenomena, the discovery of which enables us to form a conception of phenomenal[2] faculties and hence of a phenomenal character. So Kant distinguishes between the empirical character, which is just the system of laws connecting events in the empirical self as phenomena, and the intelligible character, which is the ground in the noumenal self of that empirical self we know.[3] It is the empirical character that enables us to predict human action, and with sufficient knowledge of it, Kant holds, we could predict all acts from the past with the same certainty

[1] *Critique of Pure Reason*, B., 577 (=A., 549).
[2] In B., 574 Kant says that we observe the empirical character in the shape of faculties and forces.
[3] *Critique of Pure Reason*, B., 567 ff. (=A., 539).

as we could predict an eclipse of the sun or moon.[1] Not only desires but the appearances of the will (for the will itself may " appear,"[2]) would, it seems, have to be included in that empirical character, but Kant does not make the point clear as to whether the self as agent can really appear at all as an even phenomenal agent. But, in any case, freedom is declared not to be inconsistent with the complete predictability of all human acts from circumstances and motives.

Responsibility, Kant insists, is not avoided by ascribing an act to empirical characteristics like innate badness as its natural cause, for these are the result and not the cause of the bad will. Common sense holds a man to be responsible and punishable for his bad deeds even though they may be accounted for causally as due to his empirical, natural disposition. But " this could not take place if we did not presuppose that everything which issues from his will (and certainly every deed done intentionally) has as its basis a free causality, which from early youth onwards has expressed its character in its appearances (the actions of the man).[3] These appearances on account of the uniformity of conduct enable us to recognise a natural connection (*Naturzusammenhang*), which does not, however, make the evil quality of the will necessary, but is rather the consequence of the voluntary adoption of bad, enduring principles, which only make it all the more culpable and deserving of punishment." Kant even carries out his view of responsibility with such extreme rigour that he declares that in condemning an action we may set aside altogether all natural psychological influences and previous actions, and " treat the past series of conditions as never having occurred (*als ungeschehen*), and this deed as quite unconditioned with regard to the precedent state, as though the agent thereby began a series of consequences quite independently (*ganz von selbst*).[4]...And, indeed, one regards the causality of reason as not merely a competing, partial cause (*Concurrenz*), but as in itself complete, even if the sensible motives (*Triebfedern*) were not at all in its favour but actually against it. The action is ascribed to the intelligible character of the agent ; he has now, at the moment in

---

[1]*Critique of Practical Reason*, 99. *Critique of Pure Reason*, B., 578 (=*A*., 550).

[2]*Critique of Pure Reason*, B., 580 (=*A*., 552), " Man's will has an empirical character, which is the (empirical) cause of all his acts."

[3]*Critique of Practical Reason*, 100.

[4]*Critique of Pure Reason*, B.,583 (= *A*., 555).

which he tells the lie,[1] complete responsibility." The point on which the solution depends is that, if freedom is ascribed not to particular, empirical acts of will, but to a non-temporal principle, the antinomy is avoided, because as non-sensible it cannot be determined by desire for a sensible object, and as non-temporal it cannot be determined by antecedent events in time.

The solution is sometimes expressed by saying that the noumenal self begins a series of consequences in the phenomenal world of its own accord (*von selbst*), without either the action beginning *in* the noumenal self, or the effects of the free action in the sensible world themselves beginning " *von selbst.*"[2] Thus he claims to avoid what the antithesis of the third antinomy forbids, an absolutely fresh beginning in the phenomenal world. To say that the noumenal self begins a series of consequences in the phenomenal world " *von selbst* " must mean that the noumenal self as their ground determines them independently of other noumena and, above all, independently of precedent phenomena in time. Kant held that, although thus independently determined, they yet might, and in fact must, follow necessarily on precedent phenomena in such a way as to be capable of inference from them by causal laws, so that as phenomena they never constituted a fresh beginning in the causal series. Kant may have conceived it like this—to put it in the shape of a formula—the phenomenal sequences A B C, D E F might be determined by noumenal grounds, X and Y, independently of each other, and yet occur in experience so that D E F always followed A B C under the phenomenal conditions G H, etc. This would have involved the rather awkward conception of a pre-established harmony between noumena acting independently ; but after all Kant was not bound nor indeed allowed by his own principles to advance any theory as to the nature of this noumenal action.

To pass to another aspect of Kant's treatment of freedom ; it is a striking fact that he always identifies free action with action according to the moral law. For free action consists in action by the noumenal self according to its own law, *i.e.*, the law of reason, and Kant held that the only law of action

---

[1] In a footnote on *B.*, 579 (=*A.*, 551) it is, however, said that we cannot estimate responsibility accurately because we are never in a position to know how much in action is due to the pure work of freedom and how much to natural qualities of temperament.

[2] *E.g., Critique of Pure Reason., B.*, 569, 582 (=*A.*, 541, 554).

which could be regarded as really universal and so capable of directing reason must be the moral law. He declares that the two concepts, freedom and morality, are so closely connected that you can deduce either from the other, that they are in fact *Wechselbegriffe*. It is only by regarding it as determination by the moral law that we find any positive content in the idea of freedom as conceived by Kant. In the ethical works the connection of the two is pressed as far as well possible. " A free will and a will under moral laws are identical (*einerlei*).[1] If then the freedom of the will is presupposed, morality with its own principle follows from freedom by the mere analysis (*Zergliederung*) of its concept." . . . " The two concepts are so inseparably united (*unzertrennlich verbunden*), that practical freedom could also be defined as independence of the will of anything other than the moral law alone."[2] This identification of free action and action according to the moral law, however, leads to serious difficulties. We may object that, if free action and action according to the moral law are identical, then wrong acts cannot be free, and so how can we be responsible for them ? Yet the contention that, if all acts are exclusively determined by natural causality, we cannot be held responsible for wrong-doing was the argument for freedom on which Kant chiefly insists. If it be said that in wrong acts the fault lies not in the positive commission of the act through freedom, but in neglecting to exercise our noumenal causality to stop it, this neglect is at any rate free, if we are responsible for it, and therefore freedom is still not equivalent to morality, but may actually involve immorality. Kant says that we are responsible, not for sensible inclinations as such, but only if we allow them to affect our " maxims " of conduct,[3] but to admit such a possibility at all really implies a breach with the view so insisted upon elsewhere in the ethical works that free action and moral action are identical. The same remark applies to Kant's doctrine in *Religion within the Bounds of Mere Reason*, that human badness is due to a single intelligible, supra-temporal act as the ground of all empirical wrongdoing.[4]

Nor is it easy to see how a pure and absolutely timeless reason, devoid of all desire, could be other than perfectly

---

[1] *Foundation to the Metaphysic of Ethics*, 447 (Abbott, p. 95).
[2] *Critique of Practical Reason*, 93, *ad fin.*
[3] *Foundation to the Metaphysic of Ethics*, 458 (Abbott, p. 113).
[4] *V. H.*, VI, 125.

moral, if indeed morality has any meaning when applied to such a being ; nor how reason can subsume and take up into itself as a motive something so heterogeneous as a sensible desire, if reason is conceived as pure form without content and desires as merely mechanical reactions to wholly external stimuli. Further, surely, the noumenal self must be conceived as the ground of our whole empirical character as its appearance, not only of some of its acts, otherwise my noumenal self is not in any real sense myself. But, if the noumenal self is the ground of the whole empirical self as its appearance, all action by internal causation (*i.e.*, action which as phenomenal belongs to the chain of appearances of the noumenal self of the agent) becomes in the last resort equally the work of the noumenal self. We might indeed still distinguish moral acts from other acts by saying that all other action as determined by externally caused desires had its real ground not in the noumenal self of the agent, but in other things-in-themselves, and, so, that moral action alone was action according to internal causation ; but Kant has debarred himself from this resource by his doctrine that all action, whether moral or not, can be adequately accounted for causally (phenomenally) by desires of external objects, *i.e.*, externally caused reactions of a mechanical order. This doctrine would involve the conclusion that we have no more right to call any action internally or externally caused than any other. The whole character of the empirical self cannot in any case be regarded as (phenomenally) moral ; yet, if the noumenal and empirical self are, as Kant holds, the same person regarded from different standpoints, what we call the immoral as well as the moral elements in the empirical self must belong to the " appearance " of the noumenal self.

Kant avoids the various difficulties connected with the identification of moral and free action by declaring immoral action to be inexplicable, thus trying to make it just an instance of our ignorance of the connection between the noumenal and the phenomenal, but his account makes it not only unintelligible, but positively self-contradictory and so absolutely impossible. Perfect freedom may be identical with determination by the moral law, but it does not follow that all freedom is. Kant denied degrees of freedom, and his doctrine would seem to involve the logical conclusion that, inasmuch as the evil in any act is not in any way determined by freedom, we are not responsible for it, but only for the good, and hence are never liable to moral condemnation, a view which he would have been the first to repudiate.

The proof advanced by Kant to show that free action is always moral action cannot be described as satisfactory.[1] It is to the effect that free action must be independent of empirical determining grounds, and must therefore be action according to an *a priori* law, this being the only possible non-empirical ground, and that action according to an *a priori* law has already been shown to be identical with moral action. But, in the first place, Kant's attempt to make all action according to a universal (or *a priori*) law necessarily moral action seems to break down ; and, secondly, to say that free action cannot be action determined by desire of particulars is not the same as to say that it cannot be action determined by empirical reflection on, *e.g.*, the amount of pleasure which previous experience justifies us in expecting to result from it. Of course, Kant's view of the noumenal self as pure reason practically commits him to the view that all free action, as action by the noumenal self, is moral action, but then the noumenal self as conceived by Kant seems a hopeless abstraction. But more of that later.

The question as to the possibility of giving a proof of morality independently of freedom and of freedom independently of morality is discussed in several passages. In the *Critique of Practical Reason* Kant seems at first to take the attitude that the validity of the moral law cannot be proved either *a priori* or *a posteriori*, because it is non-empirical and yet cannot, like the categories, be shown to be a condition of the possibility of experience,[2] but for all that it is declared to be given as a factum of pure reason and to be apodeictically certain,[3] whether it be ever realised in any empirical action or not. Further, though indemonstrable itself, it serves as the only possible basis for the deduction of freedom. Kant would have been on safer ground if he had stopped here, but he attempts to turn this relation into a kind of proof of the moral law. He says that this verification of the moral law by using it to deduce freedom fully serves the purpose of an *a priori* justification of it.[4] " For the moral law thereby proves its reality sufficiently to satisfy even the critique of speculative reason, because it gives positive determination to a causality that was thought only negatively, the possibility of which speculative reason was bound to

[1]*V. Critique of Practical Reason*, 29.   [2]*Ib.*, 46–47.   [3]*Ib.*, 47.   [4]*Ib.*, 48.

accept without being able to comprehend it." In the same section the idea of freedom, as regards its possibility, Kant actually declared to be not only a "need" (*Bedürfnis*) but an "analytic principle" of pure speculative reason. Yet in the *Critique of Pure Reason* he would not grant that we could know even the "real possibility" of noumenal attributes like freedom, and declared the object of the negative solution of the antinomy between causality and freedom given there to be not an attempt to show the actuality, or even the possibility, of freedom, but only a proof that it does not contradict universal natural causality?[1] Yet now he seems to argue that the moral law is verified by the fact that it makes intelligible[2] an idea that we were bound by speculative reason to accept, but yet, till we introduced moral conceptions, could not understand or describe except in negatives. Such an argument lays much greater stress on the import of the demand of reason for a "first cause" than is done in the discussion appended to the antinomy itself, but, after all, it was the unfailing conviction of Kant even in the *Critique of Pure Reason* that theoretical reason by itself forces us to conceive phenomena as having a non-phenomenal ground, *i.e.*, as based on a non-sensible type of causality, which causality *Ethics* proceeds to define further. Kant is careful to insist that this does not give us a theoretical insight into the nature or possibility of freedom or extend our theoretical knowledge in the least, but only enables us to know that our actions may be "practically" determined by a free[3] (*i.e.*, not sensibly conditioned) act of reason according to the moral law. It is the moral law that Kant generally makes the real basis of the proof of freedom. For example, in the *Critique of Practical Reason* he argues that we must know morality first and infer freedom from it, not *vice versa*, on the ground that we cannot be immediately aware of freedom, because our first concept of it is merely negative, and also that it is theoretically indemonstrable and scientifically useless, so that we cannot come to know its reality by any other means than an appeal to the moral law, which we know immediately, as pre-

[1]*E.g.. B.*, 586 (=*A.*, 614).

[2]In the *Critique of Judgment* (Section 91, 457) Kant declares freedom to be the only one of the *Vernunftideen* which can be regarded as a *Tatsache*, though established not theoretically, but practically.

[3]*E.g., Critique of Practical Reason*, 49, ff; *Foundation to the Metaphysic of Morals*, 459 ff. (Abbott, p. 114 ff.).

supposing freedom.[1] He also appeals to the empirical fact that we frequently argue from " ought " to " could." In the *Critique of Pure Reason* any proof of the reality of freedom is expressly left to the ethical works. Again, in the *Critique of Practical Reason*, Kant remarks that "freedom is the only one of all the ideas of speculative reason of which we *know* the possibility *a priori*, though without comprehending it, because it is the condition of the moral law, which we know."[2] In a footnote he adds that freedom is the *ratio essendi* of the moral law, and the moral law the *ratio cognoscendi* of freedom, because, if it were not for the moral law, we could never be justified in accepting freedom. We may say that Kant's general attitude is to take the moral law as valid in its own right without deduction from anything else, and freedom as a necessary presupposition of morality, the result of the *Critique of Pure Reason* being merely to show that freedom and causality are not absolutely incompatible, and the negative idea of freedom which it gives serving as a slight additional confirmation, not as an essential basis, of the conclusions of moral philosophy.

In one passage in the *Foundation to the Metaphysics of Ethics* he adopts a more " dogmatic " standpoint.[3] He admits the occurrence of a circle in his argument as he had proved morality from freedom and then freedom from morality. This was needed to show the two to be " *Wechselbegriffe*," but the circle is escaped by the contention that theoretical philosophy drives us to a distinction between phenomena and things-in-themselves, between the self as active and the self as passive, and that the negative conception of freedom as independence of sensible causes, thus established, cannot be separated from the positive idea of freedom as autonomy or determination by the moral law. It is obvious that such a contention is quite inconsistent with the " critical " character of Kant's philosophy ; if it be taken literally, we arrive at a wholly theoretical proof of freedom and the moral law.

In the same work, however, a more profitable line of proof is suggested.[4] It is said, namely, that if reason is to be practical, *i.e.*, to determine action, there must be freedom, because reason cannot be conceived as determining action if we are wholly dependent on mere desire or impulse. We might say that the possibility of reason being " practical " presupposes

[1]29 ff. cf., *Religion within Bounds of Mere Reason*, H., II, pp., 143-4 (footnote).
[2]4.   [3]450 ff. (Abbott, p. 100 ff.).   [4]448 (Abbott, p. 97).

both morality and freedom, morality, because, unless certain acts realise absolute values, no act can be more rational than any other, freedom, because, if action depends wholly on sensible desires or physical causation, reason does not determine action.

In the above sketch of Kant's treatment of freedom we have assumed a line of interpretation which would be absolutely rejected by one large and influential body of Kantian critics, I mean, by most or all of the "Marburger school." This school, to put it as briefly as possible, generally interprets transcendental freedom not as a cause that is not sensibly determined, but as an end that is not a mere means. According to, *e.g.*, Cohen, that is free which is an end-in-itself, *i.e.*, a rational being, and that only, and this freedom is not affected by the complete determination of what is an end-in-itself by natural causality. Such an interpretation would quite separate freedom from any kind of causality. "Freedom in its positive sense," Cohen declares, "has nothing whatever to do with causality.[1] The mode of action (*Wirkungsweise*) of freedom is not to be determined according to the analogy of causality. So *neither ought it to be described as causality.*" Thus freedom is made wholly an ethical and not in the least a metaphysical attribute. Kant is not held to believe in the actual occurrence as a fact of an uncaused causality, even in the sense of a noumenal ground which is determined, but not determined by sensible causes. So Cohen says[2] "One cannot realise forcibly enough that the freedom which one accepts for the sake of something[3] that is but an idea, can itself only be accepted as an idea."[4]

It cannot be denied that it is very tempting to accept this theory. It would explain why Kant represented the noumenal self as perfect, why he held the moral law to be deducible analytically from the concept of freedom, why he made freedom, as something positive, the subject of practical not of theoretical reason, *i.e.*, because it was a value, not a fact. It would at one stroke remove the numerous difficulties involved in the sharp division between the noumenal and the phenomenal self and in the very awkward conception of a

[1]Kant's *Begründung der Ethik*, p. 230.
[2]*Ib.*, p. 225.   [3]*I.e.* the moral law.
[4]Presumably = a valuation. Would Kant have agreed that judgments of value express mere ideas? And why, if definite grounds can be given for it, as here with responsibility and freedom, should not a judgment of value imply a judgment of fact? "Ought" implies "can," says our philosopher.

twofold causality in the self. And it would do all this without indeterminism and without " mysticism." It seems so much clearer and simpler just to say that moral acts have value as ends-in-themselves, although completely determined by natural causation, than to save a mystical and incomprehensible freedom by an awkward, nay impossible, separation between the self as agent and knower and the self as passive and known. Of the obscurity and difficulty of the Kantian doctrine, as usually interpreted, any one who has read through these last twenty pages will at least be convinced, if of nothing else.

But, without attempting to go into detail, I must say that it seems to me quite impossible to reconcile this simpler interpretation of the Marburger school with the general tenor of the text of Kant. The simplicity of the interpretation is only achieved by ignoring the close connection between freedom and causality apparent throughout the discussion of the former. Cohen says that freedom is not to be associated with any kind of causality, but that freedom is identified by Kant with a kind of causality is a fact that he cannot deny. The difficulty Kant has to face is how to reconcile this kind of causality with the absolute supremacy of natural causality among phenomena. Now the view of some event as an end-in-itself may be contrasted with the view of it as an effect of natural causality, but I do not see how it can be said, even *prima facie*, to contradict it. The difficulty is not, it seems, that it is supposed that a mere effect cannot have any intrinsic value (be an end-in-itself), but that it cannot have a particular kind of value (*i.e.*, moral value in the narrower sense), because complete determination by natural laws of causality conflicts with moral responsibility and with any causality by reason at all, as a causality by the whole self not expressible in terms of quasi-mechanical laws of any description. Simply to say that a moral act, though completely determined by natural causality, is an end-in-itself hardly seems to alleviate these special difficulties attaching to moral action. Whether an act has intrinsic value or not, the difficulty which Kant holds to be cardinal remains, namely, how can we be responsible for an act which is completely determined by past events, *i.e.*, by what is not in our power at the moment of action. Kant definitely and repeatedly says that, if actions are exclusively and only determined by natural causality and no other kind, there is no room left for morality, but the statement that moral actions are ends-in-themselves would not introduce any other kind of causal determination, while the hypothesis of a real noumenal causality, with all its difficulties, does. So, whether one can hope to save the situation by the latter expedient or not, one at any rate cannot hope to save it by the former. If the solution put forward by Kant is what this school holds it to be, he was simply ignoring in his solution the difficulty which in his statement of the problem he made of cardinal importance.

Kant laid great emphasis on having first worked out the distinction between phenomena and things-in-themselves, just because it enabled him to solve the problem of freedom, but the distinction in the *Critique of Pure Reason* is clearly not a distinction between fact and value, but between appearance and reality. The distinction between judgments of fact and judgments of value was not one that needed a Kant to discover it. If the only distinction between the noumenal self as free and the phenomenal self as determined by natural causality is that the noumenal self is the phenomenal self regarded as having intrinsic value, or in so far as it has intrinsic value, then it seems quite impossible to connect this distinction with the teaching of the *Critique of Pure Reason* as to the phenomenal character of space and time and the unknowable character of things-in-themselves, yet on this teaching it is said by Kant to be based.

If the Marburger school be right, it seems to me that the whole account of the subject in Kant's works ought to be rewritten in quite different terminology, substituting " end " for " freedom " and " means " for " natural effect." To suppose that all the subtleties of Kant's treatment are develop ments and paraphrases of the simple point that moral acts are ends-in-themselves, even though completely determined by natural causality, seems to me to be a far worse slight on Kant than to suppose him guilty of the " mysticism " involved in his doctrine of the noumenal self as usually interpreted.

Our next step must be to turn back and see in just what sense Kant really succeeded in proving causality in the *Critique of Pure Reason*, so that we may try to see if this principle really conflicts with freedom, whether in " noumena " or in " phenomena." Fortunately, however, we have already fulfilled the former task and need not repeat what we have said earlier. Kant, we concluded, has proved causality in the sense that all sequence among phenomena is necessary. Now Kant identified this necessity with a mechanical or quasi-mechanical necessity, but in so doing he seems to have

P

been wrong. For, as we have seen, all the arguments for causality show only necessary sequence and do not prejudge the question as to the nature of the necessity.

Mechanical necessity, the omnipotent deity of Naturalism, properly means necessary determination by the Newtonian laws of motion, or by other laws that make use of terms bearing reference only to motion and mass. Now it is obviously absurd to apply these laws to psychical causation qua psychical, for the simple reason that emotions, volitions, thoughts, etc., are not, as such, motions of bodies in space. Hence the only resource of the materialist, who wishes to make all causation mechanical in this sense, is to deny psychical causation altogether. But this is not the point at issue here. So let us pass on.

There is a second sense of necessity, which we may call " quasi-mechanical," and it is in this sense that Kant interprets " natural causality." It is in this sense that Kant, as it seems rightly, contends that " natural causality " is incompatible with freedom in phenomena as phenomena. The dicta that every change must have a cause and that everything happens according to laws of nature, taken literally, imply that for every event another event or set of events can be found, with which a connection can be established such that every item in the effect is connected with every item in the cause by a necessary law. Thus causal explanation of an effect, X, is obtained when it is analysed into its component parts,[1] A, B, C, D, E, and each of these connected with some precedent cause in such a way that we have the relation—if F then A, if G then B, etc. But such a method clearly presupposes that it is possible to effect a complete analysis of X. It further presupposes that A, B, C, D, E, can be isolated from the whole, which they make up, sufficiently for us to be able to say, if F then A, whatever happens to the other factors of X, whether they are all present or none at all. Now reflection seems to reveal that, however it may be with the physical, neither condition is fulfilled in the sphere of psychology. We cannot say that a man at a given moment is a sensation of hunger plus a feeling of satisfaction at the sight of food plus a volition to have his dinner plus a desire for a better dinner than he has plus a feeling of annoyance that the better dinner is not forthcoming, all these factors causally interacting together. Nor, does it seem, can we ever correlate,

[1] I do not mean, of course, to imply that the parts need be self-subsistent, they may be just qualitative or quantitative factors in the event.

for example, desires with physical stimuli so that we can say that the desire must inevitably be roused to a certain intensity by the stimulus without taking into account the direction of attention of the self, the degree of moral effort of which it is capable, etc. But these are not additional isolable factors, they are principles governing the reaction of the self as a whole to the stimulus of a part, yet it seems obvious that psychology cannot advance far without taking them into account. If so, it follows that these psychological factors cannot be isolated in such a way that we can connect them with other isolable factors by invariable causal laws formulated without reference to the causality of the self as a whole.

Now Kant conceived that he was compelled by his acceptance of universal causality to treat the empirical self in just such a way. But he was not, for he had only proved that the sequence of any two events, whether physical or psychical, must be necessary, not that this necessity must be of any particular type. His proof of causality does not, it seems, really carry with it any special objection to a necessity conceived neither mechanically nor quasi-mechanically, the necessity of a whole determining its parts. It only shows that any phenomenal sequence is necessary, not that this necessity can be reduced to a series of laws connecting atomistically isolated elements. If by cause is meant an antecedent event, Kant has not proved that every event must have a cause sufficient to determine it. He has only proved that every event is necessary. The proof does not imply that an event can be inferred with absolute certainty from any other event or events. This is quite clear even from a mechanical point of view, as far as the possibility of human calculation is concerned, because, as everything interacts, we can never know the full sum of conditions of any event, but it may be the case that this is impossible not only because we can never have a complete list of all the events required but because the whole is not a mere sum of events.

Now there are two points in which this quasi-mechanical causality seems to conflict with morality. But on neither point is there a real conflict with causality conceived as necessary sequence, *i.e.*, causality in so far as really proved by Kant. Now, to take the first point of conflict, if we treat man as a mere conglomeration of interacting desires, sensations, ideas, etc., moral action becomes impossible. Moral action implies an action of the whole self which compares its different desires in respect of the value of their objects. In moral action it is not a case of one desire or tendency to act being stronger than another, but of it being judged to be worth more than another. Such a power of judging between tendencies seems to imply a self that cannot, qua active, be reduced to a mere bundle of tendencies. To speak of a thought, etc., as a psychical event is simply a way of saying that the whole self was thinking. It seems that no psychical action can be taken apart from the whole self, as this atomism tries to take it, but in the case of morality the self as a whole is in a special degree prominent and the artificially abstracted parts or elements in the self in a special degree and sense subsidiary. This old and rather trite point conflicts with the universal application of what Kant called natural causality to the empirical self. It does not conflict with the universality of necessary connection, which is all that Kant seems to have really proved. But, because he conceived causality in an dtomistic way, he treats all states of the empirical self as aeducible from external forces and desires, regarded as another class of merely mechanical forces reacting to stimuli. Modern physical science, we may note on the other hand, is quantitative rather than atomistic in its conception of causality, but there are obvious limits to the application of a quantitative causality in the psychological sphere.

But it may be said that the greatest difficulty with regard to freedom is due to a man's present acts being determined by the past. As we have seen, this is a difficulty on which Kant lays great, perhaps the greatest, stress. But Kant's proof of causality, we must insist, in so far as really established, does not imply that every change must have a cause, or causes, in the sense of events atomistically conceived. Now the dictum of the determinist is that a man's present acts are absolutely determined by his character and his circumstances together, or perhaps rather his character reacting on his circumstances, but is a man's character merely his past acts or conscious states ? If not, we are not compelled to regard a man's present acts as necessarily determined by his past. They are determined by his character—yes, but character is a principle which cannot be identified with one's past acts any more than with one's future acts, and, though inseparable[1] from the series

[1] I do not mean, of course, to suggest that what we empirically call the " character " of a man cannot change. That it does change is an undoubted empirical fact, but all changes, however complete, may still be due to unchanging principles, just as we conceive the most complete changes on, *e.g.*, the surface of the earth to be due to *unchanging* natural laws.

of one's conscious states, past, present and future, is not exhausted by them. My character is neither my present conscious state nor the sum of my past conscious states apart from the principle of connection between them. Nor is it *merely* a system of laws which determines my possible and actual actions, for that would imply the reduction of the self to an aggregate of isolable elements connected by laws. It is not for us to enlarge on this view here, but if it can be maintained that, in a principle like human character, we have a necessary connection that cannot be reduced to causal laws and that is yet not incompatible with the proof of necessary succession which we have tried to defend, in this sense, though not in a really indeterminist sense, freedom might then be admitted even in what Kant calls the empirical self.

We thus see that the proof of causality given in the *Critique of Pure Reason* leaves three loopholes for freedom :—

1. It is not valid of the noumenal self as being that for which alone causally connected phenomena exist.

2. It does not imply that the phenomenal cause is the logical ground, or at any rate the whole logical ground, of the phenomenal effect. (That it need not be the *whole* logical ground is, of course, not in any way inconsistent with our conclusion in the last chapter).[1]

3. It does not imply universal mechanical or quasi-mechanical causation even in the empirical self.

In his ethical works Kant made use of the first two loopholes, but not of the third. So far from doing so, he insists that " natural " (quasi-mechanical) causality is absolutely supreme among phenomena, apparently because he holds its universality to have been proved by the *Critique of Pure Reason*. In this he seems to have been wrong ; the *Critique of Pure Reason* seems to have succeeded in establishing the necessity of all events, but I fail to see any justification there for dogmatising[2] as to the precise nature of the necessity.

[1] *V.*, above, pp. 181–2.

[2] In the *Metaphysical Rudiments of Natural Science* (*H.*, IV, pp.439 ff.) Kant advances a proof that all change in matter is due to an external cause. He gives as his ground that matter has no internal grounds of determination, because it has no qualities at all but external relations in space. This, of course, involves the universality of mechanism, in the sense of causation by motion alone, for the inorganic world. Kant is, however, careful to make it clear that this does not debar non-mechanical causality in living beings, but only compels us to account for such causality by the assumption of a living being conjoined to matter. However, the only point that I can find urged by him in favour of the premiss of the argument, namely that matter has no qualities but

And, as we shall see, Kant realises and corrects his mistake in the *Critique of Judgment*. He does not however give a fresh account of freedom in the light of the conclusions of the later work, yet it is just the identification of causality as proved in the second Analogy with a quasi-mechanical causality that makes the solution of the problem in the ethical works appear so unsatisfactory. It is because he makes a mechanical or quasi-mechanical causality universal among phenomena that he has to separate the noumenal from the phenomenal so completely, as the timeless from the temporal.

The awkwardness and obscurity of Kant's solution comes, no doubt, partly from the difficulties of the subject, but also from the fact that, because he supposed the only kind of necessity to be quasi-mechanical, he regarded himself as having proved in the Transcendental Analytic not only necessity but also " natural " (quasi-mechanical) necessity to be universally valid among phenomena and was consequently only able to secure freedom in another, non-temporal sphere, totally alien to the world in which we live. The difficulties of his absolute separation between the two selves, the free self and the empirically determined self, are many and hard to surmount. How can a timeless, purely rational self be conceived as acting immorally, and if it never acts immorally, how can we be said to be responsible for immoral action? How can I regard as myself a being so different from the self I know, as a timeless self must be? Again, if we are to form any sort of definite conception of the noumenal self, it seems that it must be in the last resort reduced either to God or to a mere abstraction of the fact that we know and will, and neither alternative provides an opportunity of saving human freedom, if mechanical causality is regarded as universal among phenomena and yet as quite incompatible with freedom in the man as phenomenal. If the noumenal self be equivalent to God, then God alone is free ; if it be merely an abstraction of the fact that we know, it cannot be a self-subsistent, concrete subject such as we must predicate moral action of.

If phenomena are only phenomena for the noumenal self, how can they be regarded as completely determined by each other in abstraction from their relation to this self? How can even the appearance of a reality which is a true whole be itself a mere aggregate of mechanically interacting parts?

spatial relations, is that the outer senses can only be affected by motion (*ib.* p. 366), and this can hardly be described as conclusive.

Can two such absolutely disparate beings as the noumenal and the phenomenal self be yet held in any sense to be one ? Again, how can a timeless morality be conceived ? Morality is essentially a struggle and progress, but how can this struggle and progress occur in a timeless sphere, and, if they occur only in the phenomenal world, then how can this be reconciled with the denial of the possibility of moral action by us qua phenomenal ?

Some or all of these difficulties may perhaps be avoided by a mixture of mysticism and agnosticism, but only at the cost of making the solution so incomprehensible and abstract as to be no real solution at all. It is easy enough to say that in the unknown noumenal self may lie qualities which account for the possibility of moral action in spite of universal " natural " causality ; but, when we try to form a definite conception of the noumenal self on Kantian lines, we are forced to choose between an absolutely unknowable, and so useless, entity and a mere abstraction conceived as self-subsistent, *i.e.*, the abstraction of form without content.

These defects result from taking the noumenal as absolutely disparate from the phenomenal self, and so not as including and transcending but as merely negating the temporal. This separation was forced on Kant by his belief that the phenomenal world was necessarily and universally under the sway not only of necessity but of a type of mechanical causality. Any attempt to establish a closer connection between the phenomenal and the noumenal self would have either caused a breach in the chain of " natural " causation, or given the noumenal self " sensible " or temporal content and so brought it under the sway of this " natural " causation.

Kant recognised that " natural " (quasi-mechanical) causation could not be used to explain the facts of knowledge and morality even in the sense not of logical or rational explanation but of explanation by natural, causal laws ; but he supposed that we could separate these facts from the other facts about the self in such a way that the self, as knower and agent, could be regarded as absolutely timeless, and the self, as passive and known, as completely " natural," *i.e.*, completely determined by a quasi-mechanical, atomistic causality. A better hope of a solution is provided if we recognise

1. that what Kant calls " natural necessity " has not been proved of the empirical self (though necessity in general has) ;
2. that " natural necessity " is on the contrary quite

inadequate to meet all the needs of a study of even the empirical self ;

3. that, while moral action can only be explained by a principle that is in some sense supra-temporal, *i.e.*, character, this principle cannot be separated from the concrete nature of what is known by introspection, from the conscious states of the self, though it is not thereby exhaustible in such a way that it can be reduced to a mere series of conscious states or events, or a mere aggregate of ideas and tendencies.

Kant seems to have been right in so far as freedom calls for a principle which is in some sense supra-temporal, but he made it timeless, which is a different thing. He realised that moral action must be regarded as necessary with a necessity other than that given by his quasi-mechanical causation, but he first sought the necessity in the absolutely timeless reality the mere existence of which he believed himself to have established on theoretical grounds. The attempt to work out such a conception of necessity must be regarded as a step towards the conception of organic causation established in the *Critique of Judgment*, although, unfortunately, he does not extend this conception by applying it to psychology. But in this later work he seems to break with his earlier position that all causality must be of a mechanical, or at any rate, of an atomistic type. It is not the place to deal at length with the *Critique of Judgment*, but we shall just point out briefly how he there strove to develop along more satisfactory lines the conception of a non-mechanical causality.

Now the professed object of the second part of the *Critique of Judgment* is to reconcile the conflicting claims of mechanical causality and teleology, and thus to deal with the important concept of " purposiveness " (*Zweckmässigkeit*). There are four types of purposiveness distinguished by Kant. First, there is the purposiveness displayed by beautiful objects, *i.e.*, a fitness to produce a harmony between sense and understanding in a human percipient, a "*freely*" purposive harmoniousness without a definite end expressible by means of concepts. Secondly, we are driven to regard phenomena as purposive[1] relatively to the understanding in the sense that they are capable of an indefinite amount of classification and systematisation. We have an " Idea of Reason " of nature as a systematic whole, with much more than the minimum of unity and system which is required to make experience

[1] *I.e.*, to regard them as if arranged for the purpose of being comprehended by our understanding.

possible, and this " Idea," while indemonstrable, is progressively, though never completely, confirmed by our success in dealing with experience on this presupposition.

Thirdly, we have design in the common sense of the term, that is, marvellous instances of adaptation of physical organs to the needs of animal or man. But, fourthly, Kant associates and contrasts with this the " purposiveness " of an organism qua organic unity. It is this " purposiveness " alone with which we are concerned.

Kant begins the *Critique of Teleological Judgment* by pointing out that it is clear that teleological principles, (among which he includes purposive causation immanent in an organism), can be neither discovered by mere experience nor proved *a priori* to be involved in the concept of nature. So far from the latter being the case, the evidence of design in nature is held to prove the contingency[1] of nature and point to a principle beyond and other than nature. It is because purposive causation is held to be incompatible with dead matter and merely mechanical laws that the argument from design appears so cogent. The fact that it is impossible to prove any teleological principle suggests that the principle is regulative, not constitutive. " However, it is right to apply the teleological mode of judgment (*Beurteilung*) in the investigation of nature, at least problematically, but it should only be applied in order to bring nature under principles of observation and investigation by the help of the analogy with causality according to purposes, without claiming to *explain* it thereby.[2] . . . If, on the other hand, we based the order of nature on *deliberately* acting causes, and so based teleology not on a merely *regulative* principle for the mere judging (*Beurteilung*) of phenomena . . . but on what is also a constitutive principle for deducing the product from the cause, then the concept of an end of nature would belong not to the reflective but to the determinent judgment. But then, indeed, it would not specifically belong to the judgment at all (like the concept of beauty does, as formal, subjective purposiveness), but as concept of reason would introduce a new causality in natural science,

[1]Design points to contingency in two senses; (1) as seeming to imply that nature as a whole is contingent on a divine purpose ; (2) as being difficult to reconcile with the universality of mechanism even among phenomena and so seeming to be contingent as regards (*i.e.*, not the necessary consequence of) natural laws.

[2]*Critique of Judgment*, 269-70, Section 61.

which causality we after all only borrow from ourselves and ascribe to other beings, whom we yet are not willing to regard as like ourselves."

The purposiveness displayed in organisms is described pretty fully in Section 64. An organism, it is contended, can only be understood as an end of nature (*Naturzweck*). We see that it is impossible to explain it by mechanical laws alone and are therefore driven to introduce the other type of causality known to us, the causality of the will as determined by thought. We have thus passed from the sphere of the understanding to the sphere of reason. But the causality involved in an organism is of a peculiar kind ; if it cannot be identified with mechanical causation, neither can it be identified with the purposive causation of an artist working on an external object. For the design is not external but immanent. A thing exists as " *Naturzweck*," if it is at once cause and effect of itself.[1] A tree, for instance, is both cause and effect of itself in that it generically reproduces itself in new trees. As individual, too, it produces itself, for its growth is quite different from any increase in size by mechanical laws. " The tree first transforms the matter which it adds to itself so as to give it an unique quality, not producible by the mechanism of nature external to it, and thus develops itself further by means of a material which, as to its mode of composition, is the product of the tree itself.[2] For though, as respects the constituents as acquired from nature outside, it must be regarded as merely a derivative product (*Edukt*), yet in the separation and re-combination of this raw stuff there is such an original way of division and formation to be found in this kind of natural beings, that all art falls infinitely short of its object, if it seeks to restore those organic products out of the elements which it obtains by analysis of them, or out of the material which nature provides for their nourishment.

Thirdly, the parts of the tree produce each other in such a way, that the maintenance of the one depends reciprocally on the maintenance of the others. . . . While the leaves are products of the tree, they also return its support by preserving it, for repeated defoliation would kill it, and its growth depends on the action of the leaves on the stem. I shall only mention in passing the self-help of nature in these organisms in case of injury, how the defect of one part, which was needed for the

[1] Kant adds, in the second and third editions, the proviso " although in two different senses."   [2] 287, section 64.

preservation of the neighbouring parts, is restored by the other parts ; how in abortions or malformations in growth certain parts owing to the occurrence of causal defects or obstacles assume quite a novel form in order to preserve what is there and produce an anomalous creature ; though these are among the most wonderful properties of organisms."

In describing an organism as at once cause and effect of itself Kant seems to have had in mind chiefly the relation of the whole to the parts ; in an object produced by purely mechanical laws the whole is merely the sum of its parts and in its special form merely the product of the causal inter-action of its parts ; in a work of art the whole is the cause of the parts in that it is only the presence of the idea of the whole in the mind of the artist that enables the object to be produced ; in an organism we need both conceptions. The whole must determine the parts and the parts the whole. Each part helps to preserve the health of the other parts and is at the same time preserved by them. Hence, in the formal defini-tion of organism, the terms " end " and " means " replace " cause " and " effect." " An organised product of nature is one in which everything is at once end and, reciprocally, also means."[1] Now to conceive a thing as " *Naturzweck* " means to conceive it both as " *Zweck* " and " *Naturprodukt.*" To conceive it as " *Zweck* " we must suppose that the parts are only possible through their relation to the whole. Each part must be regarded as deriving its precise nature, partially at least, from conformity to the needs of the whole. But this is not enough, for we must not regard it as a work of art made by an external intelligence, but as a " *Natur-produkt.*" We must not regard the parts as externally related by some outside principle, but as producing and mould-ing each other by a process of causation immanent within the organism itself. When we find ourselves baffled in the attempt to explain organisms by mechanical causation we naturally turn to the analogy of art, but this external teleology is still more in opposition to the essential unity of the organism than is the all-pervading mechanism of natural science.

" For a body, therefore, which in itself and according to its inner possibility is to be judged as an end of nature (*Natur-zweck*), it is required that its parts should produce each other altogether reciprocally, as regards both their form and their

[1]296, section 66.

combination, and so produce a whole by their own causality, and that the concept of the whole (in a being which possesses the power of causality according to concepts fitted for such a product) should *vice versa* be the cause of that being according to a principle.[1] In that case the combination of *efficient causes* could be at the same time considered as *production of an effect through final causes.*

In such a product of nature every part, while only there *through* all the other parts, is also thought as existing *for the sake of* the other parts and the whole, *i.e.*, as instrument (organ). But this is not enough, (for it might still be represented as an instrument of art and so as only possible at all as end), it must also be thought as an organ *producing* the other parts (so that every part produces every other reciprocally). Such a property cannot be ascribed to any instrument of art, but only to nature which supplies all material for instruments (even the instruments of art). It is only in that case and for that reason that such a product as an *organised* and *self-organising* being can be called *an end of nature."*

Commenting on Kant, we may note two essential differences between the mode of causation implied in an organism (as conceived by Kant) and that implied in a work of art. In the first place, in a work of art, while the parts only exist for the sake of the whole and so for the sake of each other (as the whole is not something that can exist independently of the sum of its parts, though it may be more than the sum of its parts), yet they do not, as in an organism, exist through each other. In a work of art (or mechanical instrument) they are juxtaposed by external causation, in an organism they actually produce each other. In the former the influence of efficient causation as operating between the parts of the whole is reduced to a minimum, in the latter such causation must be predominant if the organism is to be regarded as part of the natural order at all.

Secondly, in a work of art the final[2] causation depends on and subserves the ends of a being quite external to the object determined by it, in an organism it depends on and subserves the ends of something within the organism itself or, rather, simply the organism as a whole. The final, like the efficient causation, involved is in a work of art (or mechanical instrument) external, in an organism internal to the object deter-

[1] 291–2, section 65 [2] *I.e.*, causation determined by and for purposes.

mined. Thus in a manufactured product like a clock, because the parts cannot mould each other as in an organic being, and because the purposive causation involved depends on the intervention of a mind external to them, there is no natural reparation of deficiencies or injuries by growth, no total assimilation and transformation of material taken from outside such as we find in organic nature, no production of offspring ; and similarly such a product cannot be regarded as in any sense striving towards the fulfilment of its own end by self-development, but only as a means to what is conceived as an end by a being other than itself. In an artificial product neither can the whole be regarded as determined by the causation of the parts, nor can the parts be regarded as determined by the causation of the whole except as an idea in the mind of an external agent.

The teleological principle, Kant insists, must be regarded as supreme in all scientific study of organisms.[1] Of such beings we can say not only that " nothing is the work of chance " (*von ungefähr*), *i.e.*, (presumably) not due to efficient causation, but also that " nothing is in vain " (*umsonst*). Rather inconsistently with his sharp distinction between regulative principles and categories, Kant even remarks that the students of the organic world can no more renounce the teleological principle than they can renounce the principles without which no experience would be possible, because the renunciation of teleology would leave them without a guiding-thread (*Leitfaden*) for the study of organisms.[2]

But he insists with equal emphasis that the use of this teleological principle must not be accompanied by any " dogmatic " assertions about the supersensible. If science introduces the hypothesis of a divine intelligence to account for " purposive " natural phenomena, it is passing beyond its own sphere and the introduction of the deity would be merely an excuse for neglect or failure to attain its own end, *i.e.*, the explanation of the phenomenon in question by means of efficient causes. Science must recognise the purposive character displayed in organisms, but it must abstract from the question whether these " *Naturzwecke* " are designed or undesigned. It may speak of " Nature " as wise or provident, thus indicating the purposive character which is found in phenomena as empirically given, but it must neither adopt a " hylozoism," which would, by giving to inorganic

<hr />

[1]*E.g.*, section 66. [2]*Ib.*

matter the properties of life, contradict the fundamental concepts of physical science itself, nor introduce supernatural causes, for such do not belong to the realm of phenomena, and so we can form no proper conception of their causality at all.

The metaphysical implications of the teleological character of organisms as empirically given are discussed on agnostic lines similar to the standpoint maintained in solving the antinomies of the *Critique of Pure Reason*. The antinomy presents itself as :

" Thesis : All production of material things is possible according to merely mechanical laws.[1]

Antithesis : Some production of material things (*i.e.*, the production of organisms) is not possible according to merely mechanical laws."

The antinomy is declared to be the result of two mistakes. In the first place, it is forgotten that the principles apparently in conflict are only regulative, not constitutive. Neither can be proved to be universally valid even in the phenomenal world. In the second place, it is forgotten that the two principles may actually be reconcilable, (though not for human understanding), as inadequate or partial aspects of one supersensible principle. To point out the former of these two mistakes may be said to be Kant's solution of the antinomy in so far as it affects science, to point out the second may be said to be his solution in so far as the antinomy affects metaphysics (in the transcendental sense).

We shall confine ourselves to the former point, on account of its direct bearing on Kant's conception of causality. Now it is very important to note that both the conflicting principles, mechanism and teleology, and not teleology alone, are declared to be merely regulative. Kant says explicitly:—
" Reason can,[2] however, prove neither the one nor the other of these principles, because we can have *a priori* no determining principle of the possibility of things according to merely empirical laws of nature." This passage by itself seems to constitute quite a sufficient proof that Kant does not at this stage mean to identify mechanism with phenomenal causality (as proved in the *Critique of Pure Reason*). Causality is certainly neither a regulative nor a merely empirical principle to Kant, and he certainly held its universal validity to have been apodeictically demonstrated for the physical world.

[1] 314, section 70.
[2] 315, section 70 ; Kant also declares both principles to be regulative in 386-7, section 82.

Kant may have identified causality with mechanism at one
time, and he took a very mechanical view even of psychical
causation in the ethical works, but it seems impossible to
hold that he identified the two at the time when he wrote the
Critique of Judgment. Further, in refusing to identify
causality with mechanism, he does not only mean by the
latter causation through motion in space, but causation by
the interacting parts as opposed to causation by the whole.
That the whole seems to determine the parts as well as *vice
versa* is the distinctive mark of organisms which impresses
Kant. His attitude in this work, therefore, constitutes a
definite breach with his earlier, atomistic view of causal
necessity. He finds it impossible to conceive organisms to
have been produced by any non-purposive causality, and
purpose, according to Kant, implies that the whole or the
idea of the whole as a unity determines the parts.

Kant definitely asserts that organisms can never be
explained by mechanism. He adds, it is true, the limitation
" for a human understanding," on the ground that a perceptive understanding might discern a supersensible principle
in which both teleology and mechanism are united. But
mechanism implies time and space, and so would lose its
meaning if applied to a supersensible principle. So the limiting
clause does not save the universality of mechanism, for mechanism is only a principle for phenomena, and, if we may say
a priori that there is no possibility of a human understanding
(*i.e.*, an understanding which depends for its content on what
is given in space and time, as perceived by us) explaining organisms by mechanical laws, they cannot as phenomena ever
be explained by mechanism, (and as noumena they certainly
cannot). In saying that we cannot explain organisms by
mechanical laws, Kant does not merely mean that we cannot
see the logical intelligibility of the causal laws by means of
which we account for the development of organisms, for
we are, he has insisted, in a similar plight as regards all causal
laws. The trouble is that we cannot even describe the
development of organisms by means of mechanical laws,
because we cannot in the case of an organism regard the whole
as a mere sum of its parts. It is not merely that we have
so far not been able to discover adequate mechanical laws for
the purpose, but that we can see on principle that mechanical
laws adequate to describe organisms qua phenomena can
never be discovered, because nothing can be described adequately by such laws unless it is reducible to a mere sum of

parts affecting each other causally, but not subject to any causal determination which can be ascribed to the whole in opposition to its parts.

That teleology must be introduced somewhere Kant has no doubt whatever. He declares the view of Epicurus that all apparent design is the purposeless, chance result of the moving forces of matter to be, " if taken literally, so palpably absurd (*offenbar ungereimt*), that it need not detain us."[1] This quotation shows as clearly as anything Kant's decisive opinions on the subject of teleology in general, but, as stated, it is not made an argument for supposing a non-mechanical causality in phenomena, but only for supposing a purposing ground of nature as a whole.

In his posthumous work Kant is even more decisive than here as to the impossibility of us ever bringing organisms completely under mechanical laws. He says there that for the production of organisms is needed " an *immaterial* principle with indivisible unity of the faculty of representa-tion.[2] For the manifold, the combination of which in unity rests on *an idea of a subject working purposively (like an artist)* cannot arise from moving forces of matter (this unity of principle being lacking in matter)." It is argued that an organism displays purpose, but that matter cannot have a purpose, because purpose implies the unity of a thinking being, " because it is the absolute unity of a subject which *combines* the manifold representations in a single consciousness *whereas all matter and every part thereof is composite*."[3] Kant concludes from this that " we must accept a simple, and so immaterial, being, either as part of the world of sense, or as a being distinct from that world as *mover* either outside or within the body (for matter cannot organise itself and act according to purposes)." The apparent " dogmatism " is much toned down by the proviso that we cannot know whether the being res-ponsible for the movements in question possesses under-standing, or only a faculty analogous to understanding in its effects. Elsewhere in the same work it is said that organisms reveal an immaterial principle, and even an *anima mundi*, because without this the purposive produc-tion " cannot be, I will not say explained, but not even thought."[4] Again it is declared that " *final causes* too belong to the moving forces of nature," a remark which, of course,

[1]*Critique of Judgment*, 322, section 72.
[2]*Altpreussische Monatsschriften*, Heft 19, pp. 72 ff. ; *v.* also *ib.*, p. 586.
[3]*Zusammengesetzt.*   [4]Heft, 19, p. 584.

involves a definite breach in the mechanical order even for physics as such, since it is physics that he is discussing, and he proceeds to say that the concept of these final causes " must go before physics *a priori* as a clue to the investigation of nature."[1] So in the same passage " the concept of a system of moving forces of matter " is said to require " the concept of an *animated (belebt)* matter," although this concept is at the same time declared to be problematical and even, as viewed by us, self-contradictory,[2] unless we introduce an understanding independent of matter. Kant's views on teleology in this work are of special importance as coming at the end of his philosophical development. Considerably earlier, in the treatise on *The Use of Teleological Principles in Philosophy*, published in 1788, two years before the *Critique of Judgment*, Kant declared that " the nature of an organism as that in which everything is both means and end to everything else leaves only a teleological,[3] not a " physico-mechanical mode of explanation," open to human intelligence, and that " a curtailment of *teleological* grounds of explanation in order to replace them by *physical* grounds in the case of organised beings, as regards the maintenance of their species, is not to be thought of."[4] In *Lose Blätter* (Reicke) Kant declares that the " principle of purposiveness in the structure of organic, particularly living, creatures is as closely connected with reason (*so mit der Vernunft zusammenhängend*) as the principle of efficient causation is relatively to all changes in the world.[5] To take as purposeless any part of a creature which belongs to the species as a normal feature is just as bad as to take an event in the world as having originated without a cause."

Some, though not all, of the passages quoted might perhaps be reconciled with a wholly mechanical view of nature as phenomenal by banishing the teleology required to the noumenal sphere and allowing it no influence on individual phenomena, but only on the whole universe of phenomena taken together. For example, in the *Critique of Judgment* 331, Section 74, he says that the conception of a " *Natur-zweck*," since such a being implies as " *Naturprodukt* " determination by " natural " necessity and as " Zweck " a

[1]Heft, 20, p. 77.
[2]Since the end (effect) cannot causally determine the means to itself.
[3]*H.*, IV, p. 491.   [4]*Ib.*, p. 481.   [5]P. 137.

Q

contingency as regards[1] natural laws, involves contradictions which can only be reconciled if there is a ground both in nature for the organism and also in the noumenal sphere for nature itself. Such a line of argument would imply that mechanical causality was absolute in nature as phenomenal but that the purposive character of organisms was to be explained by a mind determining nature as a whole, in the same way as what is purposive in the inorganic might be explained.

But Kant's treatment of mechanism as regulative and his strong emphasis on the unique character of the phenomenal causality of organisms seem to commit him to the belief in a non-mechanical causality exercised by the whole on the parts as occurring even in phenomena. Teleology is constantly described as another kind of causality, and this causality is introduced, not in order to explain the purposiveness of nature as a whole, but to account for particular instances where the attempt at description by mechanical laws breaks down, *i.e.*, not as a supplement to (as in the other *Critiques*), but as a substitute for " natural " causality. If causality (phenomenal) were regarded as equivalent to mechanism, Kant would be bound to insist that it was quite impossible for teleological principles to be valid of organisms, but on the contrary he suggests the probability though not the certainty, (owing to the limitations of human understanding), that they are.

Where Kant seems to take the view that organisms may be producible by mechanism after all, his attitude may be explained by a second sense of mechanism as " a causal connection, for which an understanding is not taken as exclusive cause."[2] It was considered by him as an ineradicable infirmity of human intelligence that we were unable to form a satisfactory concept of organic causation, but were driven to have recourse to the causality of an outside principle to explain design. Hence design was for him a regulative principle, which we could not comprehend in the least except by means of the totally inadequate analogy of a work of art, and which involved the further difficulty that it could not be separated from its reference to the unknown noumenal sphere.

The close connection of teleology and mechanism is constantly insisted on. Teleology presupposes mechanism,

[1]Otherwise we should not need to appeal to the category of purpose in order to account for it causally.

[2]*Critique of Judgment*, 346, Section 77.

because it presupposes that certain organs are means to ends and so are efficient causes of the fulfilment of these ends. But any causal connection must involve mechanism in the sense of causality of the parts as opposed to the whole, although it is not therefore necessarily reducible to mechanism. The principles of teleology and mechanism are, in fact, declared to be so closely connected that they must be combined in a single supersensuous principle.[1] Mechanism, Kant insists, is absolutely indispensable for natural science and no limit whatever must be set to the use of the principle even in regard to organisms, provided we do not dogmatically assert that everything in organisms is to be accounted for in terms of mechanism. We must apply the principle wherever we can, but abstain from saying that it is applicable everywhere. Kant says that teleological principles are to be regarded not as belonging to natural science (*Naturwissenschaft*) but only to the descriptive study of nature (*Naturbeschreibung*), although they are important for natural science as helping to regulate its method of research.[2] The conception of a living matter (" *lebendig* " as opposed to " *belebt* ") is repudiated as contradicting the very concept of matter and being the end of all science. Similarly, in *The Metaphysical Rudiments of Natural Science,* the idea that physical science is coterminous with mechanism permeates the whole argument. Yet even here Kant admits the possibility that, in order to explain life, we may have to appeal to an immaterial substance, distinct from, but combined with matter.[3]

That mechanism and teleology are regarded as, in the last resort, two partial aspects of the same supersensible principle tells as[4] much against mechanism as against teleology. Of the relation between mechanism and teleology in the noumenal sphere we need not speak ; our object in considering the *Critique of Judgment* was mainly or only to emphasise the point that Kant conceived his proof of causality as still leaving room for an organic and purposive mode of causation, generically different from the mechanical causality of natural science. In insisting that both design and mechanism are

---

[1] *E.g.*, 358, section 78.   [2] 365–6, section 79.   [3] *H.*, IV, p. 437 ff.
[4] Teleology is said to be not a principle of explanation but a principle of exposition (357 ff., section 78), on the ground that we can only explain a thing by means of what is clearer than itself, but neither is mechanism conceived as a principle of explanation—Kant never holds that efficient causes *explain.*

regulative, not constitutive, Kant means that we must simply try to apply them wherever we have a chance, without dogmatising as to the limits of their possible application or, still less, categorically asserting that there are no such limits in phenomena at all.

Kant's views on the subject of teleology are not necessarily put out of court by the discovery of evolution.[1] On the contrary, if he is right in maintaining that organisms are wholes not completely reducible to mere aggregates, the process of evolution can never be described completely in terms of natural laws connecting universals, or physical atoms, or quantitative factors, though such a way of description may be quite adequate to meet the needs of certain branches of science even in regard to the organic. It can never be so described completely, because the individual organism cannot be reduced to a mere product of isolable factors of any description, and something can from the nature of the case only be accounted for by causal laws if it can be reduced to such isolable factors and each factor connected with a factor in an earlier state by an invariable law. That we are now in a position to admit the development of the higher from the lower organisms by a continuous process, and that the fact of adaptation may be scientifically accounted for by factors like natural selection without recourse to an external mind, may affect the question of design on its theological side ; but we are not concerned with this here, and, if Kant's contention be right, the hypothesis of evolution certainly does not make the organism, as it exists now, less of a true whole. But to say that it is a true whole means that it is not capable of full description[2] by mechanical laws.

We shall not press the case of organisms further, but we would insist that psychology at any rate reveals, even if biology does not, a true whole that cannot be regarded as a mere product of factors such that the self, even as empirically observed in introspection, could ever be wholly accounted for by natural laws connecting each factor with a factor (or factors) in a preceding state. Unfortunately Kant did not use the standpoint of the *Critique of Judgment* to examine the science of psychology, but, had he done so, he would surely have developed a more satisfactory account of freedom than that given in the ethical works and would not have

---

[1] A hypothesis which Kant himself suggested.
[2] We do not mean to assert that even the inorganic is *wholly* reducible to mechanism.

been driven to attempt the solution of the problem by an appeal to an unknowable, absolutely timeless, abstract entity like the noumenal self.   I do not, of course, mean to say that such an account would remove all difficulties, but it seems to me the only line of argument that could set us on the way to do so.   It is strange that Kant should relegate the purpose of man to a noumenal sphere in which it could not break the mechanical order of nature, and yet, a few years later, admit the purposive action of animals as non-mechanical within the sacred precincts of physical research ; it is strange that he should, in the ethical works, regard the empirical self as completely determined by a mechanical necessity, and yet, a few years later, liberate animal organisms from the bonds of this same necessity.

Conclusion

WE have discussed Kant's proof of causality at length and tried to show its validity in principle not only for the physical, but also for the psychological sphere. This seemed to imperil freedom, but we see that Kant has not proved mechanical causality, but only necessary sequence, of phenomena, thus leaving a more promising way open for the reconciliation of freedom and causality than the way he actually took in his mystical relegation of freedom to the noumenal sphere. In our discussion we have maintained that the essential part of Kant's message on the subject of causality is not that our mind arranges (synthesises) nature according to the category of causality, but that we can prove the universal validity of the causal principle by showing that without it knowledge would be impossible. Perhaps we have unduly neglected the subjectivist side of the argument. It is certainly plausible to say that we can only know what mind has itself produced, and that we are able to know causality because it is only the universal mind in us which has constituted a nature according to causality, but the importance of this subjectivism in the thought of Kant has been greatly over-estimated, and certainly, if we can prove causality to be valid of phenomena because we otherwise should not know them, we do not need any further help from the subjectivist standpoint. If causality has been proved to be valid of all objects as far as they are knowable, we do not need further to contend that our minds have put causality into phenomena and that we consequently know it to be there. For the proof, if really a proof at all, at once removes the special difficulty as to our knowing causality. The contention that mind can only know mind or the product of mind would apply, not specially to causality taken alone, but to knowledge in general; but our task was to prove, if possible, the validity of the special principle of causality, or necessary connection between events, not to discuss the problem how knowledge in general is possible.

236

It is sometimes asserted that science has no need of causality, because the general principle of causality does not in itself enable us to discover any particular causal laws. This seems to me rather like saying that a house has no need of a foundation, because the foundation cannot be used as a room to live in. The whole idea of a physical system, on which idea science rests, presupposes necessary connection throughout, and necessary connection is just what Kant seems to have proved in causality. The proof of causality does not indeed establish uniformity in nature sufficient for science to develop, but only uniformity sufficient for experience of objects as objects to be possible. That there is enough uniformity in nature for science to develop successfully has been shown empirically by the history of science itself, but science could never have even started without presupposing causality, i.e., seeking to account for any event by means of what is external to that event. Nor, as Kant showed, is a physical object even thinkable without necessity.

In view of the success of science in the past and the valuable effects of the assumption on the course of science, we are justified in assuming as a " regulative idea " a greater degree of uniformity and unity in nature than is empirically given ; and the importance of such ideas as supplementing the bare schemas of categories is stressed by Kant even to the point of exaggeration. " One cannot say that reason has first derived this unity according to its principles from the contingent qualities of nature.[1] For the law of reason to seek it is necessary, because without this law we should have no reason at all, but without reason no coherent employment of understanding (keinen zusammenhängenden Verstandesgebrauch), and in the absence of this no adequate criterion of empirical truth, on which account we must presuppose the systematic unity of nature throughout as objectively valid and necessary." [2]Regulative ideas that specially interest the student of causality are the principle of mechanism, the principle of design, and the belief that all the laws of nature can be deduced from either one principle or a few very simple principles.

But it is not the utility of the causal principle to science that is in question, as though science would not use the cate-

---

[1]Critique of Pure Reason, B., 679 (=A., 651).

[2]The three regulative ideas of unity, diversity and continuity are applied by Kant in the Critique of Pure Reason, B, 676–8, to the classification of species, not to the finding of natural laws.

gory of causality till its validity had been proved by metaphysicians or would abandon it if metaphysicians failed to find a proof.   A proof of causality has not the same kind of value as a proof of a new empirical fact ; it does not give us causality as a new fact which we had not assumed before ; but who can deny that by showing the relation of causality to other fundamental principles, by making explicit the implications of its common use, by defining more correctly and concisely its nature, function and limits, it does add to our understanding of reality ?   Surely it is well worth while to devote some trouble to the proof of a principle which, without being in itself logically self-evident, is the indispensable presupposition of all science, nay all rational action, which is the main, if not the only, bond of unity among phenomena, which is the one gateway to the conception of reality as a systematic whole, the conception often, if not always, regarded as the chief end of philosophy.

INDEX